SPIRIT

Transformation and
Development in Organizations

Harrison Owen

UNIVERSITY OF
GLOUCESTERSHIRE
at Cheltenham and Gloucester

ABBOTT PUBLISHING
Potomac, Maryland

Please Note The type has been reset for this printing resulting in small changes in pagination compared with previous printings. All other aspects of the book remain the same.

First published in 1987
Second Printing May 1988
Third Printing May 1990
Redesign and Fourth Printing December 1993

Abbott Publishing
7808 River Falls Drive
Potomac, MD 20854
301-469-9269

Printed in the United States of America

Library of Congress Catalog Card Number 87-70469
ISBN 0-9618205-0-0

Table of Contents

Other Books by
Harrison Owen

Leadership Is

Riding the Tiger

Open Space Technology: A User's Guide

PROLOGUE

I have written this book for friends and colleagues, known and unknown, who find themselves in the midst of a transforming world, and are resolved to look beneath the surface to the underlying source of change. This source, which has become manifest in the forms and structures of our organizations, I call Spirit. It now seems to be transforming in new ways. Although my subject is Spirit, my intent is totally practical, for the issue at hand is, how do we make sense out of Spirit, and perhaps more important, how do we facilitate its journey towards new form?

In many respects, this is a "book in progress" in that the thoughts and practice described are in continuing evolution. Discretion might dictate waiting until all the pieces fit. But that would mean waiting for eternity. I sincerely doubt that we will ever have all the pieces, and for sure they will never quite fit. In the meantime, we experience our world, and the organizations of which we are a part, as being in transformation. The old ways are passing, and the new ones have yet to arrive. We are in the Open Space between what was and what might become. And the question remains, What to do about all that?

Under the heading of *caveat emptor*, I should warn you that this is not an easy book. Its difficulty arises in part from the language, which comes from many places; and although I have tried to use words in their everyday sense, I have not always been successful. Even when I have managed to do so, you will find that the words can be understood on several levels simultaneously, and I will often play with all of them. So I can only suggest careful reading.

I suppose I should also forewarn you that some substantial portion of my language is "religious," or at least that is the way it may be perceived. However, while it is true that many of the truly "heavy words" of the great traditions of the East and West are present, I have used them because they were the right words for my intention. Of course, I might have used a different vocabulary from psychology, anthropology or philosophy. That I did not was a conscious decision. It is my conviction that when speaking of things of the Spirit, we will do well to remember, explore and utilize the powerful words of our world traditions. To the extent that this is off-putting, I apologize, but I would also ask you to look beneath the surface and consider whether those familiar old words are truly lost or do they, in fact, contain some of their age old power.

But language is only part of the problem; indeed, it is more symptom than cause. The heart of the matter lies in the fact that when seeking to make sense out of

Spirit in a world dominated by materialism, you not only end up saying some very strange things, you also require of your readers a certain conceptual shift. Whereas we have been trained since our youth to take form and matter as primary, with Spirit as a somewhat inconsequential add-on, I find it necessary to turn all of that upside down. The net effect is the sort of conceptual gymnastics similar to those employed by the physicists when they began to take the subatomic world seriously. Rather than thinking in terms of bits, pieces and things, it becomes important to play with fields, flow and force. And that is where you run into the problem of language, for English, as we have developed it, is much better at substance than flow, unless you want to enter the world of poetry. Not that poetry is bad, but it does lack a certain precision.

To be even more specific, I am convinced that it is necessary to take the kind of conceptual leap negotiated by the physicists when they moved beneath form to the essential energy, only we must do it in terms of our thinking about organizations and the individuals that constitute them. My reasons are several. In the first place, I really think there is something "there" which is worth thinking about. I also sense that we have about exhausted our ability to think further about organizations and individuals in terms of bits, pieces and things. The truth of the matter is that it is all too complex and fast moving for that sort of approach.

Thinking at the level of Spirit and flow is no longer just nice, it is now necessary. We simply must develop the means to think at higher levels of abstraction and thus rise above the confusion of particularity, while at the same time maintaining an earthy practicality which roots us in the here and now. That is precisely what I have attempted to do.

As I said, this is really a book in progress, and it is therefore also an invitation for co-creation. The effort, at least in its contemporary form, is so new that the last word is far from utterance. And if I do nothing but goad or inspire you to "take your shot," I will have succeeded.

Of course, it must be acknowledged that in terms of the history of the Species, the human attempt to make sense of Spirit is by no means novel. But contemporary man seems to have forgotten or intentionally put aside all that wisdom as being somehow irrelevant superstition. Thus, much of this book is an attempt to remember what we already know.

Harrison Owen
Potomac, Maryland
1987

Chapter I

ABOUT SPIRIT

This book is about Spirit, and the ways in which Spirit transforms and develops in organizations. The intent is not that organizations become more spiritual, but rather that we might recognize that organizations in their essence are Spirit, and then get on with the important business of caring intelligently and intentionally for this most critical and essential element.

Perceiving the centrality of Spirit in our organizations is not as strange or difficult as it may appear. Indeed, every person who has ever found occasion to remark that, "The spirit around this place is terrible," or "Got to keep the spirit up" or, "Our spirit is our most important asset," has already made the connection. The problem, however, is that we typically do not have much more to say, and worse than that, we apparently possess very little in the way of appropriate technology in order to do something with, or for Spirit.

Until recently, "doing something with Spirit" may have appeared less than a serious pursuit, and if the technology was lacking, the loss was not consequential. But as the pace of our world has speeded, and the competitive edge narrowed, high performance and the attainment of excellence are no longer just nice, they have become essential. And whatever else high performance and excellence may be based on, they would seem to have something to do with the quality of Spirit . . . human Spirit, our Spirit, the Spirit of our organizations.

In another day, it seemed that the forms and structures of our life might last forever. Indeed, if they changed at all, they changed with such glacial slowness that it hardly seemed worth while thinking about. But that day has gone, and its passing has been noted by the likes of Toffler, Naisbitt, Yankelovich, Peters, Waterman *et al.* Putting it all together, we might say "Here we are surfing on the third wave, buffeted by megatrends, playing by new rules, and in search of excellence." Whatever it is that has happened to our world, it certainly isn't the place it used to be.

The difference which we now experience is nicely caught in the turn of phrase which converted "Ready, Aim, Fire" into "Ready, FIRE, aim." The point, which now seems almost trivial is that in the "good old days" we might carefully lay our plans five years into the future with some assurance that what we imagined as future would be only a slightly evolved version of the present. We could afford to carefully get ready, aim our project, and then when we were fully prepared — let her go. No longer. We have discovered to our chagrin that in all too many cases, plans made today are out of date before the ink is dry. It is almost as if our target (the future) were racing with such speed that our projectile (our project) just can't keep up. We have no choice but to launch our projects, and then figure out how to *rendez-vous* with a yet-to-be imagined future while in flight. Confusing at best, and for sure the old rules of management just don't seem to work the way they used to. For those who run their lives (and organizations) by the old adage "Make the plan, manage to the plan, and meet the plan," frustration and failure appear as almost constant companions.

It is rather like sitting on a train, watching the trees pass by the window. A hundred years ago, when the maximum speed was perhaps 30 miles an hour, we could observe each tree in its discreteness, passing with solemn dignity. Fifty years later, the passing trees moved by with greater speed, but by turning our head and refocusing our eyes, we could still track each tree. Today, if we are to sit on a train, especially if that train is one of the new breed making 300 km/hr (180 mph), we would risk severe eyestrain and whiplash were we to attempt to keep track of every tree. We are left, sooner or later, with a blur . . . and how do you make sense out of a blur? We might close our eyes and hope for the best or failing that, reach for the emergency cord and stop the train. But if the train is our organization, neither strategy is useful. When all the world is a blur how do you make sense out of that blur? How do you leave the level of structure and form in order to deal intelligently with the energy and flow (I would say Spirit) which drives that structure and form?

Dealing with Spirit is not just nice, it is essential. For Spirit may be the only thing we have left. Then again, it may be the only thing we truly ever had. Perhaps the sages of ages gone by, to say nothing of large portions of the human (non-western) race were right. Man in his essence is Spirit, and the forms and structures of our existence are only momentary manifestations of that Spirit. Heresy, perhaps, but in the days of "Ready, fire, aim," the idea may be worthy of further exploration.

Before embarking upon such an exploration, it should be noted that the changed conditions confronting us are not simply a matter of increased speed, but also complexity. If we have learned anything over the past several hundred years that Western science has reigned supreme, it is that the simpler things appear, the more likely that enormous complexity lurks just beneath the surface. The simple and irreducible atom has given birth to the incredible world of quarks and antimatter, and the peaceful evening sky has exploded into the infinity of space and black holes. Even the familiar biological forms, in which we and the other creatures of this planet appear, are the product of a cybernetic system known as DNA, which compresses within the nucleus of a single cell the programmatic information necessary to replicate a human being or a frog, which is at once recognizably human (or "frogy") and yet different from all others.

What is true for the worlds of biology, astronomy, and high energy physics, appears to be true for our organizations as well. The simple business of doing business isn't so simple after all. Outside of the fact that we in our organizations are simultaneously part of the world of the atom, the black hole and DNA, we are also a participant in that wonderful thing called "organization" in which complexity confounds complexity. In a slower moving day, we could seemingly overlook the complications (or leave them to the academics), and in fact we did very well. Actually, we did very well in two rather specific situations. First, we managed well with simple organizations in a fast moving environment. The archetype for this situation would be the bucket brigade at a fire. We knew how to keep the water flowing even when the fire changed its course. By the same token, we did quite well with highly complex organizations in a slowmoving environment. Large corporations or government bureaucracy could exist and do the job so long as the environment for which they were designed remained essentially unchanged.

At the moment, however, we have a new situation wherein we must deal with highly complex organizations in very fast moving environments. No longer is the world just rapid or just complex, it is, what I must call, Ra-plex. Raplexity is by no means a linear extrapolation from the previous situation as demonstrated by the fact that when we apply the old "fixes," things aren't fixed, indeed they seem to get worse. For example, when events outpaced the capacity of the simple fast moving organizations to respond, the answer was quite clear — improve communications. Make them faster and more precise. And of course we now have the means for doing just that in style, otherwise known as the computer. But, we now find that simply improving communications with the computer doesn't fix anything, for as we increase speed in one part of our system — all other parts slow down relatively. It appears that Einstein was right; in the world of high energy, everything is relative.

The world of raplexity is a different world indeed. We can't continue with business as usual. Indeed, our business and the organizations which do that business are being transformed whether we like it or not. Like the dinosaurs, we are discovering that when the environment radically alters, such that the old way of being is no longer appropriate, the choice is fairly clear. Evolve, or go extinct. The dinosaurs apparently didn't get the picture, and some of our organizations appear to suffer from a similar lack of perception. But for the rest, we may hope that the search for a better way to be, now initiated, will be carried to some reasonable and successful conclusion.

There are, of course, no guarantees. The odds, however, may be improved to the extent that we possess some accurate understanding of what is transpiring, coupled with the ability to facilitate the process. At this juncture, we come back to Spirit. For no matter what else may be going on during the process of transformation, it is clear that the forms and structures of our organizations are changing with such rapidity and confusion that we almost loose track of them. Like trees viewed from the passing train, they are a blur, and it becomes important to ask and understand what lies beneath those indistinct shapes. What is it that is being transformed? The word itself suggests that it is not form, but rather something more elemental, which I take to be Spirit.

This book, then, is about Spirit, or more exactly, the process of transformation and development through which Spirit takes form in the shapes and structures of our existence. The intent is eminently practical, for it is my hope to suggest alternate ways of thinking and working with organizations under the conditions of raplexity. Were the good old days still with us, the effort might be nice, but surely not necessary. But the good old days have gone, and with them the efficacy of our standard ways of thinking and working with organizations. If this statement appears extreme, I make no apology, the days are extreme. A better way to think about our organizations is needed. The way I propose starts with Spirit, and attempts to make sense.

By making sense I mean telling a "likely story" within which the reality and function of Spirit may be perceived. The sources of my tale are manifold, and while the tale may appear novel, it is by no means new. Indeed, we shall be revisiting, and hopefully remembering many forgotten places in the human experience. The value will lie, however, not in antiquity, but rather in contemporary application. So in addition to theory, we will explore present-day practice and results through case studies. The proof of the pudding however, remains with the eating. By way of an appetizer, consider the following.

Imagine that you have been given the task of focusing the Spirit of 1,200,000 people, living in nine cities and four counties, which, for the past 300 years, have either ignored each other or engaged in a variety of hostile acts. From this disparate conglomerate of humanity, it is desirable to create a single, conscious region where

4

cooperation is the norm, and the common Spirit is dedicated to regional development as opposed to parochial turf protection.

In two years, operating as a part time consultant, you manage to facilitate the creation of an environment within which the United Ways unite, the Chambers of Commerce merge, tourism is approached on a regionwide basis, and a Regional Sports Authority emerges to begin development of a sports facility which is publicly supported by most political jurisdictions and opposed by none. Indeed, three mayors and a city manager were to be seen on television proclaiming for all the world to hear that they didn't care where the facility was built so long as it was good for the region. And last, but not least, the region moved, almost overnight, from being the 149th market area in the United States to become Number 29.

Wishful thinking? Black magic? Not at all. That is the story of Hampton Roads Virginia. Details are described in the final case study, while the theory and method are outlined in between. The starting point was Spirit, the medium was culture, and the mechanism myth. In a word, the Spirit was brought to new shape through the power of a new story.

How do you make sense out of Spirit? Or put slightly differently, how do you tell a likely story which assembles the relevant facts in such a way that the reality and function of Spirit becomes manifest and useful? The simple answer is that we must look in those places and times where Spirit is working and moving, and then develop the method or means to catch Spirit in the act. I propose that the critical time and place are those moments when the Spirit is transforming or developing. The special method or means comes from myth, ritual and culture.

PRELIMINARY DEFINITIONS:
TRANSFORMATION, DEVELOPMENT AND ORGANIZATION

Transformation is the organizational search for a better way to be. It is what happens when the environment radically alters such that the old ways of doing business are no longer appropriate or possible, and a new way becomes essential. The alternative is extinction. The thrust towards transformation is usually not something the organization itself initiates, and for good reason, for the process of transformation is always painful, and if carried to completion, results in a new organizational form (lifeform) which marks the end — we may say death — of the old way of being. Although the results of transformation appear with the emergence of new

5

organizational form, the essence of transformation lies in the odyssey or passage of the human Spirit [1] as it moves from one formal manifestation to another. The word "transformation" says as much, for the central idea is movement across or through forms.

Development consists of making an organization, located in a particular time and place, better. Development presumes a relatively hospitable and stable environment, and the issue becomes one of enhancing existing organizational form and function in order to achieve optimal performance under the circumstances.

Organization may be defined as two or more individuals gathered together for a common purpose. Given this definition, everything from a family of two, up to and including the entire planet will fit. Granted, there are significant differences in size. but considered at the level of Spirit, I am more struck with the similarities than the differences. However, most of what I will have to say relates to middle sized organizations, which others might call large social systems.

It is important to make a distinction between development and transformation, or to use the terms of Ken Wilbur,[2] translation and transformation. Although the two are in some ways similar, and indeed constitute a continuum[3], they are essentially different in effect and function.

Transformation consists of making an organization different because the environment is so unstable and/or radically altered that the prior form, structure, way of being is simply unworkable. It is important to notice that in no way is the prior form considered "bad" or inferior — for it probably worked quite well in the circumstances for which it was designed. Just so with the dinosaurs. Their lifeform was in no sense "bad," indeed it was well suited for a swampy, warm world. However, when that world radically altered, the dinosaur life form was no longer appropriate.

The present situation with AT&T is instructive. As we all know, AT&T used to be the "phone company," affectionately known as MA BELL. In its day it was

---

[1] Spirit is used here without definition, in part because it defies definition, but mostly because the meaning evolves in the following material. For openers, however, spirit may be understood in the colloquial sense of "My spirit is willing but my flesh is weak." Whatever spirit is or may become, it is initially "that which underlies all that I am or we are." Spirit is man in his essence.

[2] Ken Wilbur "Up From Eden", Anchor Press/ Doubleday, pg. 71 ff.

[3] Organizations having undergone transformation subsequently require development in order to reach their potential, which in turn establishes the ground from which future transformation may occur.

large, and largely effective. Indeed it produced and managed the best telephone system on earth, which has become the standard against which all others are measured. AT&T was also a protected, regulated organization which knew no competition.

Then on the first of January 1984, virtually everything changed. The code name was divestiture which meant that AT&T would be separated from its operating companies — the local phone companies — and thrust into the highly competitive telecommunications-computer world with no protection. Without debating the merits of the decisions which lead to divestiture, it is a fact that the world changed. It is also a fact that little in the corporate experience of AT&T prepared them for this jump. The new situation represented a radical discontinuity with what went before, and under the circumstances, development, as we were talking about it above makes no sense, for you could develop the "phone company" past all limits, and only succeed in increasing the disparity between organizational form and function and the demands of the new world in which AT&T finds itself. Development will not do it. Transformation is essential, and that is precisely the course that has been embarked on.

Perhaps the best example, or symbol of transformation comes not from the world of organizations at all — but from the world of the butterfly. As we have all known since childhood, butterflies start out as caterpillars. When the time is right, the caterpillar spins a cocoon about itself, and after a period, emerges with beautiful colors and wings to fly. That would seem to be a transformation — but it might have been development, just as the tadpole develops bit by bit into a frog, losing its tail and growing legs. Indeed when you ask children what they think is going on inside the cocoon, they will describe just such a tadpole-to-frog process.

The reality, however is startling different. Once the caterpillar is safely inside, away from the eye of the world, it literally dissolves. Were you to cut open the cocoon at that stage, what you would discover is not a funny caterpillar growing wings, but apparently dissociated protoplasm. The caterpillar has gone to its essence, which is then reformed — transformed — into a butterfly. Presuming that being a butterfly is a better way to be, it becomes clear that the only way to get there is to allow the old form to dissolve, thus freeing some essential energy, purpose, or Spirit to achieve new form — with wings.

If the example of the butterfly makes it clearer what transformation is all about, the same example also highlights the difficulty involved with thinking about transformation, or for that matter, doing something about it, for the essence of transformation is neither the caterpillar nor the butterfly, but rather what happens in between. And when we look "in between" we see precisely — nothing, for the form has been dissolved on the one side, and hasn't happened yet on the other.

So with organizations, it is interesting to note what they were when they started, or what they became when transformation was complete. But we want to gain clarity about what happened in between. What happened in the Open Space between what was and what was to become. Like the caterpillar, organizations in transformation are confusing to say the least. Forms appear, disappear, are held forfeit, and sometimes hardly seem to exist at all. What we are impressed with, if only on the level of intuition, is the incredibly complex and often turbulent energy flow — the flow of Spirit as it moves from one manifestation to another. To observe the forms is to be one step away from what really is going on, and indeed sometimes, there are no forms to observe.

It is rather like trying to make sense out of a river by looking only at the shape of the gorge and the flotsam and jetsam that were tossed up along the way. To be sure, a certain amount of sense can be made by reconstructing what happened from what is left over, but it is very second hand, and certainly does not compare with watching the river in full flight. Furthermore, if the concern is to assist the river as it flows, it does little good to consider the situation after the river has all dried up. So too with the consideration of organizations in transformation. We need to be there in some sensate and sensible way in order to know what is happening — especially if our intent is to facilitate the process of transformation. But how do you get beyond the forms in order to image Spirit? How do you think of an organization primarily as Spirit, and only secondarily as form?

The first step involves believing that you really could do something like that, and the second part requires discovering or developing the means. If the whole enterprise is discarded on an *a priori* basis — not very much can happen. Indeed, there is much in our western tradition, that might lead us to such an *a priori* judgement. However, if we can get beyond such pre-judgment, if only on an experimental basis, the possibility that we might be successful in our quest is given to us by the fact that a large number of quite intelligent human beings have, for a number of centuries, seen Spirit as primary — and form as the momentary manifestation. Of course I am referring to the traditions of the East, to say nothing of the Western mystical traditions of Judaism, Islam, and Christianity.

Closer to home, we might also take certain comfort in the efforts and success of the community of high energy physicists, who faced an analogous, if not identical problem. The issue for them was how to deal effectively with a world that you could neither see, touch, taste, nor smell, which by definition was nonsubstantial, and worse than that, did not seem to operate by the same laws as the visible, concrete world. Indeed, when you tried to describe this "other world" in terms that were generally acceptable (Newtonian physics), things came out very strangely indeed — space bent, time all but disappeared, observer and observed appeared to merge. Fritjof Capra tells us:

> "The study of the world of atoms forced physicists to realize that our common language is not only inaccurate, but totally inadequate to describe the atomic and subatomic reality. Quantum theory and relativity theory, the two bases of modern physics, have made it clear that this reality transcends classical logic and that we cannot talk about it in ordinary language." [4]

In the end, the physicists have managed to say the unsayable, and view the world at once as energy and mass. But to do so, they found it necessary to build a new language and concept in which to work, which is quantum theory and all that has followed it. They have also been fortunate in being able to create certain mechanisms with which to image the passage and presence of pure energy, such as the cloud chamber.

Were it necessary for us to start from scratch in such an endeavor, as it relates to our field of concern, we would indeed have a long way to go. But fortunately, I believe that such a language and mechanism already exists, and it remains for us only to remember it, and relearn how to use it. That language and mechanism is myth, through which we may make sense out of Spirit.

---

[4] Capra, Fritjof, "The Tao of Physics", Bantum New Age Books, 1980 pg 32.

9

Chapter II

MYTHOS — THE IMAGE OF SPIRIT

Myth is neither true nor false, but rather behind truth — as that body of material through which a culture's values, purpose and direction come to expression. Myth is not just "any old story," it is the story, which gives shape and focus to Spirit, and makes everything make sense.[5] Myth, in short is the "eyeglasses" through which a given people perceive and interpret their world. It is the vantage point from which, or by which the true is judged to be true.

But myth does more. On a deeper level, myth communicates the moving quality of the human Spirit as it seeks to become whatever it was supposed to be. In the words of Ernst Cassirer,

> . . . Myth harbors a certain conceptual content: it is the conceptual
> language in which alone the world of becoming can be expressed.
> What never is, but always becomes, what does not, like the structures
> of logical and mathematical knowledge, remain identically determinate,
> but from moment to moment manifests itself as something different,
> can be given only a mythical representation.[6]

---

[5] This understanding of myth as the marker or medium of Spirit is part of a long tradition, described by a large body of literature. The reader interested in pursueing the development of this tradition could do worse than to start with C.G.Jung's "Symbols of Transformation" (Bollingen Series/Princeton University Press, 1956). A parallel tradition, which connects at many points emerges from the fields of anthroplogy and mythology, beginning possibly with Frazer's "Golden Bough," but in the present day powerfully represented by Joseph Campbell in such works as "The Masks of God," (in four volumes, Viking Press, 1962). Most recently, the work of Ken Wilbur (particularly "Up From Eden," Anchor Press, 1981) has provided an extraordinary synthesis.

[6] Cassirer, Ernst; "The Philosophy of Symbolic Forms", Vol II, Yale University Press, 1955 pg 3.

10

Finally, myth doesn't just communicate about Spirit in its quest, but in some way manifests that Spirit in experiential terms; you can feel it. That may sound like black magic, but it is no more nor less than any good story accomplishes when "you get so into it" that the story becomes reality itself . . . or why else did you stay up until 4:00 a.m. reading it?

If you noticed the greek word *mythos* in the chapter title as opposed to the more usual word myth, you may suppose that my antiquarian interests got the better of me. That may be, but there is a purpose. To this point, I have used the word myth to indicate the primal stories which are told in the life of an organization, which may suggest that such stories are the only mechanism by which the Spirit of an organization is captured and represented. That is true only in part, for man does not live by words alone. Although the stories are primal, they do not appear just in words, but also in color, form, sound (non-verbal) and movement. This is Ritual.

It is common practice to speak of myth and ritual as if they were two separate things, but that is not so, for ritual is simply putting the words of myth into form, motion and music. Myth and ritual are two sides of the same thing, which I will call *mythos*. When it is useful to refer just to the words, I will use *myth*. And when the color, form, motion and sound are critical to the discussion, I will use the word *ritual*. But all of this is a matter of intellectual distinction. In life, you never have one without the other, and so my normal term will be *mythos*.

Having short-changed ritual to this point, it seems only fair to back up a bit to make the introduction and the connection with myth. Ritual is acted myth. Just as we cannot communicate by words alone, but use a whole range of kinesthetic expressions, so myth is but a very partial vehicle. With ritual, myth assumes shape, form, texture, color, sound, smell and motion, as all the senses are brought into play. Occasionally, of course, a story apparently may be told without the benefit of such things, but that is only apparent, for even in the private telling of a tale, the listener has the benefit of the gestures and facial expressions of the teller. Indeed, when tales are told bereft of physical expression, they are experienced as unendurably boring.

Ritual is myth expressed in the full tapestry of human experience. This expression may be quite formal as in the services of the church, synagogue or other religious body. Similar formality may also been seen in the gatherings of purely secular bodies such as the state, the military, and yes, even corporations. At the other end of the spectrum, ritual appears in less awesome terms as the greetings we offer upon meeting each other and the subtle body language through which we add warmth and color to our expression.[7] The point is simply that no part of the human experience is devoid of ritual, and by the same token ritual is never far from myth. In fact, the only time that myth ever appears without ritual is on the printed page, and even there one finds the "ritual" of format, layout, typeface and texture.

LITURGY

In organizational life, mythos (myth and ritual) appears as liturgy. Liturgy is formed from two greek words, *laos* people and *ergos* work — and means in literal translation, *the people's work* or what the people do. Liturgy is the sum of what the people do and say as an expression of their deepest being. As such, it may be highly conscious, artful, and carefully crafted to express the best of the human spirit. Or then again, it may be purely happenstantial, dull, drab, and degrading. Good or bad, liturgy is what the people do.

Liturgy, of course, is also the word used to describe religious services. As the church has grown progressively less meaningful in the contemporary world, it may appear that liturgy is extraneous to life. That, however, is the church's problem with bad liturgy. The potential for liturgy to guide, direct and enhance the human spirit exists. It remains only to do liturgy well.

Liturgy at its best is the conscious production and orchestration of myth and ritual such that Spirit is focused and directed in a particular, intended way. Traditionally, it has been the role of the Priest to craft and care for the Story of the People, and to provide the means and mechanism whereby that story may be remembered. Far from being an arcane, esoteric role of doubtful utility, the priestly role is quite fundamental to the orderly, meaningful conduct of human affairs, or as we might say, the purposeful flow of Spirit. For liturgy provides the peculiar sense of time, space and propriety indigenous to a particular people and culture.

One might suppose that time and space are everywhere the same, but a moment's reflection will show that this is not so. Westerners visiting West Africa, for example, quickly discover that the sense of time is vastly different than they had come to expect. The sense of space is also different, leading to a common western observation that it is indeed strange how Africans, who live in a vast, unpopulated

---

[7] See Edward T. Hall, "The Silent Language", Doubleday, 1959.

continent, should build their houses in such close proximity one can scarcely squeeze between.

These differences might be perceived as happenstantial givens, just the way things are. And doubtless, in some early period, at the dawn of human consciousness, the peculiar sense of time and space just "appeared." But the fact that a special sense is continued and sharpened over time is not happenstantial. On the contrary, the sense of "here and now" peculiar to any culture was to some extent consciously arrived at; the special gift of the priests, achieved through the creation and maintenance of liturgy.

And how was that done? By consciously telling the Story or myth, which is what liturgy is all about. So in the West, we mark time as B.C. or A.D. Those letters mean nothing until referenced to the primal mythology of Western Christendom, the Story of Jesus Christ. And the story has been carefully orchestrated with the great celebrations of Christmas, Easter and Whitsunday, which measure out time. Likewise space has been molded in the image of the Story. The great cathedrals provided the center, and all other human habitations were arranged about.

Time and space are (or at least can be) intentional human creations, and both are the product of liturgy. Given a different liturgy, we would have a different sense of time and space.

Martin Buber captures the idea exquisitely, although we will have to remember that *prayer* and *sacrifice* are the essential elements of liturgy in order see the point clearly.

> ". . . prayer is not in time, but time in prayer, sacrifice not in space, but space in sacrifice, and to reverse the relation is to abolish the reality."

At this juncture, you may be wondering at the utility of these arcane discussions, but my intention remains eminently practical. To the extent that we would make sense out of Spirit, and perhaps even more importantly, do something positive with Spirit, an understanding of the function and effect of liturgy is critical. It is true that in the past, such considerations were held in closely guarded secrecy by a priestly class. But the times have changed, and it is given to us to create our own time and space, appropriate to the present tasks of our Spirit. Put more directly; given knowledge of, and skill with, mythos and liturgy, we can create organizations that work in a transforming world.

MYTHOS DEFINED

Mythos may be defined as *a likely story arising from the life experience of any group, through which they come to experience their past, present and potential*. In verbal form, mythos varies greatly, ranging from large volumes such as the Old and New Testament and the collected mythology of classical Greece and Rome, to the scattered tales present in the oral tradition of contemporary organizations. But no matter what the size or manner of presentation in ritual, mythos is first of all a *likely* story, which is simultaneously spoken and acted.

As a *likely story*, mythos is not history, and any attempt to understand it as history will only result in confusion in the mind of the reader and a basic misunderstanding of the material. This is not to suggest that historical material is not to be found in mythos, because of course it is. Thus in ancient myths, it is quite possible to dig up the cities referred to, or to find reference in other, supposedly neutral sources, to the personages mentioned, and thereby substantiate their historical existence. Contemporary organizational mythos will also contain elements of history, for example stories about the "early days out in the garage when the first machine was invented."

However, material also exists which careful historical research cannot validate, and may even be able to "disprove." For example, there appears to be reasonable evidence that Joshua never fought the battle of Jericho, at least in the terms described[8]. This phenomenon is by no means limited to antiquity, for contemporary organizational mythos often contains precisely the same kind of material.

The fact that such nonhistorical (or better ahistorical) material appears quite commonly in mythos has led to the almost universal conclusion that mythos "is not true." From an historical viewpoint, such a judgment concerning mythos is quite correct; however it may also be the case that history is not the final or only arbiter of the "truth." In fact, it turns out that the idea of history, at least as we currently understand it, is a relatively recent invention, and much of mankind (historically) has never operated within its constraints.[9] This is not to suggest that history has no use, for indeed it does. However, mythos understood as history will only lead to confusion and

---

[8] See Kathleen Kenyon, "Digging up Jericho", Ernst Benn, London, 1957)

[9] See Collingwood, R.G., "The Idea of History" Oxford, 1946

misunderstanding, for mythos is neither truth nor nontruth; rather it lies "behind" truth as the *context* within which mankind is enabled to perceive truth as Truth. This last statement obviously requires considerable elaboration, but I make it only to indicate that mythos and history operate in radically different ways, each with their own utility. Never should they be confused.

Mythos *arises out of the life of the group*. That is to say, it is indigenous to that group. The language is common to the group, as are all the other means of formal representation (color, form, motion and sound). A major consequence of this fact is that somebody else's mythos usually is experienced as weird, strange or bizarre. However, from the point of view of the group that owns the mythos, it is very natural, so natural in fact that they are virtually unconscious of its presence, and totally oblivious to the fact that "others" may perceive it as strange.

Last, mythos is the mechanism *through which the group comes to experience its past, present and potential*. The past, present and potential, to which we have reference is nothing more than the journey of Spirit through transformation as it has been experienced by the group. In mature mythos, all of these elements and occur-rences may be organized in what appears to be chronological order, but the intent is not to portray history; rather it is to create the conditions in which **experiencing** may take place i.e. to tell a likely story. Telling this story is not simply a matter of ordering events in a book, although that is one expression, but one also finds the ritual enactment of these events over time, as in the Sacred Years of Judaism and Christianity. Christmas and Easter, Yom Kippur and Passover all provide occasions for the members to re-experience the significant transformative events.

The use of the word experience here may create problems, for we normally think of experience in rather passive terms as something that happens to us. And there is a sense in which mythos enables the members of the group to passively encounter what has gone before, what the present interpretation is, and how the future expectations might shape up.

I might also have used the word *understanding* to indicate that there is a certain rational content — a logic communicated through mythos. But in the final analysis, mythos takes the members of the group beyond passivity and logic into a condition where the essence of the group (Spirit, if you will) is encountered as a present, timeless reality. Mythos does not talk *about* the essence of the group — but rather represents that essence in an immediate, almost palpable way. When mythos functions well in the life of a group, it is the absolute antithesis of "unreal" and "untruth." On the contrary, it is the essential arbiter of reality itself, and as such it is "beyond" reality and beyond truth.

THE DEVELOPMENT OF MYTHOS

Mythos begins in the everyday events and activities of an organization. Early on, and even in maturity, it appears as "little stories" about the way things are around here. [10] In form, these stories are short, pointed and graphic, for in their early use, they are called upon to illustrate the life of the group to new members, and to occasional outsiders who may have the need to know. For example, when a new individual joins the group and raises the question — What's going on around here?" — a usual response will go something like, "Well, back in '81 when all this got started, we all worked out in the garage."

It is critically important to note that these "stories" are about some action, event or activity in the life of the group. And although they may eventually assume verbal form, initially, it was the act that counted. This point may seem so obvious as to be inconsequential, but the issue is that myth and ritual are together from the start. In later times, the tale may be told in words alone, but it becomes infinitely more powerful when represented in physical terms — ritual. To really tell a tale, it should be produced in such a way that you can see it, touch it, taste it, and smell it — and best of all, move with it.

As these stories are told, they improve with the telling. Unimportant details tend to drop out, colorful and important points may be enhanced or elaborated upon, and the story begins to assume the form of a well and often told tale, and certain devices work their way in which sustain interest and insure "correct" telling.[11] Correct

---

[10] There is of course some thought and evidence that mythos actually begins much before the origin of any particular organization in the collective unconscious of the species (Jung) and that it first "sees the light of day" as an activity of the right brain.(See Julian Jaynes, "The Origin of Consciousness in the Breakdown of the Bicameral Mind", Houghton Mifflin, 1976.) Such ideas are interesting and appealing, and certainly should be discussed in any broader treatment of mythos. For my purposes, however, I think such discussion would only add another layer of complexity to an already complex subject.

[11] The principles operative here have been studied and described by folklorists and others concerned with the development of oral tradition. For a brief introduction to this work, particularly as it applies to biblical material see Eduard Nielsen, "Oral Tradition", SCM Press, 1954

here means the form of the story is maintained. A very common example of such a device is the "punch line" in a Western joke. Everybody knows that the punch line must be there, and told in exactly the "right" way. In fact to "muff the punch line" has become synonymous with a variety of other uncoordinated behaviors. Other common devices include rhythm or cadence and the use of alliteration, all of which tend to enable the story tellers to stay on course, and subtly cue the teller when they are "off."

Obviously, it would be a mistake to ignore the physical (nonverbal) side of this development, although that becomes somewhat difficult to get down on the printed page. But when we watch present day stories grow, certain physical movements quickly get built in (or indeed they were there from the beginning). For example, watch carefully if you ever have the opportunity to observe pilots presenting their mythos. The words spoken are almost secondary to the appropriate hand motions and loud guttural sound effects. The same, of course, applies to young children at play, telling the tales of their imaginations.

As these stories are told, they become a part of the pool of tradition which the organization has found, in some way, to be meaningful, and their evolution continues, but within certain rather confined limits. Indeed, one of the surprising things about this evolution, is just how conservative it is — in the sense that it conserves the essence of the story. This point will become very important at a later time when we begin to use the information developed here as a basis for intervention within the process of organization transformation. To the extent that we would become midwives in that process, manipulating[12] the "mythos life" of the organization will be a most important tool. However, that may be done only with extreme caution and sensitivity. It may appear to us that some part of the tradition is only a story — but to the organization that story is their story, and as such it will be guarded very jealously.

Move Towards Brevity The evolution of mythos moves in several predictable ways. On the one hand there is a tendency towards brevity. In fact this tendency can move so far as to end up with only a single word which then becomes a key word or code

---

[12] "Manipulation" is a red flag for many people, but I use it here intentionally. Webster's 7th defines this word as follows, "to manage or utilize skillfully." Of course, manipulate can also mean, " to control by artful, unfair and insidious means." The primary definition is what I have in mind, but the second definition is a useful reminder that the very same approaches can also be used for nefarious ends.

word in the organizations. I call such words *heavy words*, because they carry a meaning and importance vastly greater than ordinary usage would suggest. Their root in the organizational mythos is indicated by the fact that outsiders will not have a clue to their meaning until they hear or see the story. An example of a heavy word is scrub as used in a medical setting. Needless to say it has nothing to do with cleaning floors, but its meaning and power will only become clear only when you hear the tale of the scrub-room and all the stories of surgical derring-do that began there. Not incidentally, the relationship of "scrub" to scrub-room is a good example of the interrelationship between myth and ritual, for the word assumes meaning only in the context of the ritual act. Exactly the same phenomenon occurs on the ritual side of the fence when a single physical motion can assume incredible communicative power, as for example the Sign of the Cross for the Christian or the spread fingers (V) in the Peace Movement.

Move Towards Complexity   At the same time, the organizational mythos tends toward greater complexity and interconnectedness. This is quite understandable given the function it performs. To the extent that the stories are adduced to let folks know "how things are around here," over time there is an increasing number of things to be covered under that heading. Some examples, all drawn from the Jonathan Corporation, may make all of this more concrete. The Jonathan Corporation is a small, but very rapidly growing shipyard located in Norfolk, Virginia. I worked with them during 1983-84, and the stories reported here were unearthed during that association.

For instance, in answer to the question, How did it all begin? there are "Creation Stories." One such story related how in the early days the president and his chief associate would meet at the International House of Pancakes with a pocketful of dimes. The dimes were used impartially for coffee and to feed the outside phone — which became the corporate switchboard. As brief as this story is, it manages to communicate to present employees an essential corporate value to wit: "We don't care what the form and setting is — just get the job done."

In times of crisis when the issue becomes, "How do we get through this one," there are stories of old battles won. An example of this kind of story from the same corporation goes as follows. It seems that on the first major contract bid, the company came in a full 50 percent lower than the estimated cost of the job, which in this case was the repair of a navy ship which had chosen to run into a tanker rather than aground on a sandbar. The navy couldn't believe the figures, and asked for a review , after which all they could do is shake their head and say go ahead if you are so crazy.

As luck would have it, the job had to be done over Christmas and in freezing conditions. Everybody worked from the president on down, and more often than not they worked around the clock. But the job got done for several thousand dollars less than what was already the low bid — three days ahead of schedule. Whenever this story is told, the value is clear. Simply put, "We can do it!"

For moments of conflict between organizations, there are "Boundary Stories" which indicate who we are and how we operate under the circumstances. The story in this case related how when the company was quite young, several of the senior officers decided that they wanted to "do their own thing" and so they left with several customers to create a competing operation. The president gathered the remaining troops, told them what the situation was, and indicated that he intended to go "nose to nose." But he also made it clear that despite everything, he was sorry that the folks had gone, and still considered them good people. As it turned out, the home team won, hands down, but the abiding value communicated was that even in moments of duress and opposition, we will respect those who oppose us even if we can't agree with them.

For newcomers (and indeed for old timers), when the question of proper behavior (values) is raised, there are stories which provide the model. The story here came to be known as Norma's Apartment. It seems that one of the secretaries (Norma) came home to find her apartment burned out. She had lost everything. Within 24 hours, with absolutely no official prodding, donations of material and money came in from all over the company. The value was pretty clear: "We care for each other."

Given the fact that all organizations have, or will have, similar needs in terms of saying "How it is around here," it is not surprising that the evolving stories appear to cluster in certain types and patterns, [13] and furthermore that organizations will tend to swap stories with the form and content remaining virtually the same while only the important names will change. For example, when working with fighting gangs in the streets of Washington, I discovered that all the gangs I knew had essentially the same story about "bad dudes and the fuzz." Only the name of the hero and number of the police precinct changed. This observation actually turned out to have real practical value, because one of my constant and painful mistakes was confusion over the turf that each gang claimed. As I learned to listen to the stories and attend to the names, I found a virtually foolproof way of determining "where I was at."

---

[13] One of the best examples of this on a worldwide basis is the so called "Hero Story" which emerges with infinite variation around the world. See Joseph Campbell's "Hero with a Thousand Faces," Bolligen Series, Princeton Press, 1949.

One last example, which comes more from the world of folk stories, appeared during some work that I was doing in West Africa and the Caribbean. While in Liberia I had the pleasure of hearing the Anance Tales which recount the adventures of a spider who is constantly in trouble, and usually gets out through some ruse. Some little time later I was in the Caribbean on St. Thomas and heard from an ancient black lady the story of "Bru Anance" who was sometimes a spider and sometimes a rabbit. Bru, as it turn out, means brother, and of course it is only a short hop to the American South and Brer Rabbit.

A great deal of useful work has been done in terms of classifying the varieties of form in which organizational mythos appears. But for our purposes it is sufficient to notice the tendencies mythic material seems to follow, and the fact that certain patterns recur. When it comes to using an understanding of mythos in a practical way, I have found that the patterning pretty much follows common sense once you understand that there are patterns. Elaborate classification schemes end up being more useful to the academic than the practitioner, if only because such schemes tend to get between the practitioner and the organization.[14]

Getting The "Right Story" The process by which material of the organizational mythos emerges out of everyday life seems to be relatively unconscious. Were one to ask why one story appeared and not another, the answer either would be a blank look or an apparently offhanded comment to the effect, "That's just what we remembered." In fact, I think this is just another example of people remembering what is significant to them. One story is "chosen" over another because it serves to re-present the organizational Spirit in a way that feels right. No votes, no editorial committees — just the collective self-understanding coming to expression in an way that "feels good."

There comes a time, when such a laissez-faire approach to the organizational mythos is no longer appropriate or possible. Sooner or later, the organization comes to realize that its stories are important, and having the "right" story is critical. The judgment as to rightness is not made on the basis of historical accuracy, although the argument surrounding that judgment may sound that way. Basically it is a question of self understanding and, to use the Madison Avenue phrase, "image." The agony of

---

[14] The literature on this subject is enormous, and appears in many fields including Anthropology, biblical studies, psychology, linguistics and, I am sure, many more. What I have presented here barely scratches the surface, but I believe it is sufficient to set the stage for our discussions. The generalities which I have provided are based in part upon that literature, but in large measure derive from my own observations of organizational mythos as it grows.

such choosing becomes apparent in the preparation of the annual report, or worse yet in the creation of the corporate film. At such a time, We have to tell our story, but who are we and what's the story? Having participated as producer in several such company films, I can readily attest that the whole process bears a much closer resemblance to corporate psychotherapy than anything as cut and dried as making a film. Telling the "right" story is painful and critical.

In older institutions, getting the story right can take centuries, and involve endless commissions and no little amount of bloodshed. A classic case is the Christian Church in regard to what is called the "Canon of Scripture." The issue was quite simply which books should be included in the Bible — or what's our story? We know for a fact that a number of books just didn't make it, and a number of people were consequently excluded from the christian organization because the "out" books were their books. A prime example are the so called Gnostic Gospels, but there were undoubtedly others. When "your story" isn't part of "The Story," you are out, or in the words of the church: you are a heretic.[15]

The growth of mythos is organic, as the organization claims certain aspects of its experience as critical and necessary for its own self-understanding. This experience is represented in words and action (myth and ritual) sometimes in isolation, but normally in union. The body of mythos may appear as an historical statement, relating "Who we are, and how we came to be at this place," but the function of mythos goes infinitely deeper. Superficially, mythos is "about" the organizational Spirit, but in reality, mythos becomes the medium through which the Spirit may be experienced. How that might be is the subject of the next section.

MYTHOS AT WORK

Mythos images Spirit in an organization in such a way that we not only learn about that Spirit, but in addition may experience the presence of Spirit in immediate, palpable ways. The true function (work) of mythos is to say the unsayable, to express the ineffable, but most important, to bring the participant into immediate, self-validating relationship with Spirit in the organization. A tall order to be sure, but a

---

[15] For a short description of the development of the Canon see "The Interpreters Bible" Abingdon, 1955, Vol I, pg 32ff.

common place experience if we stop to think about it, for mythos does what any good story does as a matter or course.

Think of your own favorite story (novel, movie, whatever), and ask yourself why and how it became so powerful for you. To be sure, you found the subject matter interesting, the description compelling, the style pleasing. But after you have identified all of these elements, and a hundred others that delight literary critics, isn't it true that there is still more? Somehow a really good story manages to create an environment into which you may move and participate. You are the hero, you cross the rivers, experience the sadness and the joy, you know the freshness of the new dawn and all the rest. And that is precisely the point, you are really there. To ask questions like "Is it really true?" — seem to miss the whole point. That story for you is neither true nor false, indeed it seems to go beyond all such distinctions.

One of my favorite stories is Ernest Hemingway`s *Old Man and the Sea*. I have read it a number of times, and each time I find myself becoming the old man. No longer am I some passive observer, sitting at the edge of the ocean, hearing extraneous facts about the battle being conducted beyond the horizon. I am there. I can feel the rough texture of the small boat under my seat. I experience the heat of the sun, the sweat running down my back, and I know all about that fish. But most of all that old man is me, and I know first hand what is going on in his soul. His spirit is my spirit. To be sure, it is just a story between two covers that occupies a very small space on my library shelves. I can pick it up and put it down, but the truth of the matter is that having picked it up once, it is always with me in a way and with a power that an infinite number of real life experiences never even come close to. Should we say that it is more real than life, bigger than life? We commonly use such phrases. Perhaps they mean something.

Needless to say, I think there is meaning here, but determining what it might be requires a closer look. Were we to operate from what might be called the "standard paradigm," in which reality is determined by a plethora of "facts," we would expect powerful stories absolutely to overwhelm us with incredible detail — facts in such abundance that we are literally buried in them. There are of course stories like that, but few good ones, and should an abundance of facts guarantee power, the New York telephone book would be at the top of the bestseller lists. More to the point, if we look carefully at a story like *The Old Man and the Sea*, it is precisely the absence of detailed fact that stands out. Indeed, considered objectively, it is absolutely amazing how little Hemingway really tells us. Not much more than an old man, a small boat, and a big sea.

Where does the power come from? For me it comes from the structured open space Hemingway has created into which I may enter, and experience the reality that he offers me. The story is real and powerful because I have really entered into its "space," and my imagination has been powerfully stimulated to create a world, the old man and the sea. The story is really real to me, because I am really there. We thus may come to the conclusion, that it is not so much what Hemingway says, but rather what he does not say that creates the conditions of empowerment. As odd as it may seem, the story says the most when it says the least — it significates in the silence.

I might push all this a little further and say that the business of art is creating those suggestive open spaces in which the human Spirit may grow. Thus in powerful graphic art, the painter opens a way for you to enter in. Picasso, was a master at this. With a few lines and some color, a whole world is created. To be sure there are details, but just enough to set the stage, and invite your imagination inside. The growth which takes place is not un-inhibited growth without shape and direction, for Picasso starts you on the way and establishes the environment which channels and shapes that growth. The net experience, however, is one of co-creation. You and Picasso create the reality that results. Furthermore, that reality is more than Picasso ever could have imagined, for it includes what you have contributed. This means of course, that art is not a static phenomenon, but it continues to grow over time as succeeding generations add their imagination — their Spirit.

In music, the story is the same. For all of the cascade of sounds in a great symphonic work, it is the silences that pull you in. On one level, of course you remember the sound of soaring strings or the crash of the great crescendo, but it is the brief pause before the thunder that makes you hold your breath, which roots you in that created time and space so that the power of sound literally grabs you. The phrase for this is "timing" and it may be the most important thing a conductor does. Too fast, and everything becomes a jumbled blur, and there is no "place" for you to fit in. Too slow, and the whole sense of momentum is lost. Just right, and the moment builds until you just can't stand it anymore, and then . . . over the edge. The quintessence of what I am talking about occurs in those "time-out-of-time" moments when a great conductor, orchestra, and music combine to take you places you have never been, and when it is all over, in the silence of ending, there is a power and meaning that literally drives beyond the capacity of any form to communicate. At such moments, the unsayable seems to hover in the atmosphere, validating its own reality by its very presence.

To be sure, such moments may be rare, and the medium need not be the symphony orchestra. But those moments exist even if they do not register on the meters and scales of present-day science. The power of such a moment resides not so much in the things that are done, but not done, for in that Open Space, Spirit grows and experiences its own growth as meaning.

That in a nutshell is what mythos does. Like art, because it is art, mythos creates the structured Open Space in which Spirit appears, grows, and experiences meaning. Recognizing this function (work) is therefore the first step in catching mythos in the act of imaging Spirit.

THE LIFE CYCLE OF MYTHOS

Mythos, as it is experienced in an organization, is not a single unchanging phenomenon, but rather an ongoing process through which Spirit is imaged. This process may be understood by considering the life cycle of mythos.

The life cycle begins in the everyday life stories of the organization, as the events of common experience are captured and retained. (See preceding section.) These significant happenings represent the collective self-understanding in ways that the members can readily understand, for the stories are told in terms that are quite familiar. For the folks in the shipyard the language was "shipyard," and when the tale is told, every manjack among them knows what is going on, if only because they have been there, or at least they have been somewhere very similar.

In the Jonathan Corporation, for example, I happened to be in the "yard" just as a new job was starting. Like much of Jonathan's work, it was a "rush job" which involved mounting a special new gun on a naval ship that could deal with the threat posed by the Exocet Missile. By chance, this job also had to be done at Christmastime, and once more the weather had turned cold. During a small break in the operation, the men had gathered inside to get out of the wind and were standing around rubbing their chapped, frozen hands. Working heavy steel in subfreezing temperatures is no fun, even if you happen to have a welding torch to warm things up. There wasn't much conversation, but such as there was tended toward bitching about the cold. After a few moments, one of the older employees, who described himself as a "runty Irishman" said something like, "you guys ain't seen nothing, you shouda' been there on the Speer." There were a few knowing nods followed by an expectant silence, and the little Irishman started to tell the tale. Some will say that it is the Irish gift of gab that enables them to weave the gossamer strands of a story with such finesse, but whatever the reason, the tale was told perfectly about how that small band from Jonathan on the first big job had worked the clock around, slinging steel off an old barge tied up next to the Speer with the wind and the cold as constant companions. Most of the folks had heard the story before, and every now and again, when the Irishman hit an open point, somebody else would say, "you know what happened then?" — and another detail or perspective would be added.

I don't think the whole thing took over 15 minutes in the telling, but the effect on the crew was powerful. Those who knew the story took pleasure in adding little bits and pieces, but mostly they found strength in the common telling of the tale, remembering how once before, "they had done it." For new men on the job, this was apparently the first time they had heard about the Speer, and they listened with an intensity that told you they were really there. The Irishman was a master: he told his part of the story with sufficient macho display, which said as no direct statement could, "You guys have a lot to live up to." But it wasn't overpowering, and the saving grace was his timing, which allowed just enough time for each person in the circle to give shape and form to the events described in their own imagination. It is not stretching a point to say that you could almost see the Spirit of Jonathan Corporation appearing in the open space.

Such telling of the tale is by no means restricted to shipyards. At the other end of the spectrum (or at least in a very different place) is the Internal Revenue Service. For a period of a year or so, I had the pleasure of working with the Appeals Division. Parenthetically, I must say that I never quite got over that rush of adrenalin when the phone would ring with the IRS at the other end. Be that as it may, you need to know that the Appeals Division is in many respects the elite corps of the Service. Their function is to work out agreements between the taxpayer and the Government which is impartial and fair to both. The Appeals Officers are a superbly trained, dedicated crew who will carry as many as three earned degrees and/or certification (MBA, JD and CPA) along with years of experience. Despite, or maybe because of this superb academic and experiential background, I found some superb storytellers. Now to be sure, you had to know (or in my case learn) some little bit about tax law in order to keep up, but when a Senior Officer sat in the company of his peers with some junior officers in attendance, and told how it was that they brought some corporate giant to the point of agreement, it was a lot better than any soap opera.

What particularly intrigued me was how unconscious this whole activity was. When questioned, the best "storytellers" did not seem to attach any particular importance to what they did, and indeed, one senior officer expressed genuine surprise after a weekend training session with new Officers — that it seemed that the most meaningful thing he had done for the new folks was to tell the story. His only complaint was that they kept him up to 2:00 and 3:00 o'clock in the morning doing just that. To check out his perception, I made a point of interviewing some of the younger Appeals Officers who had been present, and their comments were, I thought, instructive. To a person, they reported that most of the formal material presented was a waste of time (regulations and procedures) which either they already knew or could easily find out in the appropriate manuals. What they really got was that sense (Spirit) of being an Appeals Officer which came though after the formal sessions and late into the night.

There is a danger, however, in the telling of these tales, for it may appear to the listeners that the only way things may be done is in the manner prescribed. Thus in the shipyard, the story of the Speer offers a powerful re-presentation of the Spirit of Jonathan at work, but it would be a tragic mistake for the assembled group to approach the new job in exactly the same way that things were done on the Speer, down to the last technical detail. By the same token, the young Appeals Officers can benefit greatly from the encounter with the senior officer's story to the extent that they experience a sense of excellence and dedication that is fundamental to the job. However, they will assuredly get in trouble should they approach the work in detail as their senior had. These statements may appear so obvious as to be gratuitous, but the sad truth of the matter is that such literal application will often occur, and over time, the results are disastrous. When mythos is perceived through the eyes of literalism, its power for communication is radically reduced and ultimately destroyed.

Literalism and the End of Mythos   To the extent that Mythos truly captures the Spirit of an organization, and re-presents in living color what it means to live in the organization, it is no wonder that people take these stories quite seriously. For as the Spirit of the organization is integral to the self-understanding of the individual (part of their life) so mythos, as the vehicle of both, is critical. To change the story is to change life, and that can be very unsettling indeed. Hence there is an understandable effort to "freeze" mythos in every detail. That is literalism, which will eventually squeeze the life out of mythos, and render a once powerful story into a meaningless shadow of its former self.

Under ordinary circumstances, the organization doesn't pay too much attention to the stories it tells. They are, after all, just "war stories" by whatever name. However, over time, as those stories become increasingly familiar, and well worn by

26

constant retelling, their presence and form is a comfort to the members and constitutes an expected part of their life. As I noted in the previous section, eventually it becomes important to the organization that the right stories be told in the right way. That in itself is no great issue, but it is not without a cost. In more flexible form, the organizational story (mythos) provides an outlet to creativity and innovation. There is enough openness to allow for different ways of looking at things which enables the organization to adapt to changing circumstances. However, at such times when the organizational life is threatened, precise wording becomes more and more of an issue. In older organizations, where the body of mythos is large and complex, this can lead to some very interesting and destructive results. The classical example of this is the phenomenon of fundamentalism in religious bodies. Stressed by an alien world that seemed to be casting doubt on the validity of the self-understanding as expressed by Scripture, the response on the part of the believers was to place more and more weight on the literal word of the text. In a situation where all seemed to be changing, it became more and more important to be aware of what God said (what Spirit was really about), and it was no small comfort to know that the "Word of God" was all carefully recorded in literal detail in a book, and therefore, always available when need arose.

It is very easy, and perhaps understandable, to treat the response of the religious fundamentalist lightly (especially if we do not happen to be fundamentalists), but to do so is to miss the powerful dynamics represented by the response, and the cost that is incurred. For the fundamentalist, certainty and knowledge are now reduced to the objective, handy form of the printed page.[16] Thus we find the fundamentalists seeking to coerce the world at large into conformity with their story, as has been the case in Iran through the efforts of Islamic fundamentalists. Such coercion is painful to them, as it is awkward for the rest of us. But failing that effort to make the world fit "their story," the only possible alternative is to withdraw from the world. This of

---

[16] It is interesting to note that in responding to the challenge of positivistic science, the fundamentalist ends up adopting the strategy of the enemy. If truth can only exist in objective, palpable form, the fundamentalist is ready, for the truth of life is now objectively stated on the printed page of scripture.) As life moves along its evolutionary journey, the presence of such certainty is enormously useful; it guarantees stability and the preservation of life as it has come to be known. The cost, however, is not inconsiderable, for boxed within such a rigid story, each and every twist and turn in the environment at large constitutes a threat and a danger. This means that ever greater efforts will be made to resist such change. A major example is the Christian fundamentalist's reaction to evolutionary theory being taught in the schools. As strange as it may seem to the rest of us, this is not a trivial issue, nor can it be dealt with on a rational basis, for the shared foundation of rationality (a common mythos) does not exist.

course is done, and small isolated communities are established within which the world may be made to look as the story says that it should. There is no small comfort in these little communities, but there can also be something very deadening about them too, and the members are progressively cut off from the normal commerce of human existence. At this point, the story of the organization, which originated as a statement about meaningful life in the world, now becomes the occasion for the denial of the world at large.

It might be assumed from what I have said above, that the fundamentalist represents a special case of aberrant religious behavior. That unfortunately is not the situation, for in as much as each organization has its own mythos, all organizations are susceptible to the dangers of literalism. In fact, organizations do not have to be either of great size or age in order to fall prey.

Several years ago, for example, I was asked to create a senior level executive development program for a major national health care institution. The program by design was small, and limited to individuals who had demonstrated outstanding competence to date and were ready to take on large, new responsibility. The objective of the program was to prepare them for their task.[17]. The design of the program was unique in that there was no curriculum. I felt that our participants, most of whom had several advanced degrees, did not need yet another academic experience. What they did need was an opportunity to explore the world of health care in a way that granted them a maximum degree of freedom, and also required them to take full responsibility for the freedom they exercised. This last point, regarding the responsible use of freedom, was critical, for in my experience, the point where many senior executives fell apart came when they suddenly recognized that nobody was there to tell them what to do, and they experienced what I called Freedom Shock. Thus Freedom Shock was engineered right into the program by offering the participants two years and many resources, with the sole requirement being that they identify some major health care system issues and do something substantive for their resolution. "Substantive" could mean anything from drafting legislation (we had access to Capitol Hill), sponsoring a conference, or even writing a book. Beyond that, it was all open space. The only formalization of the program existed in a very brief prospectus which I had drafted for purposes of recruitment and to justify the expenditure of funds.

---

[17] The institution was the Veterans Administration which is the largest single provider of health care in the United States. My "students" were aimed not only for senior positions within the VA but elsewhere in the industry, and came with such backgrounds as deans of schools, head of congressional relations for a large federal agency.

After the program had been in operation for only a few months, certain bureaucratic rumbles were felt which suggested that the effort might be in some jeopardy. This was no small consideration for the participants, for all of them had left other jobs with no guarantee of return, and some had sold their homes and moved their families across the country. All of this produced another element of Freedom Shock which was somewhat in excess of what I had intended. The result was a large amount of anxiety which manifested itself in a variety of ways culminating in a loud and rancorous meeting in which the Scholars, as they were known, took me to task for failure to manage the program effectively. The fact that I had absolutely no control over the bureaucratic "rumble" made no difference, for the truth of the matter was that Freedom Shock was getting the better of everyone. What they really wanted to know was — what they should do? After we had gone around on that one several times, and the Scholars became aware that I really believed in taking personal responsibility for one's freedom, a most remarkable thing occurred. One of the Scholars left the room and returned with a copy of the program prospectus, and began to quote passages from it line by line, as though that booklet offered the specific direction as to what should be done, when and how. I remained silent, but when pushed said, "Well, I wrote that booklet in two hours between planes. That was a first edition, and if you would like to write another, do it. There are no rules except as you make them." That almost ended the program right there, but the point I am trying to make with this story is that any organization, even (or perhaps especially) a very young organization, when it is under duress will reach out for something that looks like the Story, and then grab on to it in literal detail. Fundamentalism is not an affliction reserved only for small religious sects, it is available to us all.

Literalism, which seeks to save mythos, in fact destroys it. For mythos, like life, exists primarily in the process, and not in the artifacts created along the way. As each form appears, it contributes its meaning, and then must be cast aside in order that new (or renewed) meaning may appear in the Open Space. In the final analysis, mythos manifests Spirit not by what it says, but in the silence, and for that reason, mythos must be broken to be made whole.

The Breaking of Mythos The breaking of mythos is necessitated by the fact that our language is inevitably less than potent when it comes to speaking of really important things. This is simply an acknowledgement of an everyday experience when we seek to put into words that which goes beyond our verbal capacity.[18] For example, should we attempt to describe the true nature of someone we love, we often become "tongue tied." Harry Chapin describes this condition rather well in his song, "A Better Place to Be." When the hero first met the heroine he "stuttered like a school boy, and stammered out some words." Stuttering and stammering is what occurs when the unspeakable tries to gain expression. What usually happens next is that we make a number of attempts at expression, even though each one seems much less than adequate.

The words might go like this (especially if we were a "romantic type")."My beloved is like the north star, constant and bright." But that doesn't seem right, so we take another stab at it. Out comes something like, "No, she is like the sun which warms me all the day through." That doesn't quite do it, so we go off on a different tack with a reference to her physical appearance, "Her eyes are like limpid pools." and so on. It may appear that we are failing, and for sure there is a feeling of frustration, but in fact we are beginning to communicate at a level beyond the literal words. The pattern we employ is instructive, for what we do is make a statement, and then just as it has been uttered, we take it back, or break it. She is like the North Star, not like the North Star, like the Sun, not like the Sun and so forth. What happens is that we take a particular image, push it just as far as it will go, until we have all but drained it of meaning. Then at the last moment we throw it away, pick up another image, and repeat the process.

Using this succession of images in a state-break pattern, we effectively create a pool of meaning, an open space, in which (if we are any good) the reality of our beloved appears. But note that the reality of the beloved appears not in the statement, but rather in the moment when the statement is withdrawn. Thus our listener is sent in a direction we want to utilize (North Starness), but before that image can be taken as a literal statement, it is broken. Obviously, the literal meaning of our statement would do us no good, and indeed it would actually inhibit the possibility of communicating what was in our mind. Reduced to rather an absurd level, we could scarcely elicit in the mind of our listener the subtle beauty of our beloved, if the listener were busy getting out his sexton in order to take a directional sighting. Literalism here, as elsewhere, is an impediment to the manifestation of Spirit.

---

[18] The same may be said for our nonverbal capacity, but all of that is rather difficult to represent on the printed page.

The effective breaking of mythos occurs when those responsible for the tale consciously and intentionally break it at the peak of its expressive power. Just as one story seems to perfectly express the Spirit and intention of the organization, a new one appears to overwhelm and extend the prior version, and thereby drive the expression of Spirit in new directions, to new heights. Under these circumstances, the experience is one of being on a "roll" as opposed to the fitful and shattering experience when mythos is destroyed by literalism.

An example of this sort of intentional "breaking" occurs when a master teller of jokes weaves his magic and drives his listeners to a level of mirth where catching the next breath seems almost impossible. The "roll of laughter" is not created by telling one joke alone, but rather in the careful (artful) sequencing of jokes so that just as the first has achieved its full impact, the second is already on the way. By varying the content and intensity of each joke, and beginning the telling of the next one at precisely the right moment, the teller maintains careful control over the quality, level and power of Spirit. The net effect is that the crowd is left gasping for breath and tears run down the cheeks.

Telling jokes may not appear to be appropriate to the serious business of handling the organizational mythos, although the truth of the matter is that mythos often appears in the form of humor, and in fact the organizational jokster can be enormously helpful to the growth of Spirit. But all of that aside, the methodology of the humorist is very much to the point, and constitutes an essential tool for leadership. Rather than waiting for the environment to break some particular version, effective leadership moves intentionally to shatter the old story, thereby creating the Open Space in which Spirit may transform into something new and more powerful. Obviously this is delicate business, and not to be entered into lightly, but done well, the Spirit is released.

Russell Ackoff tells a story which well illustrates this approach.[19] It seems that Ackoff was doing some work for Bell Labs. As Ackoff walked in the door, the client said he was terribly sorry, but that the director of the labs had just called a meeting and everybody was expected to attend. However, should Ackoff want to come to the meeting, he was welcome to do so, but he must remain inconspicuous and pretend that he was a new employee. As far as the subject matter of the meeting, nobody knew, it

---

[19] I have only heard Dr. Ackoff tell this story, and whether or not he has written it down somewhere, I don't know.

was just "a word from on high" that attendance was required coupled with the implication that the occasion was important, serious and perhaps ominous.

Ackoff and his client left the office and joined the stream of people heading towards the large auditorium. It was quickly apparent that everybody was there or arriving very quickly. It was equally apparent that nobody had the faintest idea of what was about to happen. Conversation was muted, and the atmosphere verged on being thick. At precisely the moment that the meeting was scheduled to begin, silence descended over the rear of the hall, and spread forward in the wake of the director, who strode purposefully down the center isle, looking neither to the right nor to the left. The physical appearance of the director did nothing to dispel the tension, and Ackoff relates that the face of the man looked like one who stood at the edge of war, or worse. When the director reached the front of the auditorium, he turned to stand in front of the podium. Gripping the sides with each hand, he stared down for a moment, his face a dark cloud. The moment lengthened, and the silence intensified. Just as it seemed no longer bearable, the director raised his head and looked directly at his audience. In slow measured tones he said, "Gentlemen, the Bell System was destroyed this morning, and our task is to build it totally anew." He paused for a moment, and then continued before the inevitable "buts" could even form on the lips of his startled listeners. "For the next year, we will assume nothing from the prior system. We will be guided only by an intent to create excellent communications within the limits of technical possibility. We will start now." And he left.

What happened next is now a matter of history, for in the Open Space created by the conscious breaking of the old story there emerged a number of wonderful ideas which we now take as common place, for example the "Touch-Tone" phone.

It is significant that the director of Bell Labs did not wait until the old story of the laboratory had lost all of its punch. Indeed, from all I can tell, the Lab at that point was doing good work, and its story was as strong as ever. A less courageous or less knowledgeable leader might well have been tempted to wait until things were going down hill. Or even worse, might have attempted to freeze things just as they were. In fact, the leader acted at the decisive moment to break the old story (the phone system as it was, was destroyed) and powerfully invite those in his charge out into Open Space that freed their Spirit to pursue fulfillment in a host of new areas.

Mythos Broken by Itself   Not all organizations are lucky enough to have leaders like the director of Bell Labs. And even such outstanding leaders may not always function with such decisive courage. For this reason, it is fortunate that mythos may be broken in yet another way, through an internalized self-destruct mechanism which is constantly pushing the story beyond any particular limited, finite mode of expression. When mythos comes "equipped" with such a self-destruct device, the organization discovers that its own story is perpetually driving (leading) the Spirit to new and more powerful expressions of itself. In a way, the organization is then on "auto-pilot." This does not mean that there is no role for leadership, for even the organization on "auto-pilot" needs fine tuning and midcourse corrections. The "auto-pilot," however, serves a much needed function when, for whatever reason, leadership is incapacitated.

It may occur, for example, that the leader will become so invested in a particular version of a story that he or she no longer has the ability to put that one down, and move on to the creation of something new. At that point, the organization will lie dead in the water, waiting for literalism to do its work or for the leader to eventually understand that the old story is no longer functional. In either event, the growth of Spirit is retarded, and may even be derailed. This "self destruct" device is an integral part of the story which honors or institutionalizes the process of breaking.

For example, part of the mythos of the Peace Corps is the "Five-Year Rule" which states that no individual will serve more than five years either as a volunteer or staff.[20] Concretely, this rule requires a constant turn over of personnel, which means that in essence the "story" is in an on going state of evolution. Managers from other parts of the government or the private sector perceive the rule with some dismay, for it seems to destroy organizational memory and play havoc with coherence. Both of these perceptions are correct, but my experience as an associate director in the Peace Corps led me to believe that the advantage gained outweighs whatever liabilities, for it has meant that the essential Spirit of the organization is always being cut loose in order to appear in different and more useful ways. The fact that the Peace Corps has managed to survive through widely disparate political administrations, some of which were overtly hostile to the organization, is attributable in no small part to this strange rule. It has also meant that no director (leader) has ever, or will ever be able to "freeze" the story in a particular form, no matter how elegant that form might be.

The Peace Corps is not alone in possessing such a self destruct device; a similar mechanism is to be found in our national story as represented by the Constitution which requires a changeover of office holders every two, four, or six years. There are of course those who find this passage unsettling, and who would prefer to maintain

---

[20] The actual rule is a little more complicated, but this statement will do for our purposes.

some old story by what ever name (New Deal, Fair Deal, New Frontier). But the story itself as we experience it will not permit such rigidity. This has meant a continuing evolution (transformation) of our national Spirit, mercifully spared the total dissolution which periodically occurs among people who's story does not permit such renewal, for example, in dictatorships.

A classic case of the presence and operation of the "self-destruct device" appears in the mythos of the Christian organization. At the center of the christian story is a tale of one man (Jesus) who fulfills his destiny by living, dying on a cross, and then according to the tale, being resurrected. Leaving aside all considerations of historicity, which have no place in the understanding of mythos, it is apparent that the central tale of christianity is constantly driving towards Open Space and renewal. To be sure, there are those who would see this story primarily in terms of the philosophical statements, ethical precepts or daily activities of this man, but all of that is really useful only to set the stage. Each of these elements, and all of them collectively serve to garner the attention of those who hear this tale. In short, they make it real because on some level it is familiar, and seems to ring true to life. But that is just the start, for even as the hearer (believer) becomes involved in the story, it turns out that the whole point is not some new philosophical or ethical system, but rather death on a cross.[21] The story itself then breaks itself, and drives the believer into the open space wherein the Spirit may once more be reconfigured and transformed.

Over the ages, the Church, as institution, has often sought to freeze the story and confine the believers to one true way. Yet for all of these efforts, which at times have become bloody and violent, as in the Spanish Inquisition, the essential story continues to drive onwards towards renewal. The Achilles heel of the Church is in fact its salvation, for each Sunday it "celebrates the Mass" which is quite simply the re-presentation of the life, death, and resurrection of the central hero. Those who would stop the story, eliminate the change, and thereby stay the course of the Spirit in transformation discover that it is the story itself which is constantly opening the door to the new.

In Judaism there is a similar occurrence represented in part by the total sweep of the Torah. Those who understand Torah to mean simply "law" are literally correct, but if it is law, it is a living law. More accurately it is the story of the Spirit of God

---

[21] As a matter of fact, there is very little of the recorded thoughts of Jesus as we have them in the New Testament, which may not be found in whole or in part in the sacred literature of Israel.

leading his people on a journey towards fulfillment. Each time people thought they had arrived, the Spirit moved on and required some new effort, some new way of being, and the End (*telos*) is still ahead.

In addition to the Torah, the mythos of Israel also contains the Prophets, the collected words of a most unlikely and uncomfortable crew. It is common to view the words of the Prophets only in terms of condemnation for sins past. And indeed, there is no little amount of that, but the real prophetic yardstick is not so much the abrogated standards of the past, but rather the unfulfilled potential of the future. In a word, the prophets call on the people of Israel to become everything that they could be, and point out the difference between what they are, and what they might become. From this perspective they condemn present action, and just as the people of Israel find themselves getting comfortable with the way things are, the prophets break the mold and goad them towards the fulfillment of their destiny.

In many ways, the Prophets of Israel are the prototypical organizational rebels. They speak from within the organization, out of love for the organization, but always with the sense that the organization and those who own it, has yet to fulfill its potential. A unique thing about Israel (and also Christendom) is that the words and person of the prophets have been internalized within the mythos. So it is that mythos for both of those Organizations is constantly ill at ease with the way things are, and always open in principle to some new expression of Spirit.

To conclude this part of our discussion, I would only note that the breaking of mythos, whether by the leader, or through some internal self-destruct device, is essential to the process whereby mythos becomes the medium or mechanism through which Spirit in the organization is imaged in the course of transformation. At the moment of breaking, Spirit is re-presented in open space, unconstrained by the barriers of literalism, and ready to continue the journey.

The Renewal of Mythos To the extent that mythos is alive and well in the organization, those who participate in that organization will perceive the moment of breaking as a real moment of release. Their desires for the fulfillment of their Spirit will be acknowledged and encouraged. But they will also experience the moment of breaking as fearful, for if the story has been a good one, they will once again have encountered the awesome open spaces through which the organization has moved. All of which means that the life cycle of mythos cannot end with breaking. Mythos completes its life cycle in renewal. Precisely what form the "renewed mythos" will take depends in large part on where the organization is in its own transformational

35

journey. But regardless of form, the effect will be to infuse mythos with new meaning which has been gathered (perceived) during the time of breaking under the conditions of open space. Essentially what occurs is that, as the individuals participate in the story and its breaking, they discover that Spirit has been freed to explore new possibilities, as for example in Bell Labs. The experience of exploration and the new possibilities discovered are now added to the story and become part of mythos. Thus it may turn out that the actual form of the story (mythos) is relatively unchanged, only now (post breaking) it is perceived as being much broader and deeper.

For the people in Bell Labs it may be presumed that their basic story remained the same after the meeting in the auditorium. Should someone ask, "What is it like around this place?" the answer which might emerge from the common mythos would go something like, "We do research, and some very basic research." The answer would probably not be much different than before. But now there is an added dimension, which might or might not be mentioned, to the effect that our research carries us right up to the edge of things, even to the point of imagining that the system we had always taken for granted is no longer in existence. Same old story, but with profound new meaning.

Given a different organization in a different time and place the effective change in the form of mythos may be infinitely greater. For example, in the on going saga of AT&T, we have lived through the old story when they were "the phone company." That story, as we know, was shattered along with an "interim tale" they told about being the "knowledge people." As of the moment, they are "reaching out," which says basically they have gone back to the drawing boards. What the new story will be neither we nor they have any way of knowing. But we may be sure that however it turns out, it must acknowledge the truly significant past of the organization while simultaneously establishing the direction for Spirit in its new manifestation. In the event that they do not make it, their mythos, in all of its forms, will simply add to the pile of detritus composed of ancient tales from another age. In any event, the mythos of AT&T will continue in its unique function to image Spirit either as a living reality or an historic curiosity.

THE ROLE OF MYTHOS: SUMMARY

The role of mythos relative to the transformation of Spirit is threefold. In the first place, mythos is the record of transformation. As record, mythos maintains the memory of past transformative events in the life of the organization. In this role, mythos formally appears as "history" with a listing of the significant happenings and personages. But the intent of mythos is not just to talk about what transpired, but rather to create the conditions under which those prior journeys of Spirit may be experienced. The importance of mythos in this role lies in the fact that to the extent the organization and its members have experienced the prior transformations, they will be relatively more prepared to deal with future transformations. While no transformation is without pain or fear, it is also true that having some prior knowledge of, and experience with the process is tremendously helpful in terms of knowing what to expect.

The second role of mythos is as the agent of transformation. By virtue of the fact that mythos is constantly in the process of being broken (or breaking itself), it is present in the consciousness of the organization as an uneasy phenomenon. Just as everybody has become accustomed to the tale, it shifts and exposes some new area of meaning. This ongoing shifting continually creates new open spaces which invite the Spirit of the organization to consider new forms of expression (manifestation). The organization may or may not accept this invitation, but the fact of its existence keeps the possibility of new transformations always in view. Mythos, therefore, is an unsettling reality in the life of any organization, and it is not surprising that organizations will attempt to tame mythos by "cleaning up" the story, and making it appear that the "final tale" has been told. To the extent that the organization is successful in this effort, the final tale will in fact have been told, and the organization will be well on the way to extinction.

Lastly, mythos may be transformative itself. This occurs in the midst of the process of transformation, when events pass with such rapidity and power that they appear to exist out of time, or more exactly, they define time. Clock time (Greek *chronos*) is replaced by *kairos* or meaning-filled time, which in turn defines time for the organization. Such moments appear as the "great divide" against which all other happenings are judged as in "before the merger" and "after the merger," "before Christ" and "after Christ," "before Moses" and "after Moses," "before divestiture" and "after divestiture."

At transformative moments the happening is the story and the story is the happening, and there can be little if any separation between the two. Transformation and mythos are united, but only momentarily.

MYTHOS, LITURGY AND COVENANT

When mythos is deeply and continuously integrated into the life of a people, that is liturgy. Under optimal circumstances there is no distinction, for the story (mythos) and what the people do everyday is equivalent. Under these conditions, the Spirit of a people (an organization) is coherent and powerful, accomplishing the tasks at hand with high levels of effectiveness. Each moment of the day and all aspects of the environment (all human time and space) tell the tale and do the job.

The emergence of liturgy as the custodian of time and space, and the shaper of Spirit may appear as an unconscious event, outside of our normal awareness. However, as we noted previously, the creation of liturgy can also be a highly intentional undertaking. To the extent that we would exercise responsibility for the shape and effective flow of Spirit, such conscious "liturgy-making" is much to be desired.

If the raw ingredient of liturgy is mythos, the elements for liturgy-making are form and structure. Form is the way we do things, as in the phrase "that is good form." Structure is the delineated field of operation within which things get done. To be effective, both form and structure should accord with and be expressive of the essential story — which is in turn, the image and channel of Spirit.

The real purpose of form and structure is to make explicit and almost automatic, the proper flow of Spirit. Thus when we speak of organizational form and structure, we are talking about those elements which take care of ordinary business, and remind us how things ought to be done. We structure the corporate year in terms of finances, planning and production; and within that structure, we expect that people will observe a certain form. Thus IBM does its planning in a way that seems good form to IBM, and so with AT&T, and the corner grocery store. By doing all of this, we effectively create the unique time-space sense for any particular organization.

At some point in the life of an organization this special sense of time and space, form and structure, will be given formal verbal expression. Initially, this expression will be very sparce, limited to some general agreement on how things ought to get done around here. Over time, the expression will become more detailed, eventually constituting a sort of rule book for liturgy, otherwise known as policy and proceedure manuals, tables of organization, and the like. This rule book for liturgy is what I call the Organizational Covenant. (See Chapter VI)

The covenant is very useful for establishing an orderly approach to business in the life of an organization. But it can also become inordinately restrictive, and instead of making life meaningful, it becomes stultifying and crushing. At such a time, it is necessary to break the covenant, and allow Spirit to flow in new directions, creating new forms — which is what transformation is all about.

In the amalgam of liturgy and life, time and space are shaped to conform to the nature of the Spirit, while Spirit is molded by the special liturgical time and space. We in the West might appear to have thrown all that off, and in some sense gone beyond the constraints of liturgy. At least it is certain that we have moved beyond the liturgical expressions of Christendom, except in a few residual areas. We still celebrate Christmas, but it is scarcely the Christmas of classical Christianity.

This move on our part represents a good news/bad news situation. To the extent that we are no longer a part of the liturgy-life constellation of classical Western Christianity, we have been freed to experience (think about) time and space, and what goes on there — in some very different ways. Our time-space is increasingly that of the quantum and deep space described by Einstein, Heisenberg et al., as opposed to the time-space of Newton and before him, Copernicus. By the same token, we are beginning to perceive the world less in terms of Christian time-space as opposed to all others (the "saved and the heathen"), but now in terms of the unity all time-space in the family of man, linked by the commonality of consciousness.

But there is bad news too. As we have moved out from the particular liturgy of Christianity, our Spirit, sense of meaning, self-understanding (collective and individual) has become more diffuse and less focused. This has yielded high levels of anxiety, potential for meaninglessness and loss of direction. There are those, who perceiving these conditions, recommend a return to the old liturgy on the grounds that we are a "Christian nation," and therefore should have prayer (Christian prayer) in the schools and the like. Fortunately or unfortunately, we are no longer a "Christian nation," nor is there any likelihood that we ever will be again. We are an emerging planetary society, living in the age of "parenthesis" (Naisbitt), with all the richness and confusion that implies. We stand in the Open Space.

However, just because one expression of liturgy is no longer binding (powerful), this does not mean that liturgy itself is not valid, present or useful. In fact, liturgy is alive and well, and continues to function wherever human Spirit is coherent and strong. Indeed, powerful organizations all have effective liturgies — expressed through planning cycles, production programs and the daily round of corporate (organizational) life. Liturgy is, as it has always been, — the union of mythos with real life experience. Liturgy is what the people do.

POSTSCRIPT

That there are many liturgies at the moment is not surprising. Whether or not there shall ever be one liturgy for all of mankind remains to be seen. But if we are ever to realize the full power of our common humanity, a common liturgy will be essential. The opportunity before us is perhaps different than we as a species have ever confronted before. For it lies within our power to consciously and intentionally create our liturgy and our life. The attendant risks are enormous, for the power involved is immense. Given the prior history of mankind, it is quite likely that the few will seek to gain control over the many, at the risk of all. Yet we cannot remove the risk; liturgy comes with the territory, our planet and our humanity. This risk may be mitigated to the extent that the many (all of us) become aware of the power and operation of liturgy, so that the few cannot darkly create a world for their own ends. But the risk remains, and the choice is ours.

Chapter III

JOURNEY OF THE SPIRIT
In Organizations

If mythos provides the means to image Spirit in its passage, it is now appropriate to ask, What's the Story? What happens to Spirit as it becomes manifest in the forms of everyday life, and then transforms into something new? The question, of course, is as old as man, for it is but another way of asking "Who are we?", "Where did we come from?" and "How is it all going to turn out?" In a different slower time, the relevance of the question was difficult to perceive, for who we were, are, and will be, seemed pretty much the same thing. However, in the days of ready, fire, aim under the conditions of "Raplexity," such passive certainty no longer seems possible. And what was an abstruse, metaphysical issue, best left to the philosophers and theologians, is now of immediate concern to anybody who would take responsibility for themselves, their organizations, and the world in which we live.

It would be rank presumption for me to suggest that what follows is the story, or even a definitive version of the story. It is in fact my story, albeit composed of many pieces drawn from the stories of others.[22] Whether or not this story becomes your story, in the sense that it provides a useful and effective means for understanding and facilitating the Journey of Spirit, remains to be seen. Where it is useful, I invite your appropriation, but where it misses the mark, I would encourage you to create your own. Stories are rather like maps; not much in themselves, but very helpful when crossing strange territories. Of course, we must always remember that the map is not the territory, and when the map and the territory fail to agree, we probably need a new

---

[22] The Story presented here is essentially variations on a theme established by the Great Chain of Being, and the ancient chakras. As such it is truly an image of Spirit derived from some of man's oldest myths. The nomenclature for the chakras vary, but I am indebted to Ken Wilbur (Up From Eden, Anchor/Doubleday Press, 1981, pg 8) for the basic form used in Chapter VI. The schema here in Chapter III evolved as an attempt to articulate organizational analogues to the individual levels of being.

map. But even an old map can be useful, for it brings to mind the differences between what we once saw, and the way things are now.

The Journey of Spirit may be described in a series of stages which constitute the course of transformation. Each stage indicates some different quality or mode of that Spirit, which becomes manifest in appropriate activities and forms.

The movement at first (from the bottom of the figure to the center line) indicates a passage from very high, but diffuse Spirit towards increasing specificity and concreteness.[23] The journey starts with . . .

OUT OF THE DEPTHS At the genesis of every organization there was a moment when some individual or, at most, some very small group of individuals had what amounts to the Ah-Ha experience . . . that sense that "something" might be done, and the controlling idea was born. How it got there and precisely what it might mean were not clear at the time. But the presence and energy of the thought were undeniable. This is the creative moment when something emerges

Inspired
InterActive
ProActive
Responsive
ReActive
****
Information/Data
Language
Understanding
Vision
Out of the Depths

out of nothing — it appears as it were, from Out of the Depths. One might think of

---

[23] The general schema here was suggested by the work of Arthur Young in "The Reflexive Universe",(Delacort Press , 1977) who described the evolution of the universe as a movement from high Energy "down" to earthy concreteness, and then back "up" to High Energy. Young's graphics are different than mine, but the idea is very similar. The specific terminology employed here [out of the depths, vision etc] comes in large part from the work of Will Lewis. I am not aware that Lewis has published his work, but I wish to thank him for the thoughts he has shared with me. The content, however, is drawn from my own observations. Above the line [Re-Active etc.], the terminology was suggested by the work of Frank Burns and Linda Nelson as published in "High Performing Programing: A Framework for Transforming Organizations" which appears in "Transforming Work", John Adams ed., Miles River Press, 1984.

Land, when the mere possibility of an "instant camera" popped into mind or a thousand other emergent moments when the pot began to boil. At the instant, the originator may not know precisely what to do, and where it all might lead, but the thing is definitely there . . . hot, powerful and moving . . . the great "I got it." As the moment cools it may, if fortune smiles, take increasing shape as a . . .

VISION Literally, a picture or image of what all of this might mean.[24] In color, shape and form, the idea is embodied in some descriptive way. A story is told, images are called forth. The Vision grows out of the world around it as those who have experienced that sense From the Depths range far and wide to discover new and more powerful means of expression. Rivers describe flow, mountains depict strength, the soaring eagle sketches the flight of freedom, and a small child denotes opportunity.

But the Vision is not just clothed in the garments of the world, the vision also reaches out to shape, form and change that world. Powerful Visions are inclusive, they gather all to themselves, and see everything from their point of view. The world is interpreted and becomes a different place in the power of the Vision, and those possessed of (and by) the Vision presume that world to be their own, and in some real way, part of themselves. Of course those with a different Vision may disagree, for Vision, paradoxically, is often blind. Vision thus has the potential to arm, protect and possibly blind, but in any event, make comfortable, those who come to share in it, for they will "know" at a level passing cognitive knowledge, that they are centered in some positive "truth."

The emergent thought from Out of the Depths loses some little of its initial energy, but gains specificity so that it might be shared. As a picture it is sketchy and quickly changing, but it is substantial enough that others who are open to that kind of representation, may participate. With Vision, the nascent organization expands its power base as sympathetic individuals are brought within the developing energy field. What the Vision may lack in concreteness, it more than makes up for in pure raw power. Nevertheless, before things can really start to happen, a certain ordering is required, a rational supplied, which emerges at the next phase. . .

---

[24] Present day brain/mind research will tell us that what is occurring here represents typical right brain activity, but we do not need such research to support the observation, for examples may be found through out history. In ancient Israel, the prophet Isaiah [Isaiah 66] saw "a new heaven and a new earth where the wolf and the lamb shall eat together." A compelling vision, but pretty short in the details of implementation. Nevertheless that is where things start.

UNDERSTANDING   With Understanding, the Vision assumes logical form. The drive and power which appeared previously only as images are now reduced to a rational format. Shape is measured, force is calibrated, products and goals are specified. The restrictions of time and space are recognized and dealt with. Whereas Visions may typically ignore the conditions of the everyday world and present a view in which everything is possible, everywhere, and all at once . . . the workaday world doesn't operate that way. Resources must be obtained before they are used. Markets must be developed before products may be sold. Linear thinking must be applied in order for that which emerged Out of the Depths to move from Vision to the real world. The possibility of such expression comes through the creation of. . .

LANGUAGE[25] Now to be sure, all organizations appear to be speaking in the language of whatever people they are a part . . . but in addition to that, organizations quickly develop a special language peculiar to themselves in which their Understanding, Vision and sense from Out of the Depths may be expressed. In time, this language may pass into general usage so that now we do not make "copies" but rather Xeroxes. Initially, though, all of that was "special-speak," the unique mode of expression of the Xerox Corporation. The creation of this language is a necessary further step along the road to actualization, as Spirit moves from primal thought to the point where something REALLY happens.

The key is naming. When something is named, it is literally called into existence as a conscious element in the life of the organization. Before something had a name — it wasn't, at least as far as that organization was concerned. Many items of concern to the organization already have names given by the larger culture, but even here, those generic names must be tailored and defined to meet the needs of the particular organization. Thus "everybody" has a president — but nobody has a president just like we do; the reality of " our president" becomes clear only in the context of "our vision" and "our understanding." There are also special names which

---

[25] Here we are faced with the old chicken and egg question of which comes first, logic or language, or is it the logic of language and the language of logic ? The truth would seem to be that each works against the other, both as a precondition and as a consequent. What I can say, I can logically structure, but at the same time, my logical structures further my capacity to speak, and thus "grows" language. The reader interested in pursuing these interesting, important and knotty questions might wish to consult "The Philosophy of Symbolic Forms" - Vol I on Language by Ernst Cassirer, Yale, 1955, "Philosophy in a New Key" by Susanne Langer, Harvard Univ. Press, 1982, and also "On the Way to Language" by Martin Heidegger, Harper and Row, 1971. But for our purposes here, all that discussion, while interesting is not essential, for what I have in mind is that special language which all organizations create.

are created de novo to designate those realities which are unique to "us" and thereby separate "us" from the rest of the world. More often than not, these "special names" refer to some product or process that is ours alone such as "Xerox," "hydramatic," "fluid-drive," and "PC." There are also names for particular roles that may be played within the organization: expeditor, facilitator, monitor, scraper, scrubber, oiler and the like. Taken out of context, these names don't make much sense, but in the context of the organization, they not only make sense — they in many ways make the organization. Until you know the names (speak the language) you really can not know the organization in terms of its unique sense of Out of the Depths, Vision and Understanding. Having a name is an essential part of being real.[26] Finally, it is through the names/language that the organization may identify and talk about those discrete aspects, the little things, of its world that are of particular concern to it, which must be measured and collected in order to do business, and keep track of what business is being done. Those "little things" are the. . .

INFORMATION AND DATA   by which progress is measured, plans made and changed. It is important to notice that Data and Information really lie at the end of the line, they become comprehensible only in the context of a particular Language, structured by a special Understanding, which in turn articulates a peculiar Vision. Data and Information by themselves are just meaningless. But at the same time, both are absolutely essential if the organizational Spirit is going to pass from the level of "great idea" to something that "really happened." Before we pass the great divide separating POTENTIAL from ACTUAL, it would be well to pause for a moment to reflect upon the odyssey to date. First, we should note the obvious — nothing has really happened yet — at least as the world would see it. All that has occurred, has occurred under the heading of "getting ready," as the Spirit proceeded from high levels of rather diffuse energy down to something quite specific. Nevertheless, each phase is incredibly important for the future life of the organization in the real world, if only because the process has shaped and focused Spirit so that it may hit the world in a powerful and concrete way.

---

[26] The business of names and naming has been subject of intense study by anthropologists and a variety of others for a long time. In so called primitive societies, to know the name is tantamount to knowing and in many ways, possessing, the person. In ancient Israel, for example, Johs. Pedersen says that, "To know the name of a man is the same as to know his essence" ("Israel; Its Life and Culture" Oxford University Press, 1959, page 244).

We might also note that at each level, Spirit appeared in a unique and different way. While it is true that every level is connected to, and in a sense "contains" the preceding level (Understanding is the rationalization of Vision), it is also true that Spirit, when it appeared as Understanding, was a very different beast than in its appearance as Vision. If that sounds a little abstract, just consider what happens when visionaries encounter the world of logic. The tendency is for neither side to be able to deal with the other, and each to presume that the "truth" lies with them alone. Yet from our vantage point, we can see that logic (Understanding) without Vision is hollow, while Vision without Understanding is vapid. The connection is important, but the difference is critical — for in this difference we can see the process of transformation. This is the Open Space, the "in between." And although there is a continuity of flow, the same Spirit moves on through a sequence of manifestations, there is also a dis-continuity of effect. Each appearance of Spirit must end (die?) before the next emerges. What is appropriate in the guise of Vision won't work as Understanding/logic. That is the story of the butterfly, the story of transformation.

FROM POTENTIAL TO ACTUALITY

Crossing the great divide separating "might be" from "is" brings the organizational Spirit from the level of good idea to being there.[27] No matter how powerful the sense from the Depths, how compelling the Vision, rational the Understanding, eloquent the Language, or fine the Information and Data — it all stands for nothing until it is there. Inevitably there comes that first day when Spirit must function under the conditions of time and space, business must be done. From here on out, Spirit has entered upon a new phase of its odyssey in which all that was potential may now be actualized.

On the first day of business, things are different to say the least, and not a little confusing. Events and demands pile on top of each other, requiring responses

---

[27] This phrase, "being there", is Martin Heidegger's ("Being and Time", Harper and Row, 1962) which is usually left untranslated as "Dasein". I do not pretend that my usage will equate with Heidegger's at all points, and indeed the richness of his usage is almost overpowering. But the reader should know that this is where I start.

which have never been made before, and consequently are not made with ease or certainty of result. The style of the organization[28] may be described as . . .

REACTIVE Under the circumstances, it seems sufficient to meet challenge with action, almost any action will do. Just keep things moving until there is some sense of what works, and what does not, what is appropriate, and what is just be the point. Fortunately, the organization has a resource from its Potential upon which it may draw: Data and Information. Those facts and figures, which emerged out of Language, as the organization neared concreteness, now become critical. They may not be right, nor totally accurate, but it is all that stands between the fledgling organization and chaos. The data and information suggest the direction of action, and since little time exists to think about anything else, you have to go with what you've got. At times like these, it doesn't seem to make much difference what you do — *JUST DO SOMETHING . . . REACT.* For the first days of business, reactivity is fine, indeed it may be the only way to go. But as a way of life, it leaves a good deal to be desired. Under the best of circumstances it appears that things are getting done, but what things and to what purpose is not always clear. Carried to extremes, tempers become frayed and frustration mounts as action breeds reaction and then more action, all to no clear cut end. What starts as a marvelous burst of energy, finally doing something, ends with Alice in Wonderland, where the faster you go the behinder you get. And even that is not clear, because with all the activity, it is very easy to loose sight of which way is ahead.

There must be a better way, and indeed that way may be found by fulfilling the potential held in the organizational Language. It was the language, you remember, that supplied "that special way of speaking" which made this organization unique. Products and procedures were named, roles clarified by titles — and perhaps most of all, directions established, in relatively clear and unambiguous terms. You may not know exactly what the terms meant, but at least there were words for things, and that made everybody feel better. Using the language of the organization, it is possible to begin to see the beast as a whole, as opposed to the fragments represented by the Data and Information. With this sense of the whole, some order may be restored above the

---

[28] The careful reader will note that I sometimes speak of "organization" without reference to "Spirit". This way of speaking is for reasons of economy only, for the thought I wish to convey is that organization is always a manifestation of Spirit.

chaotic act-react cycle. It becomes clearer who we are, and what the business is so that the organization may be . . .

RESPONSIVE to its own needs, and to the needs of the customer, market or world. Responsive organizations are truly a pleasure to do business with for they seem to recognize what the business is, and are prepared to make "best effort" to see that the needs of business are fully met, even if they do not completely understand all the details of the total operation. An example might be good sales unit in a department store. Let's say it is Vacuum Cleaners. When it comes to vacuum cleaners, the folks on the floor know their machines, what they will do or not do, and are obviously prepared to go all the way to insure that you the customer, get what you want. In addition, the salespeople seem to feel comfortable with who they are, and are knowledgeable enough about the rest of the organization so that they may competently link you in should you have some additional needs. Lets say you want credit. They know to send you to the second floor to the sign that says "Omni-Charge." However, should you ask, What happens then? the sales people will probably not be too helpful. But at least they have the words right, and within the confines of those words (the organizational language) the organization can function responsively to your needs. Certainly a great improvement over the old act-react cycle, but not without its limitations, for the level of comprehension may not go much deeper than the words themselves. Indeed, over time, people in the organization may become so invested in the words that they forget the meaning. Faced with some change in the language, the reaction is likely to be resistance and negativity. Given a new credit facility, for example, you might hear, "But we've always had Omni-Charge."

Responsive organizations are marvelous in a given time and place. They do what they do competently, and usually with a smile. While they may not always know what the words mean, they always know the words, and in that lies their strength. But when the times change or the words have been used for so long that they have separated from their meaning, the situation becomes strained, and the sense of competence, comfort and direction disappears.

At that point, it is not unlikely that the organization may devolve to the Reactive stage in which activity becomes its own end, on the grounds that not being sure what they should do or why, they must DO SOMETHING. There is of course another possibility, that they should draw upon a deeper aspect of their Potential, Understanding — so that once again they may go behind the words to the meaning and logic of the enterprise. Should they do this, the organization will gain a vantage point from which may be thought out purpose and direction, not only as they may appear at a particular time and place, represented by a special language, but also as that purpose and direction may relate to coming events, otherwise known as the future. In short, the organization may transform and become . . .

PRO-ACTIVE Pro-active organizations have an analytic quality about them which permits looking beyond a particular time and place to see what is coming next. Typically, they are scanning their environment to see what the market change will be, how the customers will be feeling, and what may be coming down the road. At the same time, they also look within to consider their way of doing business, the adequacy of their organization, facilities and personnel as measured against what they are doing presently, and perhaps more important, what they might be called upon to do in the future. All of this critical, reflective activity is based upon their Understanding of the logic and rationale of the business.

Pro-active organization do not stop being Responsive or Reactive, indeed, they do both, but appropriately so. Thus they respond to customer's needs fully, not just with the right words, but with some real sense of the logic behind those words. By the same token, they continue to be able to re-act quickly to particular situations when the Data and Information indicate that such re-action is critical. But most important, a pro-active organization may decide neither to respond nor react when it becomes apparent, on the basis of their Understanding, that the problem at hand is neither a matter of the words people are using, nor the data and information they have collected, but of rather something deeper.

For example, in our Department store, suppose that vacuum cleaner sales have fallen drastically. Re-active types might consult that bit of data and information and conclude that the only thing to do was to try harder. The responsive types, seeing the same data and information might conclude that they "weren't saying it right." The new credit facility just didn't feel as good as old "Omni-charge." The pro-active types, having looked at the situation and beyond, conclude that the problem lay neither with words nor activity, but with the fact that the customers had all become wealthy and moved into high-rise condos with centralized cleaning services. The truth of the matter was that they didn't need individual vacuum cleaners anymore. The solution, therefore, must come from beyond language, information or data, and be based on an Understanding of what the business is all about. Probable result? Reorganization! Do away with the Vacuum Cleaner Department and re-orient to greener pastures.

Pro-active organizations do very well. Their capacity for self-criticism and environmental assessment enables them to keep on top of things, and even to get a little ahead. What they really do superbly is identify problems, and come up with solutions on the basis of their Understanding of how things are supposed to work. There is, however, a downside to the pro-active organization, which comes from the limitations of their Understanding, and the concentration on problems.

Understanding is a specific logical structure which was built at a special time and place in order to delineate the rationale of the Organization's Vision. So long as the environment (time and place) remain relatively constant, the logic and rational will continue to work. However, should that environment change in some profound way, the logic will be less and less effective.

Consider our Department Store again. The logic of the department store is based upon an environment in which there are customers "out there" who come to shop "in here." Given that environment, the rational thing to do is to organize a series of units (departments) each to handle some type of merchandise, so that the customer "out there" may easily come "in here" to find what they want. But suppose the "out there" and the "in here" were suddenly to disappear or collapse on each other, so that there was really no difference. Everybody was anywhere, anytime they wanted to be "there." That may sound a little strange, but isn't that exactly what is happening with the advent of sophisticated, widely spread computer networks? The old understanding of time and space gets radically reworked, and if we add a few bells and whistles, such as they have already done in France with their TELATEL System (computer based videotext shopping), the prior rationale for the Department Store doesn't make much sense any more.

What does the Pro-active organization do in this situation? Ordinarily, they would look for problems and solutions. That means finding out what was happening on the "outside," and readjusting the structure of things "inside" according to their understanding of how things ought to work. But in this case, the "problem" is not the "outside" or the "inside," but rather that neither exist! In fact the problem lies in the Understanding, the very mechanism that used to define problems as problems. Very confusing, but what can the organization do?

Playing by the old rules, the Pro-active organization, will engage in a continuing series of reorganizations, changing the language (words) and increased efforts to collect more accurate Data and Information. Relying on their normal "problem-solving mode," they will look far and wide for a part of the organization that isn't working and seek to fix it. But the truth of the matter is that the difficulty lies not in some part, but rather in the whole. None of these efforts will have any effect at all except to make the total situation worse, at which point the most likely result will be *devolution*, down to the most basic levels of behavior — pure re-activity. Action for the sake of action's sake. Don't just stand there . . . Do something !

There is, of course another alternative, which is to reconnect with the Organization's potential and to actualize what may be lying dormant in the Vision. At that point, it becomes possible to rise above all the specificities of Understanding, Language, and Information-Data, to achieve some new sense of the whole. Spirit may transform and become . . .

INTERACTIVE The Inter-active organization is Vision based, and functions as a whole. Just as Vision has the capacity to image the totality in organic unity, the Inter-active organization perceives itself in its connectedness as opposed to its several parts. Whereas the Pro-active organization approached itself in an analytical, reductionist fashion, seeking to identify problem areas which may then be isolated, fixed or replaced, the Inter-active Organization approaches itself as a totality in which parts may be arbitrarily identified as separable, discrete entities, but ultimately make no sense or have separate existence apart from the whole. The working model of the Pro-active organization is mechanistic with parts that may be replaced without changing the whole. The working model of the Inter-active organization is biological, in which parts are integral to the whole and no part may be replaced or altered without changing the whole in some essential way.

The relationship of Vision to what lies beyond it also represents an enormous potential for the InterActive Organization. Just as Vision ranged broadly over the world at large seeking forms and colors with which to enrich its image of that primal idea which emerged from the depths, so the Inter-active organization melds with its environment, seeking different and more powerful ways to express itself. While the pro-active organization was concerned with boundaries which become limits ("in here" and "out there"), the Inter-active organization is concerned with boundaries which become opportunities to engage the world in new and different ways. The distinction between "in here" and "out there" is still present, but no longer rigid; indeed, the Inter-active organization is concerned to reduce the rigidity and increase the flow.

The ease with which the Inter-active organization engages the world at large comes in part from the Vision which provides a sense of centeredness and grounding which literally overrides the vicissitudes of day-to-day happenings, for powerful visions are by nature inclusive, and see each new happening as an opportunity to

51

expand and enrich that Vision. The ease of the world-organization relationship also comes from the manner of self-perception held by the Inter-Active organization. In so far as the organization perceives itself as a whole-existing-in-a-world, as opposed to a collection of isolated parts-separated-from-the-world, relationship with the world constitutes no threat. Indeed the only threat exists in the possibility of separation from the world, at which point, the organization would cease to exist in any meaningful way. The Pro-active organization, however, operating under the perception that it and its parts are separable entities, may come to the belief that existence apart from the world is a possibility.

Although Inter-active organizations may appear primarily in their wholeness, and perceive themselves as such, by no means do they "cancel out" the other modes of organizational being. Reactivity, Responsiveness and Pro-activity all have their place under the appropriate conditions. Indeed, at any given point in time and circumstance, the organization may appear in any one of these modes, but it is not limited by them. In some sense, the organization seems to choose the mode appropriate to the circumstance. Thus crisis is reacted to, customers are responded to, and the present and future are dealt with in an analytical, pro-active fashion. Overall, the organization maintains its sense of wholeness and intra/interrelationship with itself and with the world at large.

Thus in practical day to day affairs, the Inter-active organization may appear like all others, but it possesses reserves that the others have not actualized and do not have available. In the case of our Department Store, the advent of the computer net, and the implosion of "in here" and "out there" would represent no threat at all, but rather an opportunity. By returning to its Vision, the store would recognize that the issue was not the maintenance and protection of the old form, but rather the realization of its basic intent (Vision) in which the objective was (we might suppose) to serve customers by providing quality merchandise at a reasonable price with maximum profit. With this Vision, the presence of the computer represents no problem at all. On the contrary, the vista is one of limitless possibility. More customers might be reached in less time, served by fewer people per customer with the possibility of even greater profit. Of course to turn this new form of the Vision into reality, all the "old modes" of organizational being will still be necessary. Pro-activity to analyze and plan, Responsiveness to meet the customers needs, and Reactivity to handle the "glitches." But for all the change in form and function, the Inter-Active Organization recognizes itself as itself, still true to its Vision. Just doing it a different way.

Inter-Active organizations possess superb flexibility, coupled with a profound sense of self, and openness to the world. Given these elements, the organization is well equipped to deal with rapid change, as the surrounding circumstances require new forms in which the Vision may be expressed. For all of their adaptability, however Inter-Active Organizations are still form driven and form based. Everything that they do eventually comes back to some form or structure to give it substance, reality, ("being there") , which is reasonable if only because the world at this point tends to define reality in terms of structure and form. However, it is at least thinkable that a day may come when change would be so rapid and complex that form, as such, no longer has much meaning, and therefore organizations must operate beyond form and structure.

Now for the big question. How and where do we find organizations that can combine these traits, not just occasionally, but every day of the week? The answer, I believe is already given in the organizational potential. It may be found in what we called Out of the Depths. At this point, we reach the final stage in the Odyssey of Spirit as the organization actualizes the last part of its potential and transforms to become an . . .

INSPIRED ORGANIZATION The potential for the Inspired Organization is given by the experience with which the organization began. That Out of the Depths experience consisted infinitely more of power and energy erupting in some irresistible way than any neat form and structure. The experience was primal in the sense that something dramatic and new suddenly appeared as if from nowhere, with scarcely more content that the great "I got it" from the lips of the founder. What "it" was, and what "it" would become were all unknowns. In the succeeding stages of the odyssey, that primal Spirit, having emerged from Out of the Depths, became more focused and particular as it appeared in Vision, Understanding, Language, and Data-Information. It moved from high energy and little focus down to a laser-like point when it became "really there" on the first day of business. From there on out, the Spirit appeared in successive modes of being, each one of which allowed for a fuller expression of its potential. Beginning with the narrow particularity of the ReActive Organization, Spirit transformed through Responsiveness, Pro-activity and Inter-activity. At each stage, the constraints of form and structure became of less consequence, while the possibility for the full expression of Spirit in time and space increased. Yet even at the Inter-active level, form and structure were important and constraining considerations. The Inspired level brings the possibility of going beyond those constraints.

At this point, there must be a real switch in perception. Up to now we have encountered Spirit that wasn't quite "there" until the "First Day of Business." After that, it was "there" through certain modes of being which were locked, more or less, to form and structure. We are now contemplating the reverse of all of that — a situation, a way of being, in which Spirit is real and free. Pure energy. Pure Spirit.

Let me stop for the moment and pose an obvious question: Why would one even want to consider such a situation? The answer, I believe has already been given when we were talking about the Ready, Fire, Aim, syndrome and the ride on the train. The point is that it is more than conceivable our world may speed to the rate where we enter a sort of "hyper-warp" in which forms transit with such rapidity that we can no longer sense their shape, but only their passage. Then, like it or not, we will find ourselves in a world dominated by energy and flow. At such a time, and indeed that time already may be now, the Inspired Organization will be more than an esoteric curiosity. It will become necessity. Thus, even if we cannot imagine an Inspired Organization in detail, we can imagine the circumstances under which the Inspired Organization would be damn useful.

But so are Sky Hooks, and a lot of other things for which we can imagine a use and yet have little hope of creating. Still, in the case of Inspired Organizations, I believe there are factors that place them somewhat nearer to probability if not possibility. First, I think we already have some limited experience with such creatures. In my view, the Inspired Organization is nothing more nor less than one of Peter Vaill's High Performing Systems operating at peak levels. According to Vaill such systems are characterized by the quality of the energy they exude. Participants there seem to be oblivious to time clocks and physical conditions; rather they express sheer joy in simply doing what they are doing.[29]

Occasionally us rather more mundane folks have the exquisite privilege of participating in such a system as for example when we witness an outstanding symphony orchestra operating at and beyond peak performance. It is not stretching a point to say that time and space, even hard chairs, just disappear, to be replaced by a soaring sense of energy and purpose. Form, structure and physicality are all there, but they are all transcended, transformed, if you will, by the spirit of the music.

---

[29] Vaill, Peter; "Towards a Behavioral Description of High Performing Systems", published in "Leadership: Where else can it go ?" Morgan McCall ed, Duke University Press, 1978.

Chapter IV

JOURNEY OF THE SPIRIT
(In Individuals)

This story as told so far is only half told. To this point, it may appear as if transformation occurs only on the level of the collective, the group. But what happens to the group has its analogue with the individual. Indeed, the group and the individual are incomprehensible apart from each other. It is quite true that for purposes of thought and neatness of expression, the individual and the group may be dealt with separately, as I will do. But that is only a concession to the weakness of our thought forms and the frailness of our language. Were it possible to do so without massive confusion, everything should be dealt with all at once.

I take it as a given that the individual and the group, taken separately, are pure intellectual abstractions, useful for thought, but nothing more. The validity of this statement is fairly clear in terms of the group, if for no other reason than that nobody has ever seen a group that did not consist of individuals. The individual, however, at least appears to be different. An individual may wander off to isolated situations and appears to exist independently, as in the middle of the desert or on the analyst's couch. That, I suggest is but momentary aberrancy, for even in moments of isolation, the individual carries some group or groups with him or her in the form of a peculiar Vision, special Understanding and a unique Language. Even the Data and Information go out into the desert.

But more than that, an individual becomes an individual in relationship to a group. Either by identification with the Spirit of the group or by distinction from it, the individual comes to understand what he or she is or is not. A most powerful expression of this idea appears in a remarkable book by Martin Buber entitled, *I and*

Thou.[30] Essentially Buber says that I become I, only in significant relationship with an other, a thou.

Thus, in response to the perpetual question of what happens first, individual transformation or organizational transformation, the answer is neither. Both happen together, inter-actively and collaboratively. How all that might work, I will turn to presently, but first, it is necessary to set the stage by introducing and describing the journey of individual spirit. Then we may correlate the individual and the organization and move on to the heart of the matter: to consider what happens "in between" in the Open Space created by the passage from one stage, to the emergence of something new.

The journey of the individual begins in a way and place quite similar to the organization. This is not surprising, for the organization in all of its modes is both ground and field for the individual. As ground, the organization represents the basis from which the individual emerges and becomes unique. As field, the organization provides the arena in which the individual journey is conducted. Graphically, the individual journey appears as follows beginning with Out of the Depths and moving upwards to Spirit.

```
SPIRIT
SOUL
ADVANCED MIND
MIND
BODY
****************
INFORMATION/DATA
LANGUAGE
UNDERSTANDING
VISION
OUT OF THE DEPTHS
```

In this case, the Depths are those of the organization. For the "prehistory" or potential of the individual is precisely that of the organization, combined with the way that the organization may have actualized its own potential over the course of its unique transformational journey.

How this might occur is relatively easy to see in terms of organizations into which we have been born. For example, if the organization were the United States of

_____

[30] Buber, Martin, op. sit.

56

America, one might talk about the primal idea which may have emerged on the Boston docks in the midst of a tea party, a Vision which gained expression in the Declaration of Independence, an Understanding as outlined in the Constitution, and a Language which is known worldwide as "Yankee-speak" — not to be confused with English. All of this stands as potential for each one of us who are citizens of the United States. And it is out of this potential that we have subsequently worked out our own identity at whatever level our personal odyssey may have taken us to.

The situation apparently becomes more complex relative to organizations with which we may have become associated over the course our lifetime. The requirement, however, for those new organizations to become the ground and field for our own transformation remains, if that new organization is to become our organization. The difference between organizations into which we may have been born, as opposed to those with which we may later become associated, relative to becoming the ground and field for our transformation, is only apparent. In both cases the critical issue is, how do you meaningfully participate in something that occurred before you were born or while you were in a different place? The answer is: through mythos, which captures the organizational Spirit in such a way that it can actually be experienced beyond the strict limitations of time and space, allowing us to become party to (part of) the story (Spirit) of any organization in such a way that it may be our own. [31]

The process through which mythos reveals the Spirit of an organization to the individual is both holographic and iterative (cumulative). Thus when the individual joins the organization and encounters mythos for the first time, the whole story is there as a holograph, but not fully realizable by the individual until subsequently iterated. How this might work will become clearer as we describe the individual's journey, but for the moment, a general description will be useful.

At the instant of joining (presuming the organization does its job as story-teller), the individual will encounter the broad outlines of the story from beginning to the imagined future. There will be some idea (albeit vague) of what the primal motivation was, how the Vision looked, what was the rational (Understanding),

---

[31] Soren Kierkegaard has a marvelous discussion of the issue raised here as he considers the difference between what he called the "disciple at the first hand" and the "disciple at the second hand." The disciples here are the disciples of Jesus, and the question is - how and by what manner can those disciples who have come a generation later [or 100 generations] be said to know the person of Jesus. In terms of classical theology, this is the problem of revelation, but the issues raised are very close to the ones we are considering. See "Philosophical Fragments", Princeton University Press, 1936, pp 74ff.

something of the Language, and of course, the Data and Information. It is all there, but scarcely comprehensible until the story becomes integrated with the individual's own journey. All of which is to acknowledge the common experience that newcomers tend to be a little green around the ears.

Less obvious is the way the iterative process works. It is not simply a matter of hearing the story over and over again, although that is important. It is rather that, as the individual proceeds along his or her transformational journey hooks are established in the individual's experience which allow for deeper understanding and comprehension. Thus the story may largely remain the same, but the perception of meaning will grow. Same old story, but richer and deeper.

When the individual arrives, the whole story is available as potential, but it will only be actualized as the individual's journey is realized in the context of the organizations. Hence, on the first day of association the organizational story will appear largely in terms of a welter of confusing Data and Information. This will permit a certain, but truly limited degree of individual actualization in that organization. It is true that things will work, but at a very low level of effectiveness. At some point, this low level of effectiveness will prove frustrating and not useful. The individual will then experience some degree of despair and dislocation, for the old ways of being are through. The alternatives are fairly clear; leave the organization, shut up and play dumb (catatonia), or allow oneself to be driven back down into the depths of the story. The central question is, "What's it all about?" Given a taste of the Depths, the Vision will be revisited, and likewise the Understanding. But what is most likely to stick is the next level up, Language. At that point, the potential available in Language may be actualized, and once the words are comprehended, life takes on new significance.

I realize that this description is pretty barebones, but it will be filled out shortly. In the interim, several points are noteworthy. Primary is the fact that transformation begins in the Depths, and progresses through a constant return to the Depths. It is the way of development to move things along in a straight linear sequence, but transformation involves discontinuity; a break with what has been, a return to a primal state, followed by the emergence of a new state. The net effect is neatly caught in an American Indian Chant: We are the old people. We are the new people. We are the same people, Deeper than before. [32]

---

[32] I heard this chant from Antonio Nunez at the IV Symposium on Organization Transformation. I have no idea where it comes from.

THE JOURNEY BEGINS

The potential or pre-history for the Individual's transformational journey begins in the Depths, but the Depths are those of the organization that forms the ground and field for that individual's quest. The journey proceeds through Vision, Understanding, Language and Information and Data. Each level provides increasing specificity and focus until that moment when the individual emerges in time and space as . . .

BODY   It is the first day in the organization, and our individual, called Jean, is operating on a pretty mechanical level. Jean is there, but "just there" as a Body. The limits and direction of activity are given by a mass of Data and Information which almost overwhelm, and certainly do not make much sense. But slowly in the welter of facts, figures, slogans and catchwords, all presented with no reference to anything else, some very elemental cues begin to emerge. Bathroom, two doors down on the left. Cafeteria, three floors up. Desk, a place to work at (what ever "work" is). Payday, first and third Fridays of the month. It is not very much to go on, but sufficient to take care of immediate physical needs.

Life as Body has its pleasures. The demands are limited, or at least the capacity to understand the demands is limited, and most immediate needs seem to be met. And yet it is vaguely disturbing, for in the midst of this pleasant, almost dreamlike state, something always seems to be crashing in. "Please take this 1040-B up to the Expediter." What on earth could that mean? Besides, Jean was just on the way to the CAFETERIA by way of the BATHROOM. Another day perhaps . . .

On another day, it is more of the same. Somehow the environment just won't let a poor Body alone. Indeed, one gets the distinct impression that something somewhere wants a poor Body to be more than a poor Body can be — or else! The threat is there, real and disconcerting. The old way just won't work any more, and the new way has yet to appear. Jean is forced to ask himself why he came to the old Department Store anyhow, and what it's all about. In a word, Jean is on his way to a quick trip down to the Depths, otherwise known as being Down in the Dumps.

As unappealing as the Dumps may be, the position does provide a change of perspective, from which it is possible to see things in a new light. The primal Vision is still pretty murky, but the logic (Understanding) is a little clearer, although still beyond his comprehension. But the Words now begin to make some sense. Suddenly, the discrete and confusing bits of Data and Information take on meaning in the context of the organizational Language.

Language, as you will remember is that special constellation of words and names which articulate the peculiar Understanding which the organization has. Through these words and names, it is possible to comprehend more or less "what's going on." For example, Jean might consult the lexicon and begin to discover in general terms what those mysterious things, a 1040-B and an Expediter, might be. Insofar as the organizational language becomes accessible to Jean, the possibility exists that Jean may transform and begin to operate at the level of . . .

MIND As mind, Jean discovers a whole new world, or more accurately, the same old world now represented in infinitely greater texture and richness. While the meaning of the words is not always clear, there is a certain comfort in being able to call up the "right" word, and thus at least appear responsive. The 1040-B, it turns out, is a purchase order, and an "Expeditor" is somebody who can get you what you want faster. Now when the great words are spoken, "Please take the 1040-B up to the Expeditor,"   Jean knows what to do and may therefore be Responsive to the needs of the organization as it seeks to be responsive to its clients and customers.

The availability of Language also enables Jean to take a broader, more comprehensive view of the Organization and its work. It turns out that there is not just one Expeditor, but five, and that each one of them is competent to perform the function. Thus, if there are 231 1040-Bs to be taken care of in a responsive way, it makes sense to spread them around instead waiting for one person to wade through them all. Jean can now think about the organization, and effectively get beyond the narrow reactive modes of behavior that life as a Body previously dictated.

Being Mind, however, has its difficulties, for Jean discovers that while it is possible to DO more, the Organization also expects more. On some days it would be nice just to be a Body again. Physical needs were met, and expectations were very low. Now things are different, indeed painfully different, especially when the temptation to revert to Body becomes strong. Body behavior is no longer appropriate, and what once was quite acceptable, hanging out in the cafeteria, is now subject to criticism.

As Jean learns the Language, sensitivity increases to the multitude of things that are going on. Before, everything was just a great meaningless blur, with no names to create distinctions. But now there are names and distinctions, which in turn yields awareness. On one level, Jean finds all of this very pleasant, as other members of the organization begin to appreciate his competence and to trust his capacity to get things done. That feels pretty good, for as others acknowledge his competence, Jean begins to perceive himself in the same way. Somehow he is becoming more of a person, bigger and more powerful, with self-respect. Jean has a reputation to live up to.

But this reputation is a two edged sword. Positively, it is really marvelous to be an accepted, respected member of the organization. On the other hand, that reputation can quickly be lost, and Jean would find himself as being worse, a "badder" person, than he ever could have been before he gained the reputation. It becomes clear that Jean can never go home again, back to the old Body. At least he can't if he wants to maintain his self-respect.

Threats to his reputation — threats to his self-respect. That is what Jean sees now, always and everywhere, as business piles up, and expectations increase. More and more 1040-Bs to be carried to more and more expeditors, and Jean is now known as a person who can get things done. Some days it seems that you just can't run fast enough or find shopping carts big enough to move the work. There isn't enough time even to think. And it is becoming clearer that running the way he's running, even twice as fast, won't do it. There must be a better way.

Once more it is down in the Depths for a change of perspective, which may yield enhanced perception. Seen with new eyes, the Vision is clearer, but still too general for comfort. However, the logic of Understanding, now there is something you could hold on to. If you can't run faster, you will have to run smarter. And that possibility is given in the potential as Understanding, which may be actualized as. . .

ADVANCED MIND Advanced Mind is a rather awkward term. Another one, which may be worse, would be Consciousness of Consciousness. The idea, however, is fairly straightforward. With Advanced Mind comes the capacity to analyze, rationalize and critique the way things are. It is given as a potential from the organization's Understanding, which as you remember, was that logical structuring of the essential Vision. To the extent that Jean is made party to the Organization's Understanding, he may move beyond the level of nomenclature (words and names) to the more critical awareness of "why" and "how." Why do things work as they do, and how are they logically interconnected.

For Jean, in terms of his individual journey, access to the Understanding provides that platform from which his actions and the actions of others may be perceived in their relationship, and furthermore, assessed in terms of their effectiveness. Given this sense of the rationale of things, and the capacity to make value judgments based upon that rationale, Jean can in fact move to a higher and more useful way to be.

Abstracted from the immediacy of endless actions and re-actions (pushing more 1040Bs to more expeditors), Jean is in a position to ask, Why? and, Is there a better way? For example, Jean might start by looking at the elements of his job and what it entails. There are customers with needs. Those needs are described on the 1040-Bs, which are then given to the expeditors who get the customer what they need. Jean's job is to run back and forth. With a little reflection, Jean can see that there is a loop here, which starts with the customer and ends with the customer. And Jean is caught in the middle, buried in 1040-Bs and spending most of his time with expeditors.

From the point of view of the Language of the organization (which contains 1040-Bs and expeditors), what is going on seems to be what should be going on. However, when you look at it from the level of the rationale or logic, which might be phrased, "serve the customer in a timely fashion," other possibilities appear. One might imagine a computer system which connected the customer immediately with the supply room. The customer just typed in what was needed, and the supply room immediately responded by dumping the needed article on a conveyor belt, right back to the customer. Quick, easy and effective, and best of all no 1040-Bs and no expeditors.

For Jean, just the thought of doing such a thing was a mind expanding experience. Suddenly, he found himself above the words, and connected with the logic. In one fell swoop, the furniture of his world (forms and expeditors), which he had assumed was set in place on the first day of creation, now fell away and disappeared, at least in theory. In his mind's eye, Jean could look at himself not just as Body reacting to physical stimuli, or Mind responding to the right words, but in a very different way. He was above it all.

Now suppose that Jean didn't get fired for thinking the unthinkable and upsetting the way things "always have been done." Rather, senior management smiled on him, and said, "Do it." At that juncture, Jean would not only have experienced the heady sensation of seeing "reality" in a totally new way, but in addition would have received positive confirmation of the power of this new way of being. Gone were the days of running faster and faster in service of a never ending pile of 1040-Bs. And in their place came that awareness of abstract power residing in an idea. Running smarter is a better way to be.

That is enough to catch a fellow's attention, and make him think rather differently about who he is. Jean might say: "I used to be the 1040-B runner, responding to the call of the expeditors. Now I am above all of that, indeed all of that is gone.

My power and identity lie in my ability to conceptualize, to think clearly and critically in ways that nobody ever really thought before. Perhaps the major difference between then and now is self-criticism, self-critique — self-awareness. It used to be that I was so much a part of things, as either Body or Mind, that I really couldn't see the difference between me and what was not me. Now I have "third sight," and reality, or at least the part that is most important to me, is not just physical, or even the mental capacity to hear the words and respond. It lies in what I might call transcendence, being able to get beyond the immediate here and now, to see things in a logical, lucid fashion."

In truth, Jean had taken a step, and senior management continued to smile. From the position of transcendence, with all the power of critical awareness, he imagined new ways to go, ways that were rational and coherent, jumping over the limitations of the body and narrowness of the mind, or at least some minds. On a good day, it seemed that he could go forever, no restrictions except the boundaries of his imagination. But as good as it was, Jean also had to admit that something was missing. The more "real" things became in his head, the further away it seemed that he got from a number of sensations that he really had enjoyed. Purely physical things, like a good long walk, or a pleasant nap in the hot sun. Or some mental things, like being down "with the guys" saying all the right words. "Ah, but that was just the price of success," he thought. "You have to give up those sorts of pleasures and deal with what's real." And he knew what was "real" if only because management kept smiling and telling him that it was real. And to make it really real, Jean was promoted to a new office with a window, on the 21st floor. From there you could see forever, but you sort of lost touch.

For a period, life on the 21st floor had its own pleasures sufficient to mask whatever sense of pain of loss Jean may have been experiencing. The fact that his old world seemed very far away, and rather unreal, was curious, but not much more. Then this sense of separation came to have some very practical implications. Jean discovered that his elegant plans seemed to have lost their grounding in reality. They sounded great on paper, or even when presented to senior management, but when it came time to put it all to work, down there where the work got done, there was a miss. Jean scratched his head and reexamined his logic — which he found to be flawless, but still unconnected. Perhaps his explanatory memos were unclear, the graphics less than appealing. Of course, it could be that the Training Department had fallen down on the job. Or then again, the workers could be just plain dumb. All possible, but somehow or other, not quite adequate.

The sense of malaise in the world of work echoed, in a disconcerting sort of way, a similar sense inside himself. He felt hollow and disconnected, not just from his work, but from himself. No longer did the air on the 21st floor mask the longings of the Body for long walks and hot sun, or the needs of the Mind to just hear the "right words" spoken among the boys. As frustrating as it may have been, there was something very nice about those 1040-Bs and his old friends the expeditors. Wouldn't it be wonderful to get it all together, and connect again in some real way? Once more, Jean felt himself headed towards the Depths.

The possibility for "getting it all together" is given by the potential of Vision, that overarching, many-colored, multiformed view of what everything is about. A view which includes rather than excludes, and weaves a fabric of purpose and direction which underlies the rational, logical Understanding. That possibility might become actualized in Jean as . . .

SOUL The word Soul, as used here, does not refer to that disembodied wraith which supposedly pops heavenward at death. The meaning is rather more substantial and comes from the biblical hebrew word *nephesh* which is usually translated as soul. Looking at the use of the word in context, we may be surprised to find that "so-and-so went out and slew 300,000 *nepheshim*," which does not mean that a large number of celestial spirits were laid to waste. On the contrary, there were that many corpses out on the field of battle. In another place, the word may be used in the way we usually think of it, as in "my soul cries out," which might be rendered "my essence" or "central self." In fact, the several usages of soul are not contradictory in the Hebrew, but rather represent two sides of the same thing, man. Pedersen puts it succinctly: "In the Old Testament we are constantly confronted with the fact that man, as such, is soul."[33]

Actually, the contemporary street usage is pretty close to what I have in mind, as in the phrase, "He's got Soul," which usually means, "He's got it all together." So, Soul means that condition in which a person has it all together, which is precisely what our friend Jean was looking for.

The possibility of getting it all together is given by the organizational Vision, and the ways in which that Vision may have become actualized in the ongoing life of the organization. To the extent that Jean can access that Vision, and become party to

---

[33] Pedersen, op.cit. p. 99.

it, his disconnectedness from parts of the organization and from central aspects of his self may be overcome.

The organizational Vision included the whole picture, not just what it was, but as it might become. In part, the Vision is like a dream, imagining future states, depicted in images and colors that have never been part of the real world. At the same time, the Vision is built out of the forms and realities of this world so that it might communicate future potential in present terms. But most of all the Vision leaps over the narrower rationality of Understanding adding scope and energy. Vision does not do away with Understanding, but rather includes it in a broader vista. What Vision may lack in logic (the domain of Understanding), it more than makes up for in power.

For Jean, access to the Vision occurred in an apparently happenstantial way. One day, sitting alone on the 21st floor, feeling estranged, disconnected and down in the dumps, he wandered out to the executive coffee suite for a little caffeine and a change of scene. While he felt just about as low as he could go, he also found a strange new sense of clarity. The 21st floor wasn't where it was at, and while he still had Understanding of how things worked, he knew there had to be more. In short Jean was ready, and as he sipped his second cup, feeling worse with every swallow, a little old man walked in to pour himself a cup. As he turned around and faced Jean, the old man smiled in a wistful way and remarked how things had changed, and yet how very much it all followed the original dream. Jean started from his revere long enough to know that he knew the old man, not personally mind you, but he knew who he was. In fact it was old JP, the founder, who's smiling countenance, framed on the boardroom wall, oversaw every presentation that Jean had made. With some embarrassment, Jean started to go, but the old man touched him on the arm, and asked if they could talk. Said the Old man, "It's been a long time since I was around, and I am sort of curious as to what's been happening."

The unlikely pair sat down in the corner, and Jean began to tell the story as best he could. But scarcely had he opened his mouth to begin, and the old man interrupted. "You know," he said, "back in the old days we knew the world would be our oyster. There were no limits to our expectations. The customers were out there with real needs, and if we could meet those needs with a quality product in a timely fashion at a fair price, well, anything could happen. Stores in every major city, branches in all the suburbs. No limits, no limits. But it sure didn't start that way. Our first store was a small one. We never seemed to have enough stock or hands to move it with, but we survived and eventually got ourselves organized. I found that I couldn't do it all myself, so I invented some new positions to move things faster. I think we called them expediters, and special forms to keep track of what was going on, the old 1040-Bs. That's all gone, I suppose, and well it should be, for in order to be true to the Vision, you have to keep up with the times. It's a funny thing, good dreams just get better and richer. They sort of reach out to the world around, to find new ways of doing business. But on some level, it is the same dream, just different clothes. Same old Vision, only deeper."

The old man left, and Jean was alone with his thoughts... But what different thoughts they were. It wasn't so much that Jean was thinking differently, or reasoning differently, it was almost as if he were seeing differently. Suddenly, everything was connected in a fluid pattern. The parts no longer retained the same iron fixation on the past, but rather, like a kaleidoscope, the same colors kept evolving into new and different forms, all different, yet all connected. The 1040-Bs connected to the Expediters, connected to the computer system, and all that changed into — what? That hadn't come clear yet. But the sense was of connectedness and not separation, united in that old man's dream.

In the days that followed, Jean discovered some quite remarkable changes in his work. It wasn't so much that he was doing different things as that the results were different. He couldn't quite put his finger on it, but somehow it related to seeing things in connectedness as opposed to difference. For example, when Jean came up with his latest concept for improving the work of the organization down on the shop floor, he presented it to senior management, and eventually to the workers, as an extension and evolution of what they had been doing rather than as a radical new concept. At first he thought he was just playing political games, candycoating the pill as it were. But he wasn't, and he knew it. That is really the way he saw things, and best of all, others saw it the same way, as indicated by their response. Gone was the defensive reaction to the "radical new idea." In its place came an interested reception to a "logical evolution from current practice." Curiously enough, there was virtually no difference in the concepts themselves or what they purported to do. What was different was the old man's dream which linked it all together, that essential Vision that held constant even as the forms changed.

Just as remarkable was the change in the way that Jean's fellow workers perceived and treated him. Whereas they used to view him with a degree of awe, not to say fear, as the *enfant terrible* who's radical ideas were constantly stirring the pot and upsetting the organization, now they treated him as one who brought things together. Moreover, they sought him out when change was imminent as one who saw the "whole" picture, and thus could interpret the change to what had always gone on.

In a way, this change of treatment bothered Jean, for it seemed to have raised him to the position of elder statesman, yet the truth of the matter was that he wasn't that much older, or that different. But he did see things in a different way. Now he had a new reputation to live up to, as one who brought continuity and wholeness to an organization that seemed to exist, more often than not, as fragments and pieces.

The external changes induced and supported some internal changes, as Jean found confirmation and support for the new way he saw the world. As the power of Vision began to integrate the external world of his work, Jean found something similar happening to the world inside. No longer did it seem necessary to forget or put down his self as Body or Mind, for both now linked comfortably and easily to that transcendent self which had given him the keen sense of critical awareness. Once more he enjoyed the pleasure of long walks, hot sun, and the camaraderie of the Boys down on the floor saying the right words. No less did he enjoy the heady sense of elegant abstract reasoning and the intrigue of structuring a new logic or rationale. But it all flowed together, connected by the internal Vision.

Jean had Soul, which was a comfort to himself as it was a support to those around him. And in a world of no small changes and many demands, the presence of Soul made the difference between flying off in sundry pieces, and keeping it all together. When Jean looked at the world and himself, what he saw was the union of these pieces, the union of the forms of existence. Although these pieces and forms might change with the rapidity of a quickly turning kaleidoscope, they held together in the common bond of the colors they shared.

Yet Jean was not immune to the forces of the world which affected him and his organization as the Third Wave surged and the Megatrends churned. What began as a rapid passage of forms united by a commonality of color became a blur in which only the colors remained. Rather like the tigers in "Little Black Sambo," who whirled at such speed that their stripes faded and disappeared into yellowness as they melted into a pool of butter, so the forms of Jean's life seemed to dissolve before his eyes. Just as one organizational pattern would be set in place, the world would change again and make it irrelevant. Taste and styles of the customers moved with such rapidity that stock could barely be shelved before it had passed. And behind it all, the advancing state of the art technologies drove everything. What was impossible today became outdated tomorrow.

Jean, in his role as the great "connector," neared the point of despair, and once again he was in the Depths. It was all very well to see the sequence of forms and maintain the connections as long as the forms themselves maintained even a minimal discretness and separation. But when the speed of passage exceeded the possibility of delineation, the world had changed indeed. And not just the outside world, for Jean noticed that as he sought to keep pace with a world apparently gone mad, his capacity to integrate his body, mind and transcendant rationality became increasingly difficult. It seemed like everything was happening all at once, and the demands which must be addressed by body or mind or reason separately or even simultaneously came faster and closer together until no separation existed at all. At the instant, it appeared that everything might dissolve to nothingness, unless there was a better way to be.

In fact, a better way to be is given in the potential by Out of the Depths, as this potential may have been actualized in the organization as Inspired. Out of the Depths, you will recall, was that primal state of Spirit when the mere sense of possibility emerged — the moment of the great, "I got it." Just as Out of the Depths lay behind Vision as the source of power, so it now lies "ahead of Soul" as the possibility of a better way to be which we call . . .

SPIRIT Our English word Spirit comes from the Latin *spiritus* meaning breath, and it is with that root sense that I am using it here. Man as Spirit is man in his essence, beyond form, operating as pure energy outside of the limitations of time and space. For a contemporary world locked in materiality, the thought of man as pure Spirit is virtually unthinkable and possibly absurd. Yet it is not totally beyond our experience, at least as that experience is represented in some of the phrases we use. We say of some absent friend, "He may be far away, but his Spirit is very much here." Perhaps that is just a way of speaking, but quite possibly it is something more. How we might conceive of that Spirit "being here" is problematical to say the least. The explanation might be that the Spirit is here in our "memory." As an explanation, that statement is less than helpful. But for my purposes, it doesn't really make any difference how that Spirit may be here, for the experience, at least as we talk about it, is of Spirit existing apart from form and substance, operating more or less independently of time and space.

There is another way in which the "reality" of man as pure Spirit seems to push into our experience. It is in those moments, usually rare, which are referred to as "personal peak performance"[34] Personal peak performances, as described by athletes,

---

[34] See Maslow A.H., "Religions, Values and Peak-Experiences", Viking Press, 1970, - sort of the personal parallel to Peter Vaill's High Performing systems.

artists and just "plain folks," have a common characteristic of "being cut free," of moving beyond the expected limitations of form and structure to exist in a mode of flow and almost effortless motion. Explanations of these moments are interesting (endorphins acting like opium), but for my purposes, essentially beside the point. The point is that we appear to share a common sense or intuition of what man in the mode of Spirit might be like.

Whether this sense of Spirit is based upon "solid fact" or gossamer hopes remains to be seen, but in a very real sense if Spirit is not "true," it should be. Indeed it must be if we as individuals and as a species are to exist in the kind of world which seems to be emerging, where forms transit with such speed that we loose our sense of form, and retain only an awareness of flow. Should such a world come to be, our way of being, personally and organizationally must be appropriate; *Inspired* for the Organization and *Spirit* for the Individual.

Here, as in the case of my discussion of the organization as Inspired, we have reached a point where normal language fails, or at least is used in such strange ways as to become uncomfortable. To those for whom standard language represents the limits of reality (If you can't say it, it doesn't exist), these discussions can only appear bizarre. Yet as the physicists have discovered, the limitation of language does not necessarily describe the bounds of reality. And when the experience of reality exceeds our capacity to express it, we have reached a choice point. Either we may invent a new language (or stretch the old one), or deny the reality. Some may find this a challenge, others an impossible, indeed unthinkable task scarcely worth the effort. Which perception is correct remains to be seen: the validation of the enterprise will occur, not by reference to some abstract "right" or "wrong," but rather in terms of our increased capacity to imagine and create organizations that can function effectively in a world where change and flow have superceded form and permanence as the norm.

INDIVIDUAL SPIRIT AND ORGANIZATIONAL SPIRIT: AN INSEPARABLE PAIR

Organizations and individuals may be separated for purposes of thinking and description, but never in reality. To speak of the process of transformation in the organization is to imply a parallel process with the individual and *vice versa*. Having now laid out my "likely story" describing transformation on both sides, it now comes time to put it all together and point out some of the implications of the relationship.

The graphic depicts a hypothetical "ideal" situation in which there is a one-to-one correlation between the levels of Individual and Organizational Spirit as each pursues the transformative journey to fulfillment. Thus ReActive Organization provides the setting for Body level people, Responsive Organization for Mind level and so forth. In reality, however, such an ideal situation rarely if ever exists, and the common experience is some degree of "being out of phase." Within limits, being out of phase is a positive advantage. Taken to extremes, it becomes disastrous.

The possibilities for disaster are perhaps most obvious in the extreme. Imagine, if you can, what it would be like to have a Spirit level individual in a ReActive organization. To begin with, neither side could possibly understand the other,

```
Individual.......Organization
Spirit.........Inspired
Soul......InterActive
Adv. Mind......ProActive
Mind......Responsive
Body......ReActive
******************

Data/Information
Language
Understanding
Vision
Out of the Depths
```

for the perceptions of reality are radically different. While the Reactive Organization sees its world exclusively in terms of an unending cascade of discrete bits of "hard" information and data, the individual as Spirit sees only flow and energy. The individual would feel uncomfortable and out of place, while the organization would feel disrupted and put upon. The state of affairs is no better if the situation is reversed (Body level in an Inspired Organization), but as we approach equilibrium, the possibility for meaningful and supportive interchange increases. Thus if we have a Pro-active organization, individuals at the Mind, Advanced Mind and Soul levels would all more or less fit in.

The fit between Pro-active Organization and Advanced Mind Individuals is obvious, for a Pro-active Organization is just plain home for such people. Those at the lower level (Mind) might feel a little uncomfortable (negative) or stretched (positive) because the Pro-Active Organization represents their potential for growth. Soul folks, on the other hand would feel rather restricted, because they were operating from the level of Vision as opposed to Understanding, but they aren't so far away as to be totally out of touch. And best of all, they give that sense of reach to the organization.

Looking at the diagram, one might conclude that the best of all possible worlds would be represented by having only Advanced Mind individuals in a Proctive Organization. That would certainly be the easiest fit, and for a period of time, probably the most productive. But over the long haul, it would be excruciatingly dull with very little possibility for growth. All the individuals, and the whole organization would purely and simply be supporting and reinforcing a single level of being with not even a suggestion that something else might be useful or possible.

Perhaps it is stretching a point, but it seems that some general principles might be stated here that could even have practical application.

> 1) Effective, growthful organizations should contain a majority of individuals no more than three levels apart.
> 2) Extremes of individual/organizational levels are to be avoided at all costs.
> 3) Short term efforts requiring maximum cooperation and mutual understanding may best be accomplished with all individuals and the organization at the same level.

ORGANIZATION AND INDIVIDUAL: HOW USEFUL IS THE DISTINCTION?

I have observed the customary practice of making a distinction between individuals and organizations, and in everyday circumstances that distinction can scarcely be avoided. Yet I wonder how useful that distinction ultimately is, as we think further about the realities involved.[35]   Indeed, I would argue that the distinction, as we make it, between individual and organization is but an artifact of our language and logic, rooted, as they both are, in materialism. However, should we begin to perceive Spirit as primal, both the language and the logic will have to change. How all of that might come out, I am not quite sure, but I suspect that we will have to develop a "halfway technology" rather like the physicists, who have found that when thinking of light/energy it sometimes makes the most sense to think in terms of waves and sometimes particles — but in either case the object of concern is light/energy. The analogue statement for our purposes would go something like: when thinking of Spirit, it sometimes makes the most sense to think in terms of individuals and sometimes organizations, but in either case, the object of concern is Spirit.

Such thoughts may be viewed under the heading of intellectual curiosities, although it should be noted that the thoughts are not mine alone. Recently, James Lovelock has suggested that the planet Earth might best be viewed as a single organism, the so-called Gaia Hypothesis [36]. Peter Russell has taken this thought one step further and proposed a common intelligence [37]

TRANSFORMATION — END STATE OR PROCESS?

It is very important to recognize that no level, for either individuals or organizations, is in some abstract sense bad. The truth of the matter is that each of us and all of our organizations will pass through most or all levels at some time in their existence. Indeed as individuals, we will repeat the process several times over as we move from one organization to another. Thus an individual, who might normally function at the Advanced Mind level, will regress to the Body level when placed in an entirely new organizational situation. Putting it rather crudely, even the highly evolved individual will have to learn where the bathrooms are all over when an organizational

---

[35] After finishing this section, I came upon Stanislav Grof's book, "Beyond the Brain," (State University Press of New York, 1985) in which he engages in substantially the same speculations. See Chapter I.

[36] Lovelock, James, "Gaia: A New Look at Life on Earth", Oxford Univ. Press, 1979.

[37] Russell, Peter, "The Global Brain", Tarcher, 1983.

change is made, and the same may be said for learning the Language, Understanding and so forth of the new organization. Presumably, it will not take such a individual as long to make the course the second or third time around, if only because they will have a good sense of what comes next. But there is no short circuiting the process if the individual is truly to become a part of the new organization. In biological evolutionary theory the phrase "ontogeny recapitulates phylogeny" captures the idea exactly. It says essentially that each individual will go through (replicate) the stages of evolution of their forbearers. In the organizational setting this means that all new folks will have to pay their dues and learn the ropes before they can be considered part of the team.

Organizations, too, will repeat the "levels" as they negotiate the transformational journey. When the environment requires a new Vision, that new Vision must be rationalized in a new Understanding and so on down to the level of Data and Information. And once more it will be the "first day of business." Thus no level in and of itself, should be considered "bad," or somehow morally inferior.

There is much in contemporary conversation about transformation which suggests that the transformed organization or individual has in some sense reached completion. There is a sense in which that can be true, but I believe that some qualification is in order, for transformation is both a process and an end state.

As a process, transformation may be described as the movement from one way of being to another. Hence an organization, once Re-Active and now Responsive may be considered "transformed." But that in no way suggests that perfection has been achieved. Indeed, there is a long way to go, and it is entirely possible that the next transformation may be "downwards," or devolution back to Reactive.

Transformation may also be understood as an end state. As should be obvious, there is a hierarchy of "ways of being" described by the stages of transformation. At the apex, man, either as individual or as organization, appears in his essence, fully realizing all potential and appearing as Spirit/Inspired. With reference to that level, and the level alone, it may be said that completion has occurred. At present, it may be true that some individuals and some organizations have achieved this way of being, if only momentarily. But few remain there, and for sure most of us have yet to make the trip.

Chapter V

OPEN SPACE
(The Individual)

The Journey of the Spirit described in the previous chapter, indicates course and way stations, but what happens in the Open Space in between? As with the butterfly, it is interesting to note the stubby legged crawling beast and the winged creature. But our central concern, you will remember, is not so much to observe the forms through which Spirit passes, but rather Spirit itself in its passage. The difference in forms or modes of being tells us that Spirit has moved, but if at all possible, we need to get closer to that moment of passage when form dissolves and Spirit transforms. To do this, I will employ a pair theoretical constructs, or likely stories, which have their roots in some of mankind's oldest mythology. I use them here, however, simply because they seem to work. These constructs are for the individual — Life, Death, Resurrection, and New Life — and for the organization, Covenant, Rebellion, Reconciliation and New Covenant.

The passage of the Individual Spirit through the transformative process may be described by the sequence Life, Death, Resurrection, and New Life. This sequence has its roots in the ancient perception of the agricultural life cycle, and is restated in classical Christian mythology. In short, the idea is not new. However, the "ancientness" of the idea does not insure its applicability to the process we may observe in the everyday world. Indeed, it may appear that such heavy words represent a case of "overkill." I suggest that the words are both accurate and appropriate, and that there are few if any alternatives once we understand the magnitude and power of what transpires.

Part of the difficulty in using such terminology derives from the fact that in ordinary usage death is only applied to that ultimate situation where the human body literally ceases to function. Resurrection, on the otherhand is typically an article of "faith," the utility of which is apparent only to the "believer." Leaving resurrection aside for the moment, I suggest that the common view of death is much too limited, and that we have literally blinded ourselves to much that goes on in the world with this narrow definition. Furthermore, the reason we have imposed these definitional blinders comes from an understandable, but unfortunate fear of death.

The rationale seems to be that since we are afraid of death, we exert maximum effort to push it as far away as possible, until it simply can't be pushed anymore. We do this, for example through the words that we use for people who have died. Rarely if ever will we say he or she is dead — but rather, passed on, departed, gone to the other side, asleep and so forth. The ultimate expression of this phenomenon is, of course, the American funeral in which the corpse is so "gussied up" as to appear "not dead." In polite conversation, until very recently, one did not talk about death or dying without the severe risk of being perceived as morbid, strange or worse. We banish the phenomenon of death to the corners of existence until it is absolutely inescapable . . . and even then we do our best to keep on pretending that it isn't so.

This behavior in itself is understandable, and "death" after all is a word which may conceivably be defined in any way we want. Difficulty occurs, however, when our definition gets in the way, and inhibits our vision of some very important things that are going on. Specifically, by understanding death only as the end of physical life, we miss the fact that death occurs in real ways every day. On a quite trivial level, if I choose to go to New York as opposed to Chicago, the possibilities of Chicago are as closed to me at that point as if I had been run over by a large truck. On another level, death appears (or what is as final as death) in moments of crisis and separation — the end of a relationship, the end of a job, the end of a corporation. In each case that end is final, just as final as if we "croaked."

But, you say, all those things might come back. Possibly, but at the same time we recognize that nothing can ever come back just as it was before. Or you may notice that I have used that little phrase "as if," which suggests I am not really talking about death, but something like it. Again, that is possible. But it is equally possible that the little phrase "as if" is but another example of the culturally pervasive denial of death. Why not call a spade a spade and say death pure and simple? Why not indeed?

Or maybe more to the point, why should we? What's the benefit? The primary benefit would be that we could then recognize death is not apart from life, strange to life, or the end of life, but rather all mixed up with life. This inter-connection might be expressed as follows, *To live is to change, to change is to die, to die is to live*. Indeed, I would want to say that death is essential to life or at least a meaningful life. It appears to me that those who assiduously avoid the fact of death end up by evading the possibility of life in all its richness.

There is, in short, another way of looking at things which has many positive advantages. That way is to see death as the natural concomitant of life, present on a daily basis, and necessary for the orderly progression and fulfillment of the human Spirit, otherwise known as transformation. In these terms, we as individuals exist in one form, which then dies, and we emerge in a new way. On a biological level, we acknowledge precisely such a progression as our cells die and are replaced every seven years. At 49 I have already "died" seven times! If there is any validity to this suggestion at all, then the normal, natural, expected way to go is life, death, and renewal — or we might say resurrection. For those who might wish to reserve the term resurrection to some final state "in the clouds," I cannot argue except to say that I really don't know anything about that state, but my daily experience is that of "moving on," which I choose to call resurrection. In sum, to talk about transformation is to talk about the movement from life through death to resurrection.

LIFE

Life is where transformation begins. Plain, simple, old, everyday life, just the way things are at any given point in time. Life is the tedium and the joy, the cry of a small child, and the challenge of a job. It is getting up in the morning and going to bed at night, just life. The nature and quality of this life depends a great deal on where you are and who you are.

To begin with the *where*, which is your place in the environment: It makes no little bit of difference whether you find yourself in the People's Republic of China or in New York City, on the board of IBM or the proprietor of a country store. Certain things are possible in one situation and not in another. This is not to suggest that one situation is necessarily bad and another good, but they certainly are different, and create very different avenues of being and ways of expression over which you don't have a great deal of control. To use the categories from the previous chapter, your environment or organizational setting provides the Vision as to what "it is all about," the Understanding that rationalizes the Vision and simultaneously creates the ground from which your Language is built, and finally, the Information and Data upon which life is worked out in detail. Whatever else may happen with you, you start with your environment, the place where you are.

Of equal importance is *who you are*, which is my way of talking about your position along the Journey of Spirit. It seems that we all start out at the same place, as Body. What happens after that is to some degree, a matter of choice. Who you are

76

determines how you see or perceive your environment, and consequently what you are able to do in that environment given its limitations. If the Who were Jean at the level of Mind and the Where were the Department Store as Responsive, the world would be perceived by Jean as expediters and 1040-Bs responding to customers' needs by virtue of himself serving as the Interconnect, running back and forth. Not a very stimulating picture, and vastly over simplified, but it may serve to establish the concept. *Who you are, and where you are creates the parameters within which you are, and that's life.*

LIFE AS FULFILLING   Life within these parameters may be characterized in a number of ways. In the first place, it is fulfilling. For Jean, this meant taking real pleasure in the feeling of competence and comfort when he had learned the Language so that he might be responsive to the world about him. It felt good to go to work in the morning and know that there was a job to be done that required everything he had, and which could be accomplished within the limits of what he had to offer. In addition, he particularly enjoyed the acceptance and respect of his fellow workers, and the reputation which he had developed as a person "who could get things done." Given who he was and where he was . . . Life was pretty good.

LIFE AS FRUSTRATING   At the same time, Jean was not totally blind to the rough spots. Life could also be very frustrating. There were days when, no matter how hard he tried, the work just didn't move. Sometimes it was the shear numbers of 1040-Bs that were just overwhelming. The faster he went, the behinder he got, and there seemed to be no way out. Then there was the fact of his reputation, he certainly didn't want to loose that good feeling of acceptance and respect from his fellow workers. In the worst of times, Jean found himself being more concerned with his reputation than he was with the job. In order to maintain appearances, there was a strong temptation to cut corners and fudge.

SELF-UNDERSTANDING   On balance, however, things tended to balance, and Jean learned to take the good with the bad. He came to understand that given who he was, and where he was, certain things worked, and others didn't, but, over all, it seemed to fit. In short, Jean understood himself as he was, in his world — he had *self-under-standing*. This self-understanding was very useful, for it allowed him to work up to his limit but no more. Life, as he interpreted it through his self-understanding, was comfortable.

LIFE AS LIMITING   But Life for Jean had its limitations. Jean recognized that there were some other things going on in the company which interested him, but which seemed to be beyond his reach, given life as he understood it. Somewhere there were folks who understood what was going on, and who used that understanding to write organizational and procedure changes which had very direct impact on what Jean did. By the same token, Jean had a sneaking thought that he could probably do something like that too, and that it might be rather fun. But that was just a "sneaking thought," because on most days, Jean was quite content with the way things were. More than that, Jean knew, on some deep level that if some changes were made, they wouldn't just be "some" changes but a whole lot, enough to alter the way things were. Life would no longer be the easy round of 1040-Bs cycling between expediters and the customer. Given such a change, who he was and where he was would no longer be as they were. Equally disturbing for Jean was the fact that he really didn't know what it would be like after the change. He only knew that it would be different. Hidden in that knowledge was a genuine sense of loss and fear of the unknown.

Life for Jean was fulfilling, frustrating and limiting: but through it all, it made a certain amount of sense, for he knew who he was and where he was, and that was his self-understanding. He also knew that to change that life in some fundamental way would represent the end of what was, even as it also represented the possibility of something new. That end, I will say death, constitutes both a barrier and a portal to what ever might come next.

DEATH

One day that end arrived. To be truthful, it didn't arrive all at once, but rather seemed to creep in around the edges. Jean's mountain of 1040-bs grew, and his capacity to deal with that monstrous mass just didn't keep pace. Run fast as he might, with the largest shopping cart imaginable, there was no way that he could be responsive to the needs of the customers. His reputation as a person who could get things done began to suffer, for in fact he just couldn't get it done. As his reputation withered so did his self-understanding. It became harder and harder to balance who he was with where he was. To save his reputation and his self-understanding, he started to cut some corners. When everything became too much, some of the 1040-bs just seemed to get "lost." And had they been "found," tucked in the mail room, where Jean had hidden them, he would have lost the last thing he had, the respect of his co-workers.

On a grey day, Jean knew what he had suspected for a long time. . . it was all over. At least "it" was all over as "it" had been before. Ahead lay open space, fearsome and vacant, representing the dissolution of a prior state. It might become the passage to a future state. But at the moment it was death.

DEATH — A PERSONAL EXAMPLE   On the assumption that my use of the word death may still seem inappropriate in the context of "Jean's tale," allow me to raise the ante with a story drawn from my own experience.

In the early '60s, I was a graduate student at a university in the south. My field was Old Testament, and the limits of my world extended from the rather misty beginnings of the people of Israel around 1200 BC up to the turn of the Millennium. On a daily basis my life was measured out by class periods and endless hours in the library stacks. In addition, I was married, the father of three children, and working on Sundays in a rather conservative church. In terms of my own self-understanding everything seemed to fit. I saw myself as an academic living in a world which appreciated academic types. While I can't say that I was totally unaware of the major changes that were occurring in the country at large, and particularly in the South, the whole business of desegregation and civil rights by no means held a central place in my consciousness. My world was certainly not perfect, but I had no inclination to change it.

One day as I sat in the graduate student lounge watching the TV, the program was interrupted with a special announcement. There had been a bombing in a Birmingham church, and three little children had been killed. There seemed to be little question that the bombing was in retaliation for civil rights activities that had been organized there, although no suspects had been apprehended. For reasons which I did not understand then, and still don't today, my world radically changed in that moment. It all looked the same, and in many ways I was still doing what I had been doing before — but it was different, and no longer very comfortable.

I found myself in the midst of a series of public demonstrations protesting the bombing. Initially, I was only a participant trying to look as if I knew what I was doing, and frightened to death. In my first demonstration, we had gathered in a vacant lot before moving out into the streets. Down the road you could see the crowd and hear their anger. According to the plan, we were to line up in pairs and march down the sidewalk, men and larger women on the outside, and smaller folk next to the wall. I remember standing in the field looking for a partner when a small black girl, not over seven or eight, came up and took my hand saying "Can I walk with you mister?"

How could one so young be so self possessed? Presumably, I was to protect her, and yet it was her strength that made it possible for the two of us to go down the road. When it was all over, she released my hand and started to walk away, pausing only long enough to say "Thank you mister."

In the days that followed, the obvious became inescapable: my world had changed, but I didn't know how much. My studies were a shambles, but more to the point, I didn't care, for they seemed irrelevant. The pleasant sundays I spent working at the local church were terminated when it became quite clear that what I was (or at least what I was becoming) and what they were, mixed like oil and water. Most disturbing, however, was what happened to my family. There had always been some level of argument and malaise, but for all of that we seemed to get along, and I confess to have taken them pretty much for granted. Suddenly, there was silence and separation — downright fear and hostility. Had it only been my studies, or the job, I suspect I would have made it — but when my family fell apart, my world was in pieces. What was worse, I really couldn't see any way to go back, for my conscience had convicted me, and in truth there wasn't any "back" to go back to.

It didn't all occur over night, but in a period of several months the true shape of things became painfully apparent. My world as it had been was no more, and the self-understanding that I possessed no longer worked. When my self-understanding fell apart, I fell apart, quite literally, just before Christmas. The clinical description was "severe anxiety reaction," but the reality was pure hell. Sleep became a thing of the past, and rationality seemed just beyond my grasp. Two things only were clear. First, I needed help, and second my world had ended.

For a variety of reasons, the only place open for me to go was Washington, D.C. And so on a rather chilly gray evening in January, I boarded a bus from that southern city to the nation's capital. As I climbed on the bus, I turned to see my youngest son waving tentatively good-by. He didn't understand, and neither did I.

The ride northward was surprisingly peaceful, and in fact I remember sleeping most of the way. But the arrival in Washington was something else. It was 6:00 in the morning, and the temperature was in the low 30s. Dawn was just edging into cold grey being, and the bus station was deserted. If ever there was a symbol which was also reality, that symbol was the bus station and the reality was death. It was all over, and there was no going home.

When the world radically changes, and a particular self-understanding is rendered null and void, that is death. While it is true that the body seems to carry on, it does so without meaning or purpose in a condition which may fairly be called

80

"despair." Some might say this is worse than death, but I am not sure that we need to go that far. Death will do. The moment of Death is awesome indeed. At first look, it is a great emptiness, a soundless vacuum, for all that used to be there has virtually disappeared, except in memory. As nature abhors a vacuum, so does the individual, and faced with the emptiness, the natural reaction is to try and fill it up with the only thing left — memories.

Thus begins the age old phenomenon of denial and the process of grief work.[38] Faced with nothingness one remembers how it used to be, if only to provide momentary surcease to the pain of loneliness. Pretend that nothing has changed, and maybe life will go on. The reaction is natural and provides small relief, but in the long run, it is destructive. By living in the past, one is closed to the future, and it is in the future, if anywhere, that possibility lies. For me, standing in the bus station, my memories were strong, but the bus station remained its unyielding grey self.

Memories turn to anger. Why did this happen to me? And then anger turns to guilt as the if-onlies flood through. If only I had done such and such this never would have happened. Ultimately, neither memories, anger nor guilt can fill the emptiness. But all of them can start a process which leads through the Open Space to a new way of being.

The critical turning point came in the person of a friend. Prior to leaving the southern city, I had called the only person I really knew in Washington. His name was Molly. Molly was a tall, gaunt individual with the visage of a prophet. Molly also had a degenerative bone disease which caused him no little pain and weakness. But there he was at dawn to meet me. As I got off the bus, he said little more than hello, and the two of us stood waiting for the baggage doors to be opened. I turned away for a moment, and when I turned back, I saw that the baggage was being placed on the street, but mostly what I saw was Molly leaning over to pick up my bag. I knew that it hurt him, and I also knew that he shouldn't have done it, but when I offered to take the bag, he would have none of it. He carried the heavy load to the car. The symbolism was obvious, and knowing Molly it could well have been conscious, but conscious or not that act was the start of my turning point.

Half an hour later, we were sitting in Molly's kitchen with the coffee pot going, and I was telling my tale. From the very beginning to that moment, I told it all.

---

[38] The process described here is well known, and has been studied extensively. Perhaps the best introduction to the field is Kuebler-Ross's "On Death and Dying", Collier Books, 1969. For a fuller description of the process please see Chapter VI.

And Molly sat there, quietly, patiently, letting me go. Somewhere around 9:00 o'clock, Molly got up to get another cup of coffee. As he sat down again at the table, he looked directly at me and said, "What the hell are you going to do with the rest of your life?" The words hit me like a barn door caught broadside to the wind. I felt shocked, even outraged that my friend should treat me so. There I was in deep pain, and he was issuing a challenge that I couldn't even begin to think about.

In retrospect, it became clear to me that Molly had done for me what I could not do for myself. He had joined me in my pain and dissolution, thereby making it a little more bearable, and simultaneously offered me the possibility of accepting what had transpired. But Molly did not stop there. Just as I was beginning to feel some modicum of comfort, he issued a challenge that literally blasted me from where I was to thoughts about what I might become. That was the turning point. The events at the bus station and in Molly's kitchen happened years ago. Since that time, it has become crystalline clear to me that all that has happened since, which I judge to be powerful, rewarding and liberating — simply could not have occurred as a straight line extension from my days as a graduate student immersed in the world of the Old Testament. It is not that those days contributed nothing to my present way of being. Rather it is the case that my Self-Understanding in those days was simply too limited and restricted to allow what I now understand as my potential to be realized. It was necessary to go through that Open Space down into the Depths, where all that was, dissolved and ended. That Open Space became the fecund ground from which my future eventually grew. Death quite literally was End and Beginning.

I do not propose that each person must go though such an experience, nor that all occasions of personal transformation happen in precisely that way. But I must confess that with subsequent reflection, the events described have become paradigmatic for me and my understanding of Individual Transformation.

RESURRECTION

If death creates the Open Space within which new possibility may appear, resurrection provides the opportunity for the possible to become reality. The means for all of this is Love.

The individual existing at the edge of Open Space suspended in nothingness is not an appealing prospect. Indeed there is much in these circumstances that calls for backing away from the edge. But life lived in denial is no life at all, for although it may give momentary relief from hollowness, ultimately it costs infinitely more than it gives. In order to preserve the illusion that "things have not changed," familiar places must be avoided for they carry too many painful memories. By the same token old friends may not be seen, for their sympathy does not console, but only serves as yet another reminder that all is not as it was. Slowly or quickly, the little bit of life that might remain is progressively narrowed and withdrawn from. Whatever else such existence might be, it by no means represents the fulfillment of Spirit.

For better or for worse, the path to fulfillment lies across the Open Space, but that passage remains impossible until the polarities change and end becomes opportunity. It is Love that reverses the flow and provides the turning point. It is the Love of another that provides the possibility of resurrection. Having said this, I have apparently said little, for the contemporary understandings of love are various to say the least, and confusing at best. When love can mean anything from frivolous fornication to some idealized state, a closer definition is necessary.

THE TWO FACES OF LOVE   Love has two faces, acceptance and challenge. Acceptance is by far the most familiar, and if you will, acceptable face of Love, for acceptance is warm, nurturing and supportive. Love as acceptance takes us just the way we are with no questions asked. In many ways, this acceptance is without standards, for given who we are sometimes, the standards must indeed be low or nonexistent if we are also acceptable. And that is a great comfort, but it is also a profound weakness, for love without standards ends in mush. So little is demanded that the value is minimal.

But Love has another face, which is challenge. This is the sort of Love that cares enough to expect and demand the very best. Nothing less than excellence will do. Love of this kind drives us to the wall and beyond. Furthermore there are standards which at times seem almost impossible to attain. These standards are positive, but they also represent the potential for disaster, for taken to extreme they end in unendurable harshness.

The truth of the matter is that Love is neither acceptance nor challenge, but both together. Or stated more precisely, love is not to be found in acceptance or in challenge, but rather in the open space created between the two as they engage each other as paradox.

It is interesting to speculate why it should be that the two are so often separated, and once separated, one or the other becomes dominant. In the history of our country, there was a time in our puritan days when the face of love was purely and simply an angry and judgmental father. More recently, the so called liberals among us have found that distasteful and destructive, and have chosen to look upon the other face of love — acceptance. Liberalism at its extreme appears to accept anything, and any form of behavior may be excused. Then the pendulum swings again, and challenge and excellence are in.

The oscillation from one pole to the other is obvious, but why it should occur is a mystery, unless it has to do with our cultural incapacity to deal with paradox. Somehow, our linear rational minds tell us that the truth must be singular with "only one right way." Given that premise, existence within paradox is impossible, and it becomes clear why we split the paradox and seek our truth in one side or the other. Older, and possibly wiser societies do not have this problem. They understand that the only way to deal with really important issues is through paradoxical statement. China, for example understands the *yin and yang* as the dual forces through which all existence is held in being. [39]

For those who stand at edge of Open Space surrounded by nothingness, and who have come to realize that going back (denial) is fruitless, the leap forward is truly awesome, as only the unknown can be awesome. Like the trapeze artist on the high swings, there is only one way to completion, but before that way can be entered, you have to let go.[40] On the first time out, the moment of release is no small passage, and a safety net is more than an incidental. In the case of the individual, letting go is no less essential or fearsome, furthermore, it is always the "first time out," for the journey is always new. The safety net appears in the acceptance by another.

The passage is fearsome because of the unknown, but essential unless the life of denial is to be continued. What was must be acknowledged as being no longer; this

---

[39] China, of course, is not alone in this ability to live with paradox. In fact the present description of love evolved from my old testament studies when I was struck by the fact that a number of western scholars seemed to make a distinction/opposition between two hebrew concepts "mishpat" [judgement] and "chesed" [often translated loving kindness] as both of these related to God. At times it seemed that you almost ended up with two Gods - a God of judgement and a God of loving-kindness. My reading of the material suggested that this was a gratuitous effort, and that for the Israelite, God was indissolubly one, who's love ["ahab"] might best be described in the polar terms "mishpat" and "chesed" In any event, I understand Love to be Acceptance AND Challenge. One without the other won't do, especially when Love is to be understood as the means whereby Resurrection is given as a possibility.

[40] The idea of "letting go" is very central to the thought and work of Robert Tannenbaum. For more on this see Robert Tannenbaum and Robert Hanna, "Holding On and Letting Go; a Neglected Perspective on Change," in R. Tannenbaum, N. Margolies, and F. Mazorik, "Human Systems Development", Jossey-Bass, San Francisco, 1985.

implies that the past and the present must be acknowledged for what they are. The old way is over, and the present circumstances are a mess.

It is a little difficult to say which part is the hardest. Saying goodby to what was pulls at the heart strings, but acknowledging the mess of the moment can shatter the last fragile remains of the ego. It goes so contrary to what every self-respecting, red-blooded, macho type [41] has come to expect as his due. It is bad enough to be down, but to have to admit that to yourself is the last straw.

For me the possibility of Resurrection was given by Love expressed through the person of Molly. It began the instant I climbed off the bus and saw Molly picking up my bag. In that symbolic act, another person reached out and down to where I was, quietly joining me in my pain. No questions asked, no standards to meet; I found myself accepted just exactly the way I found myself. The power of this acceptance continued once we had reached the house, as Molly allowed me to tell my tale. No critique was offered, and I could let all come out, from the moment that things began to fall apart up to that very instant. In telling the tale, some of the fear ran off, the events became more familiar and less stark. There were even times when I found myself laughing at some of the more ridiculous aspects. As I talked I felt less strange, for as Molly accepted me, I found that I was able to begin to accept myself and what had happened. The past could be recognized, honored, and laid to rest. Had Molly stopped right there, and done no more than accept me as I was, the final result would have been vastly and disastrously different. For in the balm and comfort of his acceptance also lay the possibility for a pathological dependence. From so many points of view, it would have been wonderful to go no further and know that at least in that little corner of time and space, I was secure. Yet to do that would have been debilitating for me and destructive for Molly; my future possibility would have been denied, and Molly might have assumed the role of petty tyrant whose ego was fed by the weakness of another.

In fact, Molly did not stop there, and as comfort neared, he reversed the field with challenge: "What the hell are you going to do with the rest of your life?" Suddenly I found myself blasted away from a remembrance of the past, and the momentary warmth of the present to deal with the possibility of future. As I struggled to answer his question, I knew that I had no answer. But I knew something else which

---

[41] Macho types are not restricted to the male of the species, although the form is somewhat different with the female. Example: "super-mom" that indomitable Amazonian type who manages to balance career, family, and a million community activities with nary a hair out of place, and no help needed.

was much more valuable, there might be an answer, indeed there must be an answer. At the moment it existed only as possibility, but that possibility was sufficient to draw me across the Open Space. The turning point had occurred, the polarities switched. The possibility of Resurrection was available.

NEW LIFE/RADICAL SELF LOVE

If the possibility of Resurrection is made available through the Love of another, where does the reality come from? The answer is, *Its already there*, resident in the unfulfilled potential of the individual. In my case, all that I had learned in my "prior incarnation" as academic stood as potential for a new life which has been unfolding. It needed only unlocking through the acceptance and challenge of Molly. But moving from potential to actuality requires another element: self-love. Actuality is given only when a person loves him or her self enough to make it so. In the final analysis, only the individual can make the difference by accepting his situation just as it is and then challenging himself to move beyond.

CONCLUDING THOUGHTS — REFUSAL OF THE RESURRECTION

But why doesn't it work? Why is it that the process of transformation so often seems to abort? If everything is truly there in the cocoon, so to speak, what goes wrong? The glitch occurs not in the process of dying, nor in the possibility of resurrection as given by the Love of another, but rather in the apparently unlikely behavior I call Refusal of the Gift of Resurrection, which is itself a manifestation of the lack of self-love.

To refuse the Gift of Resurrection appears most unlikely, considering the real pain of death and the given possibility of a better way to be. Why on earth would anybody do that? The reason is simply that resurrection always comes as a gift that is needed. In our society, accepting a gift is not something we do with a great deal of grace. Accepting a needed gift is done only under duress, if at all. To accept a needed gift implies some lack or weakness, something that we can't do for ourselves. For a people who have been raised in the shadow of the great heros of the west (the Lone Ranger, for example) or the rugged individualists of industry, showing weakness is something we would just as soon do without. In one way or another we choose to make it on our own, and there is much value in that ideal, but there are also exceptions. Transformation is a prime example.

Molly did for me what I could not do for myself: through his Love as acceptance and challenge, he opened the door for me to acknowledge the end and powerlessness of the way I had been, and simultaneously goaded me to become infinitely more than I was. But in the process we had to wash some dirty linen labeled POWERLESSNESS. If being powerless is bad, even morally inferior, knowing that one is powerless is worse, but worst of all is having someone else know you are powerless. Yet it is precisely with that knowledge, or more important with the acceptance of that knowledge, that there comes the possibility of actualizing the gift of the resurrection. This is the first act of genuine self-love. But it in itself is not sufficient. For acceptance left at that point quickly becomes self-pity, and the confirmation of powerlessness. The critical next step is self-challenge, through which the pain of the moment is cast off and transcended. Those who preach the gospel of "up by your own bootstraps" have a point. There comes a time when only you can make the difference by seizing the opportunities as they appear. New Life is ultimately a product of radical self-love.

To the extent that transformation is more than a difficult passage through a rocky moment of life, but rather the essential movement by which our lives as individuals reach fulfillment, becoming a person is not something we can do completely by ourselves. At this point, I return to the thoughts of Martin Buber. An "I" becomes fully an "I" only in meaningful dialogue with a "thou." That gnomic statement means quite simply that my transformation exists as a possibility only in the context of the Love of another who becomes "thou" to me, even as I am "thou" to him or her, a dearly beloved brother or sister to whom I may acceptably reveal my powerlessness, even as I am challenged to go beyond it.

The implications of this thought are profound, for if true, it means that not only are we our brother's keeper, but he is ours. Furthermore, our status as "keeper" is not just a "nice thing to do," but rather constitutes an essential condition for the continuance and fulfillment of mankind as a species. We will all make it together or not at all.

There is another implication which is critical for our thoughts about organizations. If an organization is any group of two or more gathered around a common purpose, then by definition we live our life in organization. That much you would expect, but the corollary is that our life in organization is essential for our fulfillment as individuals, for it is in dialogue with others that we are enabled to negotiate the journey of transformation. Essentially, that is the argument of this chapter to this point.

The next step may be a little obscure, but it represents the critical link between what I have just discussed, and what is to come under the heading of the process of transformation in the organization. The thought is this: Insofar as organization is the "setting" in which transformation of individuals occurs, it becomes the prime site of person making, and in that fact lies the organization's *raison d'etre*. So if one were to ask, What is the point of an organization? — the answer would be to provide those circumstances in which individuals may reach fulfillment. Everything else is secondary including showing a profit, making a product and providing a service. Not that those aren't important goals, for obviously they are. But to the extent that any of those "hard" outcomes replaces the "people making" business as primary, all of them stand in jeopardy. A different way of looking at things perhaps, but it is not without precedent, even on the contemporary scene. For example, the president of AT&T, Charles Brown was reported to have said to his assembled vice presidents, "Gentlemen, you have one thing to do, develop your people. The rest of the business will take care of itself." Perhaps that report is apocryphal, but if it is, nobody should tell, because it is precisely that kind of thinking and priority that may bring AT&T through its present transformational journey.

Chapter VI

OPEN SPACE
(The Organization)

The passage of an organization through the Open Space of transformation is closely analogous to that of the individual; indeed the two are totally interconnected. But the organization's passage is more complex with a different flavor, hence I will use a different terminology. Covenant, Rebellion, Reconciliation, and New Covenant are the terms.[42]

COVENANT

The process of transformation begins with a Covenant, which may be understood as the charter of organization. At the beginning, when the individuals first gather, there emerges a relatively unstructured agreement as to the way things ought to be done. It is based on the organizational potential as that is expressed through the common Vision, Understanding, and Language, and such Information and Data as may have been collected at that point. To the extent that the Covenant is written down, it is only a bare outline to remind people of the sorts of things that need to get done and by whom. Eventually, the Covenant will achieve a more structured form as in Laws, Policy and Procedure, the forms and structures of organizational life. At that point, the Covenant becomes the rule book of liturgy, specifying in fine detail what the people do and should do.

---

[42] These terms originate in the Old Testament, which I understand to be the story of the stages of transformation as experienced by the people of Israel. Each stage began with a covenant in which God and the people agreed to get along in a prescribed way. That covenant was then abrogated by some form of rebellion, necessitating a subsequent reconciliation which became manifest in a New Covenant. At each point along the way the people of Israel transformed from one state of being to another — from nomads to tribes, tribes to a confederation, and confederation to a kingdom. The validation of this interpretation is a subject for a different time and another book.

The value of Covenant in its initial loose form is undeniable, for it offers an openness and flexibility which is quite appropriate and necessary to the organization is its early stages, when it is unrealistic and pointless to legislate every move and expected behavior.

However, as the organization gains experience with itself, operating in the environment, basic things become clear, and may be standardized. This move towards formalization usually occurs at those points where it seems that "little things" are getting in the way of doing business. For example, travel expenses. At the beginning it was simply enough for each person to keep track of what was spent and request repayment in any way that seemed to get the job done. Then one day, the people in administration hit "tilt." After processing 42 requests for repayment submitted on the backs of envelopes, they said, there must be a better way, and out came the Travel Voucher. A small step to be sure, but now everybody had to do it the same way, and it was all written down.

This move towards formality and writing things down is by no means bad, and indeed performs a necessary function by taking care of the "little things" — the routine — so that people can concentrate on the important business at hand. In our department store, when it existed as a Responsive organization, having all the right words carefully defined, and displayed in their interrelationship was essential. For Jean and his cohorts, it was important to know what an expediter was, and the nature and function of a 1040-B. If they didn't know that, the job could not be done. It was also important to know the right words and relationships at some remove from any particular part of the action. Thus the folks in the vacuum cleaner department needed to know that Omni-Charge existed, roughly what it did, and how to get there. Not that they were going to handle the credit arrangements themselves, but in order to be responsive to the needs of their customers, that knowledge was critical.

In response to these needs, policy and procedure manuals, tables of organization, and functional statements emerge, which collectively constitute a conscious articulation of liturgy (what the people do). Each useful in it own way, but not without some built in dangers, for all are really abstractions from the life of Spirit within that organization. To use the word of anthropologist Edward Hall, they are "extensions" built by organizations to take care of business in an orderly way, but they, in themselves, are not the business.[43] So long as the distinction is maintained between "exten-

---

[43] Hall, Edward T.,"Beyond Culture", Anchor Press/Doubleday,1977.

sion" and the business, danger is avoided. However, these extensions may take on a life of their own. In that case the organization will experience the unpleasant effects of what Hall calls "Extension Transference"[44] in which the abstracted systems, designed to assist the business become more real and important than the business itself. At that point, form and structure displace Spirit as the perceived center of reality.

Covenant, even in its increasingly formalized appearance, is intensely useful. For the organization as a whole, the Covenant provides the essential guide for doing business indicating who does what, where, when, how, and to what standards and for what reward. Operating as the articulated collective self-understanding, the Covenant literally holds everything together.

The Covenant is also very useful to the outside world of customers, suppliers, financial institutions, and even competitors. For it is the Covenant that defines who and what the organization is and, of equal importance, keeps the organization within some general boundaries. Obviously the external players have no need to know all the details. However, if business is going to be done, it is important to know who you are doing business with, and have some reasonable expectation that the *who* will remain more or less the same over time.

For example, suppliers need to know in order to schedule production and maintain inventory. Financial institutions must know in order to have some confidence in the credit they extend. Even competitors need to know in order to plot their own strategy. Covenant is therefore important not only to the organization, but also to the external world, for it establishes and maintains the Organization's place in that world. But there is also a downside.

The external world's perception of the Organizational Covenant can actually imprison the organization in a place it no longer wants to be. For example, customers can get awfully upset when a particular product line is discontinued, and obviously banks become perturbed when some new, unexpected venture adds potential risk to their loans. Competitors are very uneasy when the organization indulges in some unexpected behavior. The point is that the external world has some considerable stake in the organization's Covenant, and generally exerts a very conservative pressure to keep things just as they are.

Lastly, the Covenant is enormously important to the separate individuals who exist in the Organization. For it is the Covenant, as collective self-understanding, which provides the context within which the individual's self-understanding is worked

---

[44] Hall, E.T.,op.cit. pg 28.

out. This is not to suggest that every individual will understand him/herself just as the Covenant prescribes, but the individual self-understanding will be crafted as some variant of the collective, either by way of elaboration, or by going off in some new directions. Some individuals will understand themselves as "company men/women," and others will perceive themselves as somehow "different," but in any case, they will all start with the organizational Covenant as a baseline.

For all these reasons, the organizational Covenant is essential, but it should never be forgotten that Covenant is a secondary phenomenon, an abstraction from Spirit. It is the rule book of liturgy, which in turn is the product of mythos, the image of Spirit. Reality lies at the level of Spirit, and to the extent that the Covenant protects and enhances the capacity of Spirit to fulfill its task, it is useful. However, when and as the external environment changes, so that the needs are somehow different, the old rules no longer apply.

THE SLIDE TOWARDS LEGALISM

Legalism might be described as the hardening of the covenantal arteries. It is what happens when an Organization begins to mistake the forms of its existence for existence itself. The beginnings of this "slide" are quite natural and barely perceptible. Under the heading of "getting ourselves organized," more and more things are formalized and written down in order to take care of the details. However, what begins as an effort to make life in the organization more useful and effective can end by having precisely the opposite effect. Covenant, which was intended to define and preserve life in the organization becomes, in legalistic form, the restricter and destroyer of life.

The early stages of legalism are quite subtle and therefore insidious. Take the matter of planning. A young organization is so busy doing business that it scarcely has time to look ahead. In its Reactive, and even in its Responsive form, the press of business is such that next year, or five years ahead is beyond consideration. But with a few stubbed toes, and "opportunities missed," the organization comes to understand that the business today is inexorably related to the business of tomorrow, hence planning for tomorrow is a useful occupation.

So far so good, but the next step is often the creation of a planning department in order to provide a center of expertise. Still not bad, but getting dangerous, for planning departments will often assume that their task is to do the planning as opposed to helping the organization perform this task. This tendency is exacerbated by virtue of the fact that most of the other folks in the organization are still too busy to do any planning, and would just as soon leave it to the "experts." The experts, not willing to loose the advantage, and seeking to expand their turf, accept the task, and the slide towards legalism is begun.

The next step is almost predictable. Once the experts have taken over the planning function, it then becomes essential to tell everybody else what to do in order to collect the appropriate Data and Information in a standardized manner. To this end, forms and procedures are developed, compiled, and published. The resulting manual becomes bigger and bigger, and filled with more and more expert-speak. Eventually it becomes so big that folks outside the planning department don't want to deal with it, and even if they did, it is incomprehensible, given the specialized language.

The impact of this latest iteration can be devastating for any one of several reasons. To the extent that folks in the organization see planning as something so specialized that they can't participate, they will forget it entirely, in which case the whole planning function is pushed over to the side, and the organization is denied an essential forward look. Another possibility, which is equally grim, is that the Planners will assume total control, and business in the organization is then expected to conform to the Planning Cycle. All of this may sound like an extreme caricature, but I remember a young executive in a client organization who was informed by "the powers that be" that he couldn't have any more "bright ideas" because they were "upsetting the planning cycle." If ever there was a case where a system intended to preserve and enhance life under the Covenant had precisely the opposite effect, that was it. And my experience tells me that the case is not unique.

The example has been planning but before the planners of this world assume that I am "anti-planning" (which I am not), let me hasten to add that any system in the organization may end up in precisely the same place, and the sad truth of the matter is that most of them do at one time or another. The tendency towards legalism is no respecter of persons, departments, or organizations. It happens to all of us.

It is also important to note that the tendency towards legalism is not necessarily the product of some nefarious scheme, contrived by "bad" people, in order to take over the world (Planners are OK). What turns into legalism is, at its inception, a good and useful idea. How, then, does it get perverted and pushed so far from its original intention? The "Devil Theory" of the advance to legalism is a convenient but quite superficial explanation, which says that "some bad people" took a good thing and perverted it to their own ends.[45]

But if not the "Devil Theory," what then? The answer is that the tendency towards legalism is the product of the natural inertia and conservatism built into the organization through the expectations of its several constituencies; those people inside, and those on the outside. Were we dealing with physical reality, the proper word would be entropy (locked up energy) and the operative principle, The Second Law of Thermodynamics.[46]

To the extent that the organization has become important for all concerned, it is critical that the organization remain as it was, "Don't Change the Covenant." In fact, the more steps taken to legislate the Covenant into "permanent existence," the better. In this way, the external world always knows what it is doing business with, while the individuals may depend on the collective self-understanding as a continuing and stable basis from which they may work out their own self-understanding.

This search for permanence is understandable, and in stable times, it is not particularly overpowering or damaging. People just sort of assume the organization will remain as it was; and in fact it will, if only because there is no particular reason to change. The result is an easy symbiosis which becomes more and more comfortable.

However, in turbulent times, such as we are experiencing at the moment, the situation is radically different. On the one hand, the organization finds it necessary to change fundamentally in order to meet an altered environment (the AT&T scenario),

---

[45] A very common example of this is the view that the early days of the Christian Church (or any other ancient and large institution) were filled with light and love. However, in subsequent generations, things became infinitely worse as the original purity got messed up in the petty battles and egomania common to mankind. The solution proposed is to go back to those pristine days. Such a return is of course impossible, and further, when those pristine days are closely considered, it turns out that things weren't nearly as perfect as we might have hoped.

[46] The analogue with physics is very close in my thinking, and the apparent dead-end of entropy is only that. I think that organizations can and do go beyond entropy with a sort of "pop" that takes them from a level of complexity which doesn't work - to a higher one which does. Indeed that is what transformation is all about. The work of Ilya Prigogine described in "Order out of Chaos", [Bantam/New Age 1984, see chapter IX] is particularly helpful in this area as a paradigmatic statement. However, I am not attempting to argue from Prigogine's findings in the physical world to the world of organizations. That is a large jump, even for me. Rather, I came to this understanding from a consideration of the process of transformation in the life of Israel and with subsequent observations within the organizations I have served. Prigogine's theoretical statement has turned out to be a marvelous image of what I had in mind. The fact that we both arrive at more or less the same theoretical statement is not, I think, happenstantial, for in both cases, the issue of concern is energy/Spirit. If it turns out, as I suspect it will, that not only are the dynamics equivalent, but also the object of concern, so much the better. In fact, Prigogine takes large strides towards making that connection in his final chapter.

94

while at the same time, those on the inside and the outside cling ever more desperately to what was, if only to protect themselves from the chaos they experience.

In the case of the external world, the example of the suppliers will make the point. For years, these suppliers have depended upon the old department store to market their goods. Their five year plan mirrored the plan of the department store, and their expectation for profits depended not just on their own efforts, but upon the success of the department store. That is the way the Covenant had worked for them. Is it any wonder then that when the times get rough, these same suppliers will make every effort to encourage the organization to establish the Covenant in concrete? Long term, irrevocable, carefully spelled out contracts are the name of the game. Otherwise known as protect your market and your life.

The pressure towards legalism and conservation from the outside is matched, if not surpassed, by an equivalent pressure from within. As the world changes, and as the individuals perceive the magnitude of that change, the temptation to hang on to what is becomes irresistible. For what is, is not some inconsequential thing, but the very life of the individual as they have come to understand it. Change the Covenant and they will change, which means in essence they will die. The awesome potential of Open Space appears before the individual, and it is known, if not understood, that once over the edge, there is no going home.

Dramatic talk? Perhaps, but how else do you explain the level of intensity and anxiety present in contemporary labor management negotiations. The code words are "job security," but that means infinitely more than a paycheck, it is a whole way of life, indeed for many it is life itself. This is not to suggest that money is not important, but that is just the tip of the iceberg. In fact, in case after case,[47] individuals will give up money (payback schemes) just to maintain the fiction that the old Covenant has not changed. Following the closing of a steel plant in a one industry town, a middleaged worker was interviewed. The off camera voice asked the painful question, "What will you do now?" The answer was barely audible and came out almost as a sob. "I don't know — I just can't think. I am a steel man, as was my father, and my father before him. It is all over. I don't think there is very much left. But somebody gotta do something, like raise the tax on all that imported steel that drove us out." Looking for somebody to prop up the old Covenant is quite understandable.

In a different time and place the issue was the same. In the middle 60's as the civil rights movement boiled to a crescendo, I heard many white southerners saying,

---

[47] e.g. Eastern Airlines.

"But you don't understand, you are destroying the Southern way of life." They were right. The fact that the "Southern way of life" was miserably destructive to millions of black Americans did not obviate the pain felt by many whites. Their life was at risk, the old Covenant was changing, and they knew (correctly) that the end was at hand. That the old Covenant must pass in the interest of justice, equity and the future may be true, but that did not, and could not diminish the anguish that many felt. It is no wonder that the policy of Massive Resistance emerged and was written into law. When the Covenant is threatened, life is threatened, and virtually any tactic to preserve the old seems justified.

The slide towards legalism may begin as a subtle, natural, barely perceptible drift, which at the time seemed to be a very good idea. In fact it is the only idea, because getting organized and adopting some "uniform procedures" make the difference between going around in circles and getting things done with some dispatch. But under turbulent circumstances, this drift becomes a massive flow as individuals within, and institutions without seek to shore up the Covenant in some permanent way. The stakes are high, and the motivation completely understandable, but the results for the organization are disastrous. At precisely the time when greater flexibility and freedom of movement is essential, there is less. Caught between the thrust of an external environment apparently gone wild and an internal rigidity which dictates that things must remain as they have been, the pressures build. And these new pressures effectively feed the cycle one more time around, the greater the pressure for change, the more adamant the resistance. However, if the organization is to survive, the locked up Spirit must be released in order to find new and more appropriate form. Legalism and entropy must be overcome. The conditions have been set for Rebellion.[48]

---

[48] In Prigogines's terms, this situation is Called "Far from Equilibrium"[op. cit., pg 140] His research has shown him that systems at rest or near equilibrium seem to coast on their way into entropy. However, when the tensions are strong enough and the vacillations are great enough, they tend to produce a chaotic circumstance which may create the ground for a whole new order or way of being. Prigogine uses the example of boiling water. As the water heats, the flow patterns are apparently random and chaotic and increase in intensity as the temperature rises. Suddenly the random behavior converts to the orderly roll of a hard boil. Rebellion is precisely the chaotic state which may precipitate a new order.

REBELLION

It is a curious and, so far as I know, a universal fact, that Rebellion, to the Rebel, is perceived as a natural, justified and necessary activity which is entered into only as a matter of last resort with the hope that somehow the essential Spirit of an organization may be re-expressed in new and more meaningful ways. Doubtless there are trouble makers who enjoy trouble for trouble's sake, but I think they are in the minority, and in any event, they are not the sort of folks I am concerned with here. A true Rebel comes from the heart of the organization, is deeply affected by the Vision and Understanding of that organization, and indeed has crafted his or her Self-Understanding in relationship to the organizational Covenant. In short the Rebel cares passionately for the organization and what it stands for, and the act of rebellion is understood to be a movement towards life.

Precisely the same action and person is perceived by the organization and all those who hold a major stake in the organization in diametrically opposed terms. Rebellion is seen as unnatural, unjustified, and unnecessary — an activity that can produce only destruction and death.

Both points of view are correct. Rebellion does in fact lead to the up-ending of all that was. It is destructive of the old Covenant, which described a way of being and doing things which worked very well and gave large comfort to all those who participated in it. Rebellion is therefore painful, disorienting and chaotic. At the same time, Rebellion contains within it the seeds of renewal, the possibility of being in a different and more productive way. It is ultimately life-affirming. But before that affirmation can become real, the old Covenant must be honored and laid to rest as the necessary pre-condition for the emergence of the new. Open Space must be entered and transversed for transformation to occur.

Rebellion begins in the dissonance created when the organizational Covenant is no longer capable of meaningfully holding the organization together in the world. The Covenant says one thing, and the world demands something different. In between stand those individuals who's lives have assumed their present shape and meaning in relation to that Covenant, and now find that meaning stretched and uncomfortable. Initially, the tendency is to overlook the dissonance and warp of meaning. So much is at stake that it is not only easier to look the other way, but also very difficult to look in the right direction. To the extent that the Covenant has become the baseline from which individuals have worked out their own self-understanding, the Covenant is also an integral part of the "eyeglasses" each individual wears, through which he or she sees and interprets the world. If "something seems strange," it is almost impossible to gain sufficient distance from the eyeglasses to understand that the problem resides in the eyeglasses themselves. And obviously there is little inclination to do this, if only because to doubt the eyeglasses is to doubt the very thing that mediates reality.

If Rebellion has its roots in the dissonance created by environmental demands conflicting with inappropriate Covenantal responses, Rebellion first appears concretely in the action of a single person who is then known as the Rebel. This may be the common experience, but it is a mistake to view Rebellion only in these restricted terms. For the activity of the Rebel is but a single manifestation of a broader malaise. What is significant about the Rebel is that he or she is forced, for whatever reason, to articulate and act upon perceptions of change which are shared, however unconsciously, by many others in the organization. The results of this rebel activity will be destructive to the Covenant as it has existed. It is natural, therefore, that the Rebel should be resisted and possibly banished. It is also natural that those who attempt to remain within the Covenant as it was, should perceive the Rebel's actions only in terms of negativity and evil. But do not lose sight of the fact that in the context of the whole transformative process, the rebel is the emergent edge of a quest for a better way to be.

REBELLION IN THE DEPARTMENT STORE In our department store, you will recall, there was a time when the organization, functioning at the Pro-Active level, began to perceive that the world wasn't working the way they understood that it should. According to that Understanding, the customers with a cluster of needs *out there* may be served by coming *in here* to shop. The way things were, it was quite natural to create a series of departments, staffed by responsive individuals who could bring need and product together. The Covenant, or collective self-understanding specified how things should be, and what should be done. There needed to be sufficient space to display the merchandise, a pleasant ambience to put the customers in a positive mood, courteous sales personnel appropriately dressed, maintenance folks to care for the space, and a host of other things that, woven together, created the nutrient environment in which the department store existed. Beyond the physical appearances, there were also powerful rewards and recognitions that made life in the Department store meaningful. Personal definition was provided by title and function; Joe is head of Vacuum Cleaners. Personal worth was established in important ways by recognition within the Covenant; William is the best sales person we've got. And of course at the Executive level, brownie points were to be made by conceiving the best possible ways to get the most people out there to come in here to buy. This involved careful planning to insure that the appropriate merchandise was available in sufficient quantities. But then the world began to change. It didn't happen all at once, but the small computer had arrived and was spreading. Folks on the outside discovered that they didn't have to go anywhere to get what they needed — *inside* and *outside* collapsed into one thing, *Here*. Furthermore, folks on the outside discovered that time was no longer divided into *store hours* and *not-store hours*, for that too had collapsed into a common Now, or anytime you want it.

Intimations of this change reached the department store in bits and pieces which seemed to make sense in terms of the old Covenant. Putting it simply, sales were down, and for those who still operated on a Reactive level, that meant only one thing; try harder, move faster. Responsive types looked to the words they used and instigated a move back to good old Omni-Charge. Pro-active individuals assumed that there must have been some error in their planning: perhaps the merchandise wasn't right or in sufficient quantity. Needless-to-say, all their efforts produced little result except frustration, which only increased the growing sense of malaise.

Now suppose that our friend Jean bought himself a small computer. After playing all the games, he decided to try out this new thing called "computer shopping." At first it just seemed like another game, and it was a lot of fun. He didn't have to go anywhere, and he could shop any time he wanted to. Then a light went on. This was very different than the world he was used to, and miles apart from the way the world was supposed to work according to the Covenant. As the light spread out, it revealed something that he might have suspected, but never thought of before. The problem back at the store was not that they were doing something wrong, but rather that they were doing the wrong thing. The world that used to be wasn't that way anymore, and in fact time and space now meant something quite different. An exciting idea, but not without some elements of risk.

You can imagine the reaction when Jean walked in with the news. "Guess what folks — the world has changed. Time and Space are not as they used to be." The immediate response, of course, would be "He's crazy." And that response is quite appropriate, for insanity, after all, is seeing the world in a radically different way than everybody else does. [49] The label insane is the accepted way of dealing with the aberrant ones in order to protect them from themselves and, not incidently, to protect

---

[49] For an interesting and possibly extreme discussion of this idea consult Laing, R.D. "The Politics of Experience, Ballantine Books, 1967, in which the author argues that in fact it is the whole Western world that is crazy.

us from them. Crazy people are, by definition, not to be held responsible. Hopefully they will get over it, but in the interim we will make some allowances. Calling our incipient Rebel "crazy" is the perfect way out, for as long as he is not responsible, we do not have to take him seriously. And of course "taking him seriously" would put the whole Covenant at risk.

There is also much within the context of the Covenant that would lead Jean to accept his craziness, for if he is right and not crazy, virtually everything that he has taken as "given" up to that point will be up for grabs. The essential understanding of who he is and where he is starts with the Covenant. Absent the Covenant, and Jean is in deep trouble. So when you look at the situation "objectively," it is greatly to the self interest of the individual to be "crazy." At best he will get over it, and at worst the Covenant will continue to stand as some sort of comfort. Incipient Rebels are not out to do bad things.

We may imagine that Jean tried very hard to get over his craziness. Yet, each night when he sat down before his little computer, that new world just refused to go away. What started as a mild curiosity became a major infatuation, because Jean could see in that little box some major possibilities for the old department store. It was just conceivable that rather than fighting this strange presence, the store could utilize it to great advantage.

On his own and very quietly, Jean began to gather some facts. How many computers were there; who owned them; what was the potential market; and how could you set up a business that would take advantage of that market? One thing for sure, whatever that business would look like, it would be a very different. No more display areas, no more salesmen on the floor, no need to be dressed appropriately, because nobody from the "outside" would ever be "inside."

As Jean pursued his interest, it became clear that this new idea was no longer just an idea. The more he looked, the more convinced and excited he became. In fact, he was becoming something different than he was. He still felt part of the team, under the old Covenant, but for all of that he was different because he had a Vision of what might be. Driven by that Vision, he could no longer sit easy. Something was breaking out for him, a new potential, a new direction.

The next time Jean raised his "crazy idea" at work he did it differently. Instead of baldly announcing what he had discovered, he came armed with facts and figures, the outline of a plan. But most of all he spoke with the conviction of one who held a Vision. And that got peoples' attention. A very few of his co-workers were captured by his logic and excitement. While they did not grasp all the details, for indeed the details were pretty thin, they did begin to share the Vision.

The majority of the people had a very different reaction. No longer could they push Jean to one side because he was crazy. He had now become dangerous. While they did not understand everything Jean had to say, what they did understand told them more than they wanted to know. If Jean were allowed to push ahead with the new idea, essentially everything they all held dear and in common would be shoved out of the way. And that simply could not happen. Incipient Rebels, with the best of intentions, are dangerous to the health of old Covenants.

The organizational response was automatic and virtually instantaneous. Cut off the resources, get rid of the threat. As the human body reacts to foreign bodies with antibodies, so the organization reacted unthinkingly to Jean and his small band of co-conspirators. Suddenly the small time and space that Jean had been allowed "because he was crazy" disappeared. He sat alone in the cafeteria and met furtively with his fellows in the basement. Such resources as they needed, they "borrowed" in surreptitious ways.[50] In a word, they were down in the dumps, but they followed their Vision.

Down in the dumps (or basement, as the case may be) is not exactly appealing, but it does yield a new sense of perspective, a clear sight of the basics. From this place, they discovered a remarkable thing, their Vision, while new, was not unique. Indeed, it shared much of the thrust and power of the founder's original Vision. Jean recalled the incredible day on the 21st floor when old J.B. told the story. In that story, conspirators recognized a Spirit kindred to their own, which added power to their venture and gave wings to the new idea. Something was going to pop.

---

[50] At this point, Jean and his fellows have become a "skunkworks," an epi-phenomenon recently discovered and marvelously described by Tom Peters in a paper entitled "The Mythology of Innovation", Palo Alto Consulting Center, 1983. The point is that skunkworks are not an epi-phenomenon at all, but rather a natural result of the presence of Rebels in the Organization, which in turn is an integral part of the process of organization transformation. The surprise is not that skunkworks were discovered, but rather that they had not been noticed before. The reason I suppose, is that in more stable times, the given order is presumed. In the present, that presumption is no longer valid, and so it becomes critical to ask what is going on. Skunkworks are at least part of the answer. From my point of view, Skunkworks have always been with us even as organizations have always been transforming. Those interested in the early history of Skunkworks might consider the motley band of the Prophets who persisted in living "off line" out in the desert, while at the same time challenging the people of Israel to live up to their ideals.

AT THE EDGE OF OPEN SPACE   The line is now drawn, and the prospects are not appealing. On the one hand we find Jean and his small band possessed of an idea which has the potential for breathing new life into the organization, but not without a price. To fully utilize this Vision, the organization will have to undergo substantial changes, indeed it will have to transform from the old way of understanding itself and its business (the old Covenant). Should the organization elect to follow this route, not only will it have to change, but all those who have defined their lives in terms of that organization will also have to change, which needless to say, they will be less than anxious to do. In fact, all things considered, they would rather die first, which is essentially what they will have to do. Transformation initiated in any part of a system eventually effects the total system or none of it. We all go together or not at all.

At the same time, Jean and his fellows are no longer at liberty to back off and give up their Vision, which has long passed the status of Good Idea, and has assumed the intensity of passionate concern, for Jean knows that there is no going back, and he believes that his Vision will lead to a future state that is not only possible but fulfilling.[51] The situation is rendered more difficult and complex by the fact that the organization has much that Jean needs to bring his Vision to reality in terms of resources and history. By the same token, Jean has precisely that which the organization needs to enable its collective Spirit to reform and make it in a new way in a new world.

The choice is no longer for or against transformation. Transformation has already been initiated by a changed environment. The choice is rather, evolve to a new way of doing business or go out of business. No matter what, the old form of Spirit, which has served so well, is no longer functional. More than that, everybody knows it. Each employee understands at some level that things really are different, the old days are over. Indeed, the violent, though predictable reaction to Jean and his idea is almost certain proof of their knowledge. It is but a contemporary example of the age-old principle — kill the messenger who brings the news. And Jean has some news.

---

[51] The capacity of organizations to deal effectively and profitably with their Rebels is a subject that has received little serious attention. Much effort has of course been devoted to bringing folks back into line — ordinarily talked about as conflict resolution, which usually means maximum change on the part of the Rebels with minimum disruption to the organization. But the present question goes much deeper, for here the issue becomes, how do you maximize the potential resident in the rebel even if, or better, in order that, the total organization may face, pursue and successfully complete the process of transformation ? Some of the most exciting work in this area is being done under the heading of "Intrepreneurship" as conceptualized by Gifford Pinchott and practiced by the Foresight Group from Sweden. The intent is to provide supportive organizational environments for rebellious (read innovative) spirits.

On the positive side, Jean's news has the potential for breaking through the noisy desperation of an organization caught in legalism and headed toward entropy[52] in order to gain attention and focus the sagging, dissipating Spirit in new and profitable directions. The News could become a "difference which makes a difference," [53] so radical and striking that it may effectively catch the flagging Spirit, and vector it toward a yet to be realized future. Making real news out of noise, especially in a way that has lasting impact, is no easy task. The message must be clear, acceptable and accepted. This means laying to rest the anxious defenses, noisily shouted about, so that the news can get through, while simultaneously shaping the message so that it is no longer discordant and jarring, but rather the basis for a new shared Vision which has the capacity to galvanize Spirit in powerful and productive ways. And then, to the extent that the difference created becomes a continuing difference, the new Vision must be firmly anchored in mythos as the ongoing image and channel for Spirit. The means for doing all of this is reconciliation.

RECONCILIATION, GRIEFWORK AND LEADERSHIP

Reconciliation is effected through Love by which the organization and the participant individuals are enabled to accept what they were and are presently, while simultaneously being challenged to fulfill their potential. The primary mechanism is griefwork, which allows the organization to cross the Open Space, created by the act of Rebellion. Reconciliation is the supreme act of leadership, [54] which lovingly creates a new story wherein all may find completion to their transformational journey as expressed in a New Covenant. The collective response to the experience of Open Space as end is not only analogous to, but identical with the response of the individual in similar circumstances. The reason is not hard to determine, for in addition to the

---

[52] The distinction between "news" and "noise" comes from the world of information theory. For a brief introduction see Jeremy Campbell, "Grammatical Man", Touchstone/Simon and Schuster, 1983, especially Chapter 14, "The Clear and Noisy Messages of Language."

[53] See Gregory Bateson, "Steps Towards and Ecology of Mind", Ballentine, 1972, pgs. 272-274.

[54] I have used the word *leadership* as opposed to "the leader" to emphasize a basic point. In the world of Spirit, leadership is the capacity to focus Spirit, and is not automatically linked to title or position. Thus, anybody who exercises that capacity is, by definition, the leader. Hopefully, titular leaders will also possess the capacity of leadership, but that is not necessarily the case.

total organization having to come to terms with the fact that things are no longer as they were, each individual must come to a similar realization. To the extent that the organizational Covenant provided the ground and field upon which each individual crafted his or her own self-understanding, the end of that Covenant constitutes the end of the individual's self understanding, in short Death.[55] Future, to the extent that there will be a future, requires both the individual and the organization to acknowledge that end, and move on. Transformation for the organization and for the individual become interactive and co-terminus. Neither can occur without the other.

In theory of course, each individual has the choice of leaving the organization and finding new meaning on their own. And in fact, many of the individuals will do that, but those individuals will be ones who had been relatively less invested in the organization — peripheral players and hangers on as it were. Such individuals are obviously important, but they are not my central concern here. Because of their peripheral status, they do not by definition constitute the core, or what we might call central Spirit of the organization. For those who do constitute that "central core," the choice of just leaving is not a real choice. The investment is too great. They are the ones for whom the organization has become their life, and their life the organization. It is because of their investment that they must work the whole business through in their own self interest. For the organization, those invested, dedicated individuals provide the critical resource of Spirit from which a future may be made. For the individual, the organization and its transformation provide the context within which their several spirits may find renewal and transformation. Moving on becomes a possibility.

GRIEFWORK   Moving on requires griefwork. To this point griefwork has largely been studied and understood in terms of the individual's response to death.[56] But the process in the organization is parallel to, and perhaps identical with what takes place in the individual. Griefwork may be described as a series of stages, each one necessary in itself and contingent upon the successful completion of the one preceding. In short, there can be no rushing or short circuiting the process. The stages are as follows.

---

[55] In the interest of simplicity, I have written as if only one organization were involved. Obviously, each of us participates in many organizations, and so my statement may appear extreme. However, if you will think of the central or primary organization with which you are involved, I think the point will hold.

[56] See Kuebler-Ross *op. cit.*

Shock and Anger At the moment of death or its imminent approach, the reaction is shock and anger. Verbally the response will often come out, "I just can't believe it. Those SOBs!" The shock is drawing the breath in, and anger is letting it out. The pyrotechnics may be considerable, but at least the patient is still breathing.

Denial/If-Onlies Given the initial shock and consequent anger, the reality of the situation begins to set in, and the pain for all those involved is acute, so acute as to be unbearable. At this point the collective psyche (if there is such a thing) cuts in an essential damage control mechanism, denial and the "if-onlies." To all outward appearances, it is "business as usual," although the truth of the matter is that there is very little business to be done, but it seems to be better to be doing something, anything at all, than just sitting there. Of course there are those inevitable moments of inaction and silence, and in order to fill the silence, and avoid the pain, the "if-onlies" begin. If only we had sought more capital, not hired so many folks, listened or not listened to so and so . . . None of it makes any difference now, but it does somehow keep the emptiness and pain at bay. As a long-term strategy, denial is not very effective, for it insures that the organization will continue to live in what was, giving no thought to what might be. However, in the near term denial has a very positive effect; it provides a breathing space to let the new reality sink in. Carried to extremes, denial will guarantee the permanence of death. Cut short, the wounds will have no chance to heal.

Iteration The healing process, begun under the protection of denial, accelerates with iteration. In Iteration, members of the organization tell the tale again, and again, and again, *ad nauseam*, or so it seems to an outsider. Beginning at the point of ending, and moving out in ever increasing circles, people begin to explore what it will be like without the "old" department, organization, institution. They recall, in detail, what each one was doing the moment the "bad news" came through . . . and then the week before, and the week before that. Salesmen may be found going over their old routes, imagining what it will be like now that they are no longer called upon to deliver the "goodies." Employees will actually leave home and travel up to the plant gates and then return, just to see what it is like now that the plant is shut down.

The process of Iteration is, in part, just an extension of the process of denial, for people will fill the emptiness they feel with the memory of what was. But if the process goes on long enough, and with a little help, memory will eventually give way to imagination as people begin to project towards some future. *What future* is, of course, the issue. Left to their own devices, the group will generally scatter and imagine separate futures. However, with skillful leadership, the group may begin to imagine a common future, which builds upon the strengths they possess and yet appears in a form appropriate to the changed environment.

From Memory to Imagination The moment of passage from memory to imagination is critical and difficult to perceive, for usually the words are the same in both cases, yet the feeling is very different. In memory, the feeling is nostalgia, while in imagination, the feeling is hope, faint hope, thin hope, but hope nevertheless. For leadership, being there with feeling at the moment of passage is essential. In the previous stages (Shock/Anger, Denial/If Onlies), there is little to be done except to listen and let it happen. At the moment of passage, when the time is "right" (a rather imprecise statement to be sure) there will occur the opportunity to "fan the flame," to take that little spark of hope, link it to other sparks, so that life is renewed.

LOVE AND THE PROCESS OF GRIEFWORK Love, as we have noted, has two faces, acceptance and challenge. Both are essential to the successful completion of the griefwork process and the achievement of Reconciliation.

Love as Acceptance When griefwork starts, the pain is real, and no amount of well intentioned exhortation to forget the past and move to the future can cover that fact. The stages of griefwork must proceed, and love as acceptance allows for that to happen. The initial shock and anger must be expressed, and that will be followed by some form of denial, if only to provide psychic distance from the pain. Then comes the process of iteration as the story is told and re-told, acknowledging the old and moving, potentially, towards the new.

Simple to say, but perhaps more difficult to do, if only because in the life of organizations at such times, frenetic activity seems to alternate with deadly silence -- neither of which are conducive to such conversation. The activity is almost a death spasm as folks try one more time, to "push it over the wall." The silence exists because nobody can bear to talk about what has happened. Leaders will often become exasperated with all of this and react with some version of, "Stop crying over spilled milk." That reaction is understandable, and ultimately to the point. Eventually, you do have to move on. But at this point the thought has come too soon, for it is quite appropriate to cry over spilled milk when that milk is your whole life. Here again, the image of the macho individualist does us in one more time. As we all know, "Big men

106

don't cry." But big men who don't cry will very often discover that they end up with nothing to cry about. By hiding their passion, they lose their world. The writer of Ecclesiastes put it rather well.

> For everything there is a season,
> and a time for every matter under heaven:
> a time to be born,
> and a time to die;
> a time to plant,
> and a time to pluck up what is
> planted...
> a time to weep...
> (Ecclesiastes, Chapter III)

Creating that time is a first order task for leadership. How it is done, and what form it takes will vary from organization to organization. But whatever its form, it will probably be some variant of the ancient and honorable institution, the Irish wake. For all of our inability to deal with death, there still exist, fortunately, within our culture the ritual forms to help us through. We have only to remember what they are, and use them in appropriate ways. Perhaps the idea of having a Wake in the context of contemporary organizational (to say nothing of corporate) life appears bizarre, but it can be done, and more to the point, it works.

Several years ago, I had occasion to work with a super high performing group in the U.S. Army known as Delta Force. Delta Force was not a combat unit, at least in the ordinary sense, and it came into existence following the Vietnam War when a small group of senior officers concluded that the Army's problems in that far off place were not simply the product of bad press and disaffected draft card burners. Indeed, the Army had a number of problems of its own making. Specifically, it became apparent that the war the Army was trained to fight was not the war in which it found itself engaged. Some major changes were required in leadership style, approach, and method of organization. Delta Force was created to discover any possible new approaches to these subjects, and bring them to the Army's attention.

The net was cast far and wide, from the groves of Esaalen to the halls of academe. And along with new ideas came new people, and they conspired to create a marvelous, rich, working group where innovation and excitement were commonplace. That was the good news. But it must also be admitted that some of the ideas, and some of the people could only be described as "kooks," and certainly not what one might expect to find in a green suit. While the positive effects of Delta Force were many, it is also not surprising that the institutional antibodies should arise to get rid of this aberrant beast.

And so it came to pass that Delta Force was through, not because it did a bad job, indeed just the opposite. And, had the work been completed, it would have been possible to hang the colors in the corner and move out. However the job was by no means done, but it could no longer be done in the "old way." Therein lay the problem, for it was precisely the people who had invested so much (were committed and motivated) in the "old Delta Force" who must witness its dismemberment and provide the skills and resources necessary for what ever might come next.

As the institutional antibodies rose, and the fate of Delta Force became clearer, the anger, shock and denial mechanisms came strongly into view. Much ink and many phone calls were expended on justifying what had been done and blaming others for the demise. But the end was there. It was clear that we had to get all the significant folks together to launch the new venture, but it was equally clear that until the old Delta Force was given a decent burial, the new form could never emerge. Hence we had a wake.

The design evolved went something like this. The critical players were invited to a three day "off-site." At dinner on the first night an order from the commanding general was read officially dissolving Delta Force, and inviting the participants to imagine and design something new which would do the job. That evening we spent no time on the future; rather we honored the past. Specifically, we adjourned to the bar. With the exception of a few startled guests the place was ours. For the next many hours, into the wee small ones in the morning, the history was recited and heroes honored. If there was any aspect of the Delta Force past that was not told by story and saluted with a cup, I am sure I don't know what it was. There were moments of deep solemnity, and big men cried for the things they had done, and would never have the chance to do again, for the friends they had made, the thoughts they had thought, the schemes that were hatched but never saw the light of day, and never would. It all came out. And it was funny too. We laughed as some of the impossible situations we had gotten into, and the strange way things worked out. Over the course of the evening, the memories poured forth and were shared. I heard stories I had never heard before, and I am sure that all the rest could say the same thing. By the end, we knew it was the end. It was sad, but I think we mostly remembered the good parts.

Perhaps it was the hour, the alcohol, or simple exhaustion, but when we left, there was a wholeness about the experience, and a sense of completion. The past had been acknowledged, but the future remained to be created. And that was the order of business for the next two days. [57]

The process of reconciliation begins at a point where time and space has been set aside for the organization to grieve over what has been and is no more. Creating the conditions under which this griefwork may take place is a special responsibility of leadership, and is rooted in the love of the leader expressed as acceptance. Whether the organizational grief takes place in the formalized setting of a wake or in some other way is immaterial. The critical point is that each person individually, and all of them collectively, have the opportunity to openly and honestly face things as they are, to honor the past, and to move beyond. Essentially, there must be a common acknowledgement of weakness and powerlessness. "We gave it our best shot, and good as it was, it wasn't good enough. There is absolutely nothing easy in this action, either in the doing of it, or in the creation of the conditions under which it may be done. As with the individual, washing the collective dirty linen labeled "powerlessness" goes against the grain of virtually everything we have been taught about life in the world of work. Few, if any, of our heros are remembered for the times they cried in failure, and more's the pity. The temptation is always to try and "tough it out" one more time and failing that, to cover up the fact that things didn't work out the way we planned. All of those reactions are understandable, but ultimately self-defeating. For as with the individual in the face of death, those reactions are only various forms of denial, which do nothing except further isolate us, and make it less and less possible that we can create a positive and useful future. Organizations that avoid the fact of death, evade the possibility of life.

Love as Challenge   If the process of reconciliation and griefwork begins with acceptance, it can only reach fulfillment through challenge, for it is challenge that can

---

[57] It should be noted that the process of griefwork in an organization will not always move with such speed and effectiveness as was the case with Delta Force. Indeed, Delta Force, and the Army as a whole, may well be a special case in that there is built into the army culture the mechanisms to deal with death in large numbers on a fairly rapid basis, if only so that one may patch up a shattered unit, and move on with the business of fighting. Having said all that, it might also be pointed out that if the Army, as an organization, can create such mechanisms, so might any organization. The point in this example is not the short time it took, but rather that it is possible to institutionalize the process, and thereby do in a more orderly way, with more assurance of positive results, what would probably happen anyhow over a longer period of time with less likelihood of a positive outcome. In short, with griefwork, there is no magic bullet.

meet the organization at the critical point of turning from memory to imagination in order to create the possibility of healing, and the evolution of something new. That new thing will be a New Covenant, which merges the dynamism of the Rebel with the resources and experience of the rest of the organization, to create a powerful, renewed form, appropriate to the Spirit.

This New Covenant is not to be confused with a totally new organization, for to be effective, it must link to the past and embody the strengths and power of the old Covenant. Hence, there is no possibility of simply wiping the slate clean and starting over. At the same time the New Covenant must, by definition, be broader and more commodious to allow for the vital aspects of the Rebel's innovation. Like the crab in its yearly molt, or the caterpillar on the way to butterfly, old form yields to new form as the organization transforms, at once related with its past, and open to the future.

The steps along the way are not unfamiliar, for the transformed organization with its New Covenant will replicate the steps of all prior organizations (ontogeny recapitulates phylogeny). Specifically, this means that leadership must guide the organization along a path which begins with that primal sense of Out of the Depths and proceeds through Vision, Understanding, Language, Information and Data. Initially, therefore, the challenge will appear in the form of an intimation from the Depths. As before, the experience is hardly specific, and surely not on the level of verbal expression. It may be nothing more than a powerful feeling of "it can be." Precisely what "it" is remains obscure, but as a first statement of the leader's challenge, the feeling is critical, for it contains the essential energy necessary to change the polarities, reverse the field, and provide the initiation of future possibility.

How this Out of the Depths awareness might be communicated is problematical. Some words may be spoken, but at the time they will appear to have little if any significance. The senior staff in an organization which recently had undergone such a transformative experience reported to me that, "they didn't know when or why things had changed," but collectively they, "recognized that something was different." Some members associated the change with the day that their leader arrived in a flaming red sports car. The car was so out of character with the leader's past behavior that they were initially concerned that he had "gone 'round the bend." Gradually they began to see the car as a positive sign of hope. Other members were largely unaware of the car, but they did notice a difference in walk, and tone of voice. Less frenetic and strident, more purposeful and at ease.

The initial statement may be sufficient to turn Spirit, but obviously there is much further to go. The original inchoate expression of possibility lacks the substance it must have to be truly effective. The next stage is Vision through which the broad outlines of future possibility are sketched in color and shape. But building a vision for an organization in the process of transformation is not like the relatively more simple task of creating a Vision for a new organization, if for no other reason than that the organization now has a substantial history which must be acknowledged.

If the details of the Vision are not clear, the general specifications are. The emergent Vision, whatever its final form must be: 1) *Big* enough to include everybody 2) *Attractive* enough to energize and motivate 3) *Do-able*, in the sense that those who will be asked to join that Vision can see some possibility of making it work

On the first point — Bigness. If the Vision is truly going to provide the common ground on which or around which a new Covenant and collective understanding will emerge, it must be large enough to hold all the participants. This means that there must be a place for the old heroes and the new rebels, and everybody in between. The theory and the practice is to literally outframe all of the other stories, and limit conflict simply by creating sufficient "turf" so that conflict is not necessary.

There is another aspect to bigness which relates to getting and holding peoples' attention. In the midst of the sort of chaos that surrounds an organization in the Open Space of transformation, "little plans" are very likely to get lost. Hence the vision must have the aspect of awesomeness and boldness.

The second point is to make sure that this Vision is truly attractive. A "wimpie" Vision just will not do when you are attempting to energize all those folks. The attractiveness of a Vision is generated not only from its own terms, but also from its capacity to liberate individuals and the organization to see themselves in different and more dynamic ways. What a Vision does is to context and position individuals and groups in such a way that they see what they possess as being infinitely more than they had ever thought of before. Implicit in a powerful Vision is the possibility of allowing the Spirit to expand and reach for its full potential. To the extent that a Vision starts as an expression of love by leadership, it reaches its full potential when it generates a resonant response within the organization such that the organization as a whole comes to love itself, what might be called collective self-love. Empowered by Vision, the organization may be confident enough to accept things as they are, and bold enough to challenge themselves to meet and realize the opportunities available.

Big attractive Visions represent a useful start, but that is not sufficient to really turn the field. The Vision must also be do-able, or at least perceived as do-able. This is both a general and specific statement: generally the Vision must appear to be workable within the "present state of the art" or what might reasonably become the state of the art. Far-out science fiction can be very big, awfully attractive, but everybody knows that we aren't "there" yet. The Vision must also be seen as do-able in the specific setting of those who might be encouraged to hold the Vision. This is more than a question of having the necessary resources available, although that is certainly important. It also relates to the necessity that the Vision link meaningfully and positively with the history of the people. It must connect in real and powerful ways to what they have been.

This is an uncomfortable point for many visionaries who may tend to see *what was* only in terms of obstruction. In fact *what was* is the necessary precondition and opportunity for what *might become.* This may appear a simple and obvious point, but during a period of work in West Africa, I watched the sad fate of a number of marvelous, visionary Western technicians and Western trained Africans who came to grief simply because they forgot the power of history. By seeing it only as the "dead hand of the past," they separated themselves from the very people they were seeking to serve, and in addition cut their Vision off from the vital "juices" that history can supply.

To be effective, a Vision must be big, attractive and do-able, all three, and all at once. Creating the Vision is the first tangible step to be taken by leadership. In itself, however, this step is insufficient. As long as the Vision remains the private property of the leader, it cannot create the conditions under which Spirit may transform. Vision may realize its power only to the extent that it is shared, and the means for that sharing is Collective Storytelling.

LEADERSHIP AS COLLECTIVE STORYTELLING

Describing the leader as a teller of stories may appear a rather anemic role, but as you may suspect, there is more behind the word "story" than immediately meets the eye. In fact, the story is the organizational mythos.

Paradoxically, in the role of storyteller, what the leader does not say is of equal or greater importance than what he or she does say. For the objective is not for the leader to tell the whole tale, but rather to create the conditions under which each individual and all components of the organization may effectively contribute their piece. In the final analysis, the tale cannot be the leader's, but rather it must belong to the total organization.

This statement may appear counter-intuitive, and certainly at variance with much that we think we have learned about the role of leader. It almost seems axiomatic that the strong leader tells the folks what to do, what the story really is. Many leaders attempt to do just that, and while their efforts may have short term positive impact, over any time period at all, that impact wanes. The reason is quite simple: when the tale is the leader's tale, and only that, there is no room for anyone else. This means that real ownership and allegiance are impossible, and creative thought and contribution virtually excluded.

Once, I found myself in the president's office of a rapidly growing but small corporation. There was no question that the organization had done very well, but there was substantial question as to whether that level of performance could be maintained over time, if only because the organization had doubled each year in terms of almost every standard measure. The expressed concern was that they might well fail by succeeding. As the president talked, it occurred to me that such a possibility was by no means an idle concern, but for reasons quite different than those the president had considered. When I asked him what he was doing to keep things moving, he stiffened, became somewhat red in the face, and looking me straight in the eye said, "I tell them exactly what to do, and they do it." To all outward appearances, this was a perfect picture of the executive who had "taken charge." But what the president could not see (or didn't choose to notice) was one of his trusted and dedicated subordinates sitting in the corner with his head in his hands, wincing with every word. People who try to tell the whole story end up with the whole story to themselves. That turns out to be very lonely and nonproductive.

So the name of the game is Collective Storytelling. This process may begin with the leader's tale, his personal understanding of how things might go, but in telling this tale, the leader, if wise, will say infinitely less than more. The intent will be to create sufficient structure and direction so that the outlines of the Vision, in terms of size, attractiveness and do-ability are apparent, but no more. Artfully done, the leader will actually create a vacuum which not only invites participation, but demands it. Elements of the tale are introduced by title, just a suggestion will do. If the organization's story were a work of art (which it should be), the name for this phase would be minimalism, just enough to get things going, but no more.

Effectively practicing the art of Collective Storytelling is rigorous and demanding business. It is also, potentially, painful. For the leader must have sufficient investment in the tale that he tells in order to tell it with conviction and feeling, but the leader must be prepared to let it go. This is no straw man, and if the story is ever perceived as such, it will lack the essential power necessary to challenge the organization to move across the Open Space. The leader must then invite participation. And when that participation comes, it must be accepted with the certain knowledge that the additions will not only add to the tale, but also change it in some essential ways such that it is no longer his tale.

In order to understand the full cost of this activity, imagine that the leader has effectively plumbed the depths surrounding the end of the organization as it used to be. He, perhaps most of all, experiences the pain of loss and failure, for ultimately the responsibility lies with him. Yet in the midst of that kind of darkness, he saw a small ray of light, the faint hope that the vision of the Rebel might effectively combine with, and enliven the rest of the organization. How this might work is by no means clear in detail, but it appears possible.

Then it happens. Suddenly the flicker of hope clicks. The vague possibility assumes some shape. Now the leader can shift to high gear; facts may be added, plans made, structure created as a phantasm assumes substance in his mind. Should you ask where the leader is "really at," the answer is pretty clear; he is totally immersed in this idea. He is it, and it is he. It is impossible to separate the two. And the reason is straight forward, for that idea constitutes the very core of who and what that leader understands himself to be. It is no wonder that he holds it with passion and is inclined to defend it in the same way. It is equally understandable that the leader should resist any and all attempts to materially alter the idea, for to do that is to confront him precisely where he lives.

Cooler heads may feel that I have overstated the case, for after all it is only an idea. Yet ideas born in passion and held with passion are exactly the sort that can challenge the organization to pursue the quest. But note the cost. For in as much as the leader would offer his vision to empower his organization, he must simultaneously offer it for change, which means modification, which means an end to the Vision in all the pristine clarity with which he envisioned it. It also means an end to the self that assumed meaning as the one who created and held that private vision. The critical bind comes when it is clear that, in order to exercise the role of leadership, he must essentially let go of something that has become very central to himself. To fulfill himself as leader, he must be prepared to lose himself.

It is no wonder then, that some leaders tend to hold on at such a point. Nor it is any wonder that true leadership is such a rare commodity. But having said all of the above, I do not mean to suggest that the leader should let go uncritically. To do so would cheapen the product and impede the process. The leader must offer his vision accepting the possibility of change, but he must also offer that Vision with the challenge that those who propose such changes do so with the intention of making the Vision better, richer, and deeper. There is obviously a fine line here, and no cookbook on leadership can possibly spell out precisely the right recipe. But when the leader powerfully and effectively offers his Vision in such a way that it may truly be appropriated and inspire the organization to complete its quest, a number of things occur simultaneously.

First for the leader, there is a quintessential moment when he knows what leadership is all about, and is fulfilled by that knowledge. For him, that can only be described as a moment of personal transformation in which his Spirit is made full and set free.

Likewise for the Rebel, to the extent that he is challenged to bring his innovative ideas to fruition within the organization and simultaneously experiences the acceptance of his co-workers in spite of the pain that he may have caused, his own transformation will have taken a quantum jump.

As for all of the other individuals who have made their home in that organization, they too can know that giddy burst of freedom when the past is truly accepted and the future exists as open challenge.

Finally, for the organization as a whole, the stage has been set for the completion of the journey. Business as it was, is no more. Open Space has been transversed, and the possibility of a meaningful future has been established in principle. In the power of a shared Vision, which has emerged from trial, been empowered by passion, and now held by all, there is the foundation of a New Covenant. The organization may once more become that place where people find meaning and personhood for themselves, and fulfillment in their collective activity. A New Covenant is at hand, but not yet there.

NEW COVENANT

Making the New Covenant actual requires another step, which is the appearance of what we might call "Collective Self-love." Just as the individual must love him or her-self enough to convert the potential for new life present in Resurrection, into New Life itself, so also with the organization. Under the best of circumstances, love manifest by leadership will excite a resonant response in the organization as a whole, but there is no guarantee.

115

Why or how genuine self-love appears in the organization is a mystery to me, but that it must appear for the actualization of the New Covenant, is clear. Only when an organization loves itself sufficiently to radically accept what is and what used to be, while simultaneously challenging itself to realize the opportunities present, will New Covenant and new organizational life become a reality. In the words of the old saw, you can lead a horse to water, but you can't make him drink.

It is now the first day of business all over again. But it is a new day for sure. Naturally the passage from the Vision to the "first day of business" does not occur overnight, nor without effort, but it is essentially a repetition of what the organization has done before, so we need not follow it through again. We may be sure though that the transformation now completed is but the starting point for transformations yet to come.

CELEBRATION

The arrival of a New Covenant, and the experience of a new "first day of business" is indeed a cause for celebration. In fact, the first day back on the job very often takes the form of a celebratory event. Old friends are now seen in new ways, and the same space is somehow different. There is a sense of triumph and accomplishment, but most of all a soaring sense of futurity and movement. Perhaps it is sufficient to just enjoy the moment, and it may well be that the press of business is such that there is little time to spare. But taking some part of that precious time for a little formal celebration will not be wasted.

Exactly what such a "formal celebration" looks like will vary from organization to organization. There is no right way. But taking the time to acknowledge those who completed the course and led the way (the heroes) and those who did not, will pay handsome dividends. Some of these dividends will be immediate as in the warm feelings generated when time is taken to say "thank you" to those who gave so much and who could not be thanked before under the circumstances.

But the long term benefits are even greater, because the formal celebration will lock the transformational journey just completed into the consciousness of the organization as a resource for the future. Just as certainly as the moment of transformation confronted the organization in the past, so it will recur in the future as new environments demand new responses, and the New Covenant becomes the Old Covenant. At such a time, it will be more than a little comforting to know that the organization has successfully faced such challenges, and may reasonably expect to do so again. That expectation is preserved in the moment of celebration, and is remembered and rekindled each time the celebration is performed.

REBELS AND THE PAIN OF TRANSFORMATION

Rebels and rebellion are most often glorified in the abstract and condemned concretely. The fact that the history of our country is firmly rooted in a tradition of rebellion does not seem to mitigate the fact that every time rebellion appears in our midst or close to our borders, we become distinctly uneasy and seem to take virtually any steps to quell the outbreak. The reason is clear and understandable, for rebellion in all of its forms constitutes a clear and present danger to life as it exists within a covenant. It makes no difference whether that rebellion is large or small, very close to home or in some neighboring country, the danger is real and the possibility for pain and destruction genuine.

Having said all that, it must also be acknowledged that the impact of rebellion is positive and constitutes a powerful and necessary aspect of the ongoing process of transformation. Viewed positively, rebellion is nothing more nor less than the breaking out of Spirit from the confines of a too-restrictive covenant. The immediate result is chaos, but this chaos may be seen as the fecund ground for future possibility.

Ordinarily, we tend to think of rebels and rebellion in political terms, but Thomas Kuhn has looked at the same phenomenon in the context of the development of science. In his book, *The Structure of Scientific Revolutions* [58] Kuhn argues that science has evolved, not in a placid straight line manner, but rather as a series of quantum, revolutionary steps in which an old way of seeing things (paradigm) was shattered and dissolved, eventually giving way to something new which permitted a larger and more powerful view of reality. At each step, the process was initiated when an individual, or a relatively small group, discovered that the old way of seeing things was no longer adequate to explain reality as they experienced it. It should be noted that the "revolutionaries" were not "bad" people, but rather thought of themselves as very much a part of the scientific community of their day. And their intent was not to destroy science, but rather they were following their noses, and being honest with what they saw. In fact, these same people spent a considerable amount of time seeking to explain the anomalies of their experience in terms of the older scientific view by proposing exceptions and twisting the standard theory to fit. Einstein, for example,

---

[58] Kuhn, Thomas, "The Structure of Scientific Revolutions", University of Chicago Press, 1962.

who initiated the contemporary revolution in physics, apparently went to his grave believing, or hoping, that things weren't as different as he had made them. Yet the difference was there, and the paradigms shifted. In the Open Space created when the shift began, but was not complete, there was confusion, pain, and chaos, much of which we continue to experience today as the shock waves from Darwin and the quantum theorists spread out. Yet in retrospect the journey seems to have been worthwhile.

When considering the reality of rebellion in the organization and death in the individual in terms of the disruption and pain that both create, it is tempting to seek a better way to go. Why should it be that transformation can only be achieved at such great cost? There are those, of course, who offer transformation without pain, but I think that offer may be on the order of snake oil. This is not because I enjoy pain or feel that it has any inherent virtue but rather that given our current level of evolution, pain is an almost inevitable by-product. I would agree, however, that transformation without pain is a theoretical possibility.

This may appear to be intellectual fence sitting, but consider the source of the pain. The pain that we experience through rebellion or death does not reside in the rebellion or death *per se* or, for that matter, in what may occur afterwards as Resurrection or New Covenant. The pain is in us as we exist in Open Space experienced as loss or end. It localizes around the phenomenon of "holding on" to what was but is no longer, with the natural but mistaken understanding, that should we "let go," we would no longer be. The pain ends, and indeed may be transmuted into a positively exhilarating experience (Maslow's Peak Experience) when we are enabled to "let go," at which point Open Space is experienced as Opportunity. Beginning on the yonder side of Open Space we can acknowledge that "we" somehow exist independently of what was, and although our being has been enriched by what we have left behind, our fulfillment is emerging in what lies ahead.

This is not some unique experience reserved for the mystical few, but the common experience of every individual who has ever existed upon the face of the earth. That is a bold, and obviously unprovable statement. Yet I submit it makes a certain amount of sense, for each one of us has more or less successfully navigated the transformational journey from infant, to child, to adolescent, to adult. Some of us may have managed better than others if only because we have more completely honored and relinquished the past in order to appropriate the future, but the majority seem to have made it. To be sure, it may have appeared, at the advanced age of 16, that life was definitively over at 30, but when we reached 35, that turned out not to be the case. What is the case, however, is that life as a 16-year-old, with all its forms and fetishes, has ended. The real sadness lies with those who are unable to acknowledge that fact, and continue at 35 to exist as if at 16.

The real issue then becomes, can we learn from our experience? If the pain resides in our anguish over "letting go," it becomes clear that we must learn to "let go" more quickly and effectively. In theory, the time devoted to "letting go" might be progressively reduced until there is no time at all, and we literally flow from one way of being to the next with out interruption. At that point it would become evident that our essence was Spirit, which only came to manifestation in form as occasion might require. That realization, of course, is where I understand the process of transformation to be headed, and in theory we might jump the intervening steps and acknowledge our primal and final state as Spirit. To the extent that we already are Spirit and don't know it, the possibility for such acknowledgement exists right now, as indeed the spiritual masters throughout the ages have told us. But we seem to be a little hard of hearing. Theoretically, therefore, transformation without pain is a possibility, which I suppose some of us have already realized. But for most of us, certain considerations appear to stand in the way.

Chapter VII

SPIRIT MECHANICS

The words, "Spirit Mechanics" may appear not only odd, but contradictory, for how can Spirit be mechanical? My phrase is analogous to the physicist's as in "quantum mechanics," which describes the function and effect of the quantum or unit of energy. So Spirit Mechanics concerns itself with the function and effect of Spirit. My intent is to describe a theoretical model within which to understand how Spirit works, and of equal importance, how we might work with Spirit. This model is both summative of our explorations to this point, and transitional to the balance of the book, where we shall consider the practicalities of facilitating the transformation of Spirit in terms of approach and results. In the interest of brevity, previously developed words and concepts are used without further definition.

Imagine that the organization is no longer a group of people, buildings and machines, but a flow of Spirit heading towards a set of definable objectives, jobs if you will. The problem then becomes one of molding and shaping that stream of energy so that it focuses in a powerful and direct manner upon the task at hand. If Spirit moves at less-than-needed force, the tasks cannot be accomplished, but by the same token, unrestrained force will "blow the deal." Under the circumstances, drag and turbulence must be eliminated or brought down to lowest levels, for anything that sidetracks or impedes Spirit will reduce the efficiency of its work.

But notice that there is not just one job ahead of Spirit, but a number, and if we have learned anything from our present world, it is in truth the day of "Ready, fire, aim." Which is to say that about the only certainty we hold is the constancy of change, and we may be sure that whatever the job of the day, the work for the morrow will be different. So Spirit must not only be focused for today, but also — and perhaps more important, reshaped for tomorrow. The military has a phrase, to redeploy the force, and that is exactly what is required here. Somehow the vital energy of the organization must be re-shaped, redirected, redeployed so as to turn from the immediate task at hand to something quite new. When caught in the flow, we must learn to manage the flow, but how do you do that ?

At this point, we may borrow a leaf from the physicist's notebook, for they discovered that to manage energy, one must use energy. Thus they constructed linear accelerators and cyclotrons which have the capacity to speed and focus energy by creating energy (magnetic) fields which successively drive and shape the quantum in ever increasing levels of intensity. The analogue to the cyclotron, for our purposes, is the organizational culture.

CULTURE

Anthropologist Edward Hall[59] says that "Culture is man's medium." Culture is not to be confused with its artifacts (particular pieces of music, art drama, architecture or social forms), for culture is all of these and more. It is the ethos or envelope within which humanity in general, and specific people, in concrete organizations, comes to being. *Culture is the dynamic field within which Spirit is shaped, formed and directed.*

---

[59] "Beyond Culture", Doubleday/Anchor Press, 1977, p. 16. I am aware that Hall's definition of culture is not the only one, and may not be the best, but it strikes a very responsive chord with my thinking, which is obviously why I like it. More than that, it seems to me that Hall has gone beyond the specific manifestations of culture to think of culture in its essence. He says, "Technically, the model of culture on which my work is based is more inclusive than those of some of my colleagues. My emphasis is on the nonverbal, unstated realm of culture. While I do not exclude philosophical systems, religion, social organization, language, moral values, art and material culture, I feel it is more important to look at the way things are actually put together than at theories."

How one might actually "get a hold" on culture in order to utilize its formative powers is suggested by the word culture itself, or more exactly in the first four letters CULTure. The dictionary informs us that "cult" comes from the latin *cultus* which in turn is the past participle of *colere* which means to cultivate, care for, nourish or grow. All of this may be on the order of "chop logic" (actually chop linguistics), but I believe the sense contained in the word suggests that the function of the "cult" in the context of the "culture," is to care for, nourish and grow. . .humanity or more exactly Spirit.

Thus Culture is the "medium of man" in which the Spirit grows under the guidance of the cult. At the heart of any organization one will find some entity (and it may be very informal) which functions as the cult does. Somebody, or some several somebodies, will assume the role of the cult, establishing values, standards of behavior, the "way things get done." This function may not be performed consciously, although in large organizations such functions are quite conscious and are ordinarily institutionalized. By understanding the "cult in our midst," we may avail ourselves of the "tools" of the cult, by which Spirit is grown and shaped.

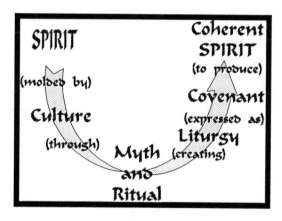

The "tools" of the cult are essentially two: myth and ritual, known collectively as *mythos,* which becomes operationally manifest in life as *liturgy.* (Chapter I) The rules of liturgy, in turn, are formally expressed as *Covenant*, the charter of organization. In a word, the cult manages the culture through mythos, by creating effective liturgy in order to provide a rich nutrient environment for Spirit [60]. We now have the elements for a general model which appears to the left.

---

[60] There is a dark side to all of this, for the level of control exercised by the cult over the spirit of man is truly awesome, and may in fact be used for purposes other than good. The fact that the mechanisms of this control are largely discounted by contemporary man only increases the power, for now it operates almost totally beyond the normal purview. By consigning such things to "pure superstition," modern man is only playing ostrich. In truth, the power of mythos does not disappear when the head is stuck in the sand. In fact, while the head is covered some very strange

BASIC MECHANICS

The basic mechanics will become clearer with an example from the Jonathan Corporation considered a little time back. You will remember that the Jonathan Corporation was a small shipyard experiencing very rapid growth. There were five major stories which collectively functioned to image and shape the Spirit of Jonathan. These stories were: 1) "The International House of Pancakes," which described the early meetings of the President as he put the company together; 2) "The Phoenix," which described how a dissident group left Jonathan to create their own corporation (Phoenix Marine); 3) "The USS Speer," which told the tales of "derring do" as the young corporation battled winter winds to bring its first contract in under budget and ahead of schedule; 4) "Norma's Apartment," a story of the corporate community effort to relieve the suffering of a secretary whose apartment had burned down; and 5) "The Spirit Wagon," recounting how in the early days every work week ended with the arrival of a pick-up truck loaded with several kegs of beer. All hands "stood down" and joined together for several "mugs of suds," all the while problems were solved and community built.

It is tempting to view such stories in a linear fashion as descriptive of the history of Jonathan, however they do not function in a linear way at all, for each story is always present (to one degree or another) in the consciousness of the Jonathan folk. The function here is that of a field as opposed to a linear progression.

Jonathan Corporation is no longer a set of buildings, bodies, piers, machines and ships. It is the focused flow of Spirit through a field (culture) defined by mythos. To understand how this works, it may be helpful to think of the field as a drum head with each myth acting as a "tuning handle." Each myth contributes its own special pressures and tensions (flavor and meanings). Thus the story of the "International House of Pancakes" provides that sense of beginning as the president and his immediate associate drank coffee and cut deals on the pay phone. But most important, this story is expressive of the corporate value that style is infinitely less important than product. By the same token, the story of the "USS Speer" offers the macho can do element which manifests the corporate willingness to take on the really tough ones,

---

things can happen, as for example the rise of the Third Reich. Whatever else Hitler may have done, he clearly tapped into the Teutonic mythos of Blood, Iron and Race and turned all of that to his own ends...which was very nearly our end.

and do well. "Norma's Apartment" contributes the sense of caring and being responsible one for another.

Note, however, that no myth is "the whole story," and indeed, should any one myth assume dominance above all others, the field (drum head) would be severely warped and possibly nonfunctional. Thus, for example, if "Norma's Apartment" were to become primary, the net result would be something akin to a welfare state with everybody taking so much care of everybody else that no work got done. To be effective, "Norma's Apartment" must be balanced by the "USS Speer" which communicates toughness, excellence, and getting the job done despite all odds. By the same token however, the USS Speer alone would also be destructive, for Macho/can do is great, but ultimately it tends to chew people up if not balanced by some real element of compassion.

In balance, the several myths operate with and against each other, to create a resonant tension — or we might say the "sound of Jonathan." Well tuned, the field provides the harmony which enables the Spirit of Jonathan to sing. . . or more to the point, get the job done.

The first step in understanding Spirit Mechanics is to perceive the organization as a flow of Spirit through culture, and focused by mythos.

LITURGY

Developing and maintaining the field of a organization, over time, is obviously no small concern, for should the field become warped or flaccid, the effect upon Spirit would be disastrous. Such development and maintenance is the function of Liturgy through which mythos is made manifest in the life of the people, as "what they do."

124

Some forms of Liturgy are quite *ad hoc*, and provide only a momentary way to "tell the story." In the case of Jonathan, at the beginning of a major new effort demanding the very best from each and every employee, the story is the USS Speer, and that myth needs to resonate strongly across the whole field setting the tone, establishing the pattern, molding the spirit. Creating that resonance might be done in a variety of ways, some of which will seem quite trivial, such as "Speer teeshirts" for all hands, and short videos on "How We Did It Before."

For the "longer haul," Liturgy must have a more durable form, which is what organizational *form and structure* are all about. Form is the way things get done, including manners and style (as in the phrase "that's good form"). Structure is the box within which things get done, the playing field so to speak. Liturgy (form and structure) creates the special time and space in which to do the job.

EVOLUTION OF FORM AND STRUCTURE The evolution, utility and limits of form and structure, may be described as follows. If we begin with our basic model of Spirit as focused in the field of culture through mythos, at some point the "job" being done becomes sufficiently routine that it may be rationalized. In other words, we might articulate the basic logic or rational of the work in order to understand it better, and do that job more efficiently. Graphically, the process of rationalization may be depicted by placing a grid or matrix "over" the field.

While it is clear that not all elements of the process of Spirit at work fit neatly within the logical structure, most do, and we are thus provided with a useful, albeit

125

arbitrary way of talking about how the work flows from point A to Z. From this rationalization it becomes possible to measure the process and outcomes, establish schedules and firm up procedures. We can, in short, describe the special time and space which is appropriate to The Story, and fits the organization.

COVENANT

Given some reflection on our measurements, schedules and procedures, we may then localize (locate) authority and responsibility in definite centers, and shortly we have emergent structure and procedures, which may be formally expressed through the Covenant.

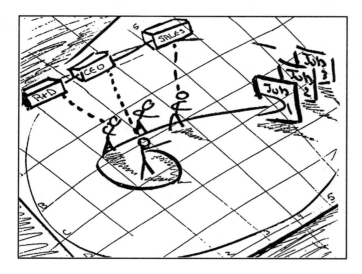

It should be noted, however, that the Covenant (and the underlying structure) is a complete abstraction based upon the field. The utility of this abstraction exists only so long as structure is aligned with the field in which Spirit flows. Should this alignment be broken, either because the direction of flow has changed, or its nature has in some way been modified, then problems will arise.

If the changes in the nature/direction of flow are minimal, minor adjustments in the Covenant will be sufficient to re-establish alignment. But note that the Covenant must be re-aligned with Spirit, and not the other way around. Should one attempt to force Spirit into alignment with a pre-existing Covenant, the result will be frustration (Spirit won't work that way), or in extreme cases, the power of Spirit will be extinguished because it is "shoehorned" into inappropriate rules and procedures. Starting

126

with structure and tailoring Spirit to fit is rather like buying a pair of shoes with out measuring the feet. It may happen that the shoes will fit, purely by chance. It is more likely that the shoes will pinch or fall off the feet.

BEING "OUT OF SPIRIT"

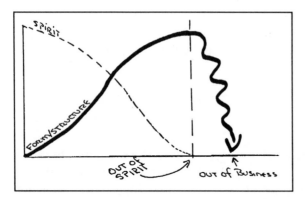

In the natural course of events, Spirit and Covenant will become dissociated. At that time, the organization finds itself "out of Spirit," and the only recourse is transformation. For those who perceive the form and structure expressed by the Covenant as the sole reality, these occasions will be confusing at best, and lead to a variety of unproductive behaviors such as re-organization and other technical adjustments. However, since the problem does not exist at the level of form and structure, such activities will be ineffective.

The dis-spiriting tendencies of organizations is depicted on the graph which indicates that as structure and form increase, Spirit is eventually controlled to the point that everything is "routinized," and the possibilities of innovation and inspired behavior are limited and eventually precluded. This graph may also be seen as a representation of what we have called the "slide toward legalism," or in different terms, the increase of entropy.

It is important to recognize that the course of organizational life depicted on this graph is inevitable[61] and not totally bad. In the interest of efficiency, we introduce

---

[61] In saying "inevitable", I do not mean to suggest that there are no other alternatives, only that there are no other alternatives at this stage of our evolution. Should the day come when all our organizations are Inspired, and we, as individuals, exist as Spirit, then it will occur that the 2nd law of thermodynamics will have been voided, and the Slide towards Legalism prevented. But as long as form and structure are considered to be necessary for organizational and individual life, then we will join the caterpillar on the way to becoming a butterfly - through chrysalis.

controls. We achieve efficiency, but at the cost of innovation, and the free flight of Spirit. Under "normal circumstances," the developed organizational liturgy is not only efficient, but also effective, in that it allows Spirit to operate congruently with the environment. However, when that environment changes, both efficiency and effectiveness diminish, and the stage is set for transformation.

MESS OR OPPORTUNITY ?

Organizations at the edge of transformation are messy. To managers, and others for whom the established liturgy (form and structure) is everything, it is not only a mess, but disaster, for the old form is in disarray. The Spirit of the organization appears as random, disorganized bursts of energy. Chaos. That is the bad news.

The good news is, that for the first time in a long time, Spirit is in evidence. The question is how to convert a mess into an opportunity. Or, how do you bring order out of chaos? The initial response is likely to be an attempt to "slap" some arbitrary structure "on top" of the chaotic Spirit, but the chances that this arbitrary structure will also be appropriate and fit, are not very high. It is more likely that Spirit, now on the loose, will continue on it chaotic way until a structure may be grown which is in conformity with the new flow of Spirit. Form must follow Spirit, just as shoes must fit the feet. The evolution of

128

appropriate form, and the creation of New Covenant, is what transformation is all about.

TRANSFORMATION

To understand the process of transformation, it is necessary not only to go beneath Liturgy and Covenant, but also the surface of the Spirit Field — down into *the Depths*. We must see the whole picture which includes not just what has become actual in the life of an organization, but the potential as well.

As organizations evolve, *the potential becomes actualized* in time and space. Thus on the "first day of business" (in a Bucket Brigade, for example), the potential of Data/Information ("there is a fire") becomes actualized as a Re-Active Organization. Spirit is focused in the existing culture through mythos (the Story is "Put out the Fire"), and liturgy (the bucket line with leader) is created, and formally expressed by the Covenant, which says, "Follow the leader and pass the buckets."

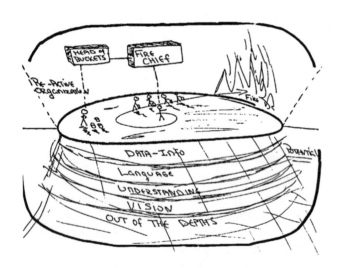

But when the environment changes (the fire has been put out), the focal point of Spirit is lost, Open Space created, and Spirit reverts to chaos (a mess). At this juncture, Spirit will either dissipate or may be refocused (re-formed, transformed) into a new way of being, which actualizes some previously unrealized potential (eg *Language as Responsive Organization*). We might then have a Volunteer Fire Department instead of an *ad hoc* Bucket Brigade.

While it is thinkable that the new way of being is simply a *development* from the old, that is not likely, for Volunteer Fire Departments, who play by the rules of *ad hoc* bucket brigades are not apt to be responsive to community needs. There must be some deeper sense of what has transpired, and what is likely to transpire over time. This sense does not appear at the level of *Understanding,* which provided the rational for the Bucket Brigade, or even at the level of *Vision*, which saw the possibility of controlling fire episodically. It comes from *Out of the Depths* as a great "Ah-Haaa. . . fires are always with us."

Transformation begins in earnest when Spirit is driven down into the Depths. As the old way disappears and the new has yet to arrive, the experience is that of being down in The Dumps.

Despite the pain, it is only from the Depths that one can perceive clearly what is basic and what is incidental. And it is a function of *leadership* to "take point"[62] on the trip. With this perception comes perspective, which in turn provides the possibility of seeing things in a new way. Hidden potential, previously locked away in the old way of doing business, as expressed by the old Covenant, is unveiled; the seed of a new idea, a new vision. Although it may look very much like the old Vision, it is deeper and richer.

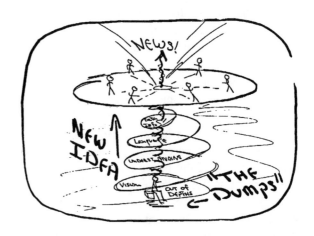

When Spirit is galvanized by a new idea, transformation progresses. As the New Idea emerges, clothed in the colors of Vision, rationalized through Understanding, expressed in Language, and Data/Information, Spirit stands on the threshold of a new way of being.

When the New Idea breaks through the mess and chaos, it appears as *News* as opposed to *Noise*, and there is the possibility that the random Spirit will once more be vectored into a coherent flow. For News catches people's attention. But the News is also uncomfortable news, for it is a word from the *Rebel*. The Rebel's word contains

---

[62] Army phrase for the person who takes the lead position on a dangerous patrol.

the seeds of renewal (a new way of being) but it is also a source of dis-ease, for it stands in stark contrast to the way "things have always been done." Nevertheless, in the midst of the randomness of Spirit, there is a "difference which makes a difference," and in this instant, the Open Space, created by the dissolution of the prior way of being (as bucket Brigade), may be converted from Mess to Opportunity.

NEW COVENANT/NEW CULTURE

Making the switch from mess to opportunity is not automatic. It is the function of leadership effecting reconciliation through *Collective Storytelling* in love, accepting what was, and calling forth which might be by challenge. If met by the resonant response of genuine, *collective self-love* , possibility and meaning may appear where formerly there was none, and Spirit can get on with the business of doing the job — a new job.

Whether this News will be more than a "flash in the pan" will depend upon the degree to which the new configuration of the Spirit is stabilized through the development of an appropriate Culture. Critical to the process of stabilization will be the conversion of News into The Story (mythos). Should the News exist only as a FLASH, it will be superceded by other News, eventually becoming noisy, until chaos returns. However, if the News becomes embedded in the Culture as an integral part of The Story, a new dynamic field will have been created that maintains the shape and flow of Spirit over time. The process of conversion is begun through Collective Storytelling, but it is brought to completion when (and only when) the Love manifest by Leadership excites a resonant response in terms of Collective Self-Love. At that point the "new story" becomes "our story" which we (as the organization) care enough about to make real and permanent as a new culture.

Given a continuing field, with relatively predictable dynamics, existing in congruence with the external environment, it is possible to orchestrate a Liturgy (form and structure) which makes life efficient, effective and, therefore, productive. Time and space may be defined (named) and articulated in terms appropriate to the new way of being, formally expressed in the New Covenant.

INITIATION AND CELEBRATION — CARING FOR THE STORY

Maintaining the shape of the field over time will not occur without care. Old members must remember the Story, and new members must be enabled to make The Story their story. The means are initiation and celebration whereby members, old and new, may experience and re-experience, through Liturgy, the organizational mythos in which everything is held together and makes sense. Although Mythos may appear as the Data and Information descriptive of everyday life under the Covenant, Mythos is constantly linking the members to their Depths (Vision, Understanding, Language) thereby providing a continuing reminder of where they came from, where they are going, and therefore, where they are at the moment.

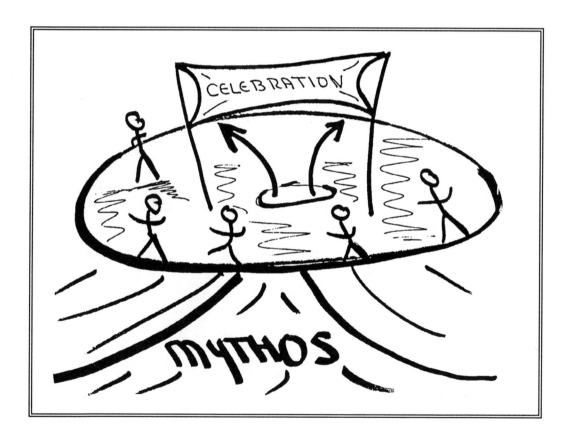

Chapter VIII

FACILITATING THE JOURNEY
OF SPIRIT

Facilitating the journey of spirit requires the conscious, informed presence of the would-be facilitator in the arena of transformation which is the organizational culture, and *mythos the key.* Simply put, the question is "What's the story, and how is it represented?" Finding mythos will be made easier by keeping clearly in mind its nature and habitat if only to insure that we are looking for the right thing in the right place.

By nature, mythos is the story, or more accurately a collection of stories which may look like history, and indeed may contain history (or historical elements), but does not function as history. Furthermore, when viewed (heard) as history, mythos will make little if any sense, and will probably be discarded or overlooked as being insignificant. The following description highlights the nature of the quarry, in contrast to the object of historical research.[63]

MYTHOS	HISTORY
Time is Kairos	Time is Chronos
Reality is the field	Reality is the "fact"
Context changes meaning	Has permanent meaning
Objectivity is impossible	Objectivity is essential

---

[63] In all fairness, I must say that the view of history [historiography] presented here is, to a degree, a straw man, for the field of history has been, and is, undergoing a number of changes which has made it infinitely more broad and various than the rather one-dimensional representation offered here. Nevertheless, there remains in the lay public a strong residue of what was called "scientific history" in the late 19th century, which continues to pursue the ideal of "pure historical facts." This description was developed as a direct derivative of my thinking about the strange world of quantum physics. The original form of this table also included columns labeled "classical physics" and "quantum physics", and in fact what I had done was to take some of the standard statements made about the world of the quantum [for example, concerning the impossibility of objectivity or separation of observer from the observed], and used this as a guide to my own thinking about mythos.

Meaning is in the void	Meaning in statement
May become truth	Describes truth
Not space-time dependant	Bound by time

TIME   Time in mythos is rather a different creature than time in history. The difference is caught in the greek word *kairos* which may be contrasted with the more familiar *chronos* from which we get words like chronometer. Kairos, to the best of my knowledge, does not appear in English, which represents a distinct loss. Kairos means "meaning-filled time," or in the phrase which translates it in the English New Testament — it is the "right time." Kairos refers to those moments of human experience which stand "out of time" so to speak, a moment when "time stands still." In essence, kairos is its own time, or maybe better, a moment which defines time. A classical example of this in the West is the birth of Jesus, which from the Christian point of view, defines time as "before Christ" and "after Christ." Judaism does not measure time the same way nor do other major world cultures, and the reason is simply that they start from a different kairos.

Chronos, on the other hand, is clock time, sun time, or star time. It is time abstracted from the human condition. This is the time of history, which represents "historical events" strung out along a continuum, a "time line." With chronos there is a very clear cut sense of "before" and "after," or past present and future. Kairos, on the other hand only knows an "eternal now."

This distinction between kairos and chronos becomes very important in our search for, and understanding of, mythos. For the time of mythos is kairos, and although it may often sound like chronos, we will quite mis-understand what is going on if we "think" chronos. For example when we have identified a myth, it is quite natural to ask, "When did that happen?" "Was it before or after such and such?" Those are the questions of history and chronos, and they simply do not apply to mythos. In mythos, there is no "before" or "after," only NOW, which either expands to include all time (chronos) or simply exists out of time.

REALITY IS THE FIELD   For mythos, reality is to be found in the field. For history, reality occurs in the fact. Thus when you approach a given body of material from the viewpoint of history, and ask the question, "What's really real?" — the answer comes out something like, "The really real appears in the cold, hard, irreducible facts." The job of the historian is to determine what the elemental facts are (by a process of reduction), validate these facts by inference from "independent sources" and then build the "historical picture." But the core of reality is contained in the "hard fact."

In mythos, the situation is very different. It is not so much that there are no "facts," but rather that fact as fact doesn't make that much difference. Indeed, as we have seen, mythos will very likely contain material descriptive of events that never happened at all. From the point of view of history, this situation renders mythos suspect at best, if only because it does not have the facts right. But what is right for history is quite beside the point in mythos. For the "real" in mythos does not localize in the fact, but rather appears in the field of meaning created by the constellation of stories within the organizational culture. When the story is told, the meaningful question is whether or not the "right" spirit has been properly imaged in the tapestry of meaning created by the interaction of the various elements which constitute the field. The validity or non-validity of these elements is irrelevant. Indeed, an outright historical falsehood may do an excellent job in imaging the spirit.

This distinction between fact and field as the center of reality becomes important in our search for, and understanding of mythos; for if we spend all our time questioning the validity of the "facts," we will entirely miss the meaning of mythos. The only legitimate question is whether or not some particular element appears in a body of mythos, and if it appears, how does it function in order to create the field of meaning through which Spirit is imaged.

MEANING CHANGES WITH CONTEXT In mythos, a given body of material can change its entire meaning depending upon the context. In history, the material is understood to have some sort of permanent meaning. For example, the historical statement that "Columbus sailed the ocean blue in 1492" is presumably true no matter where or when it may be said, or in what context it might appear.

This idea does not apply in mythos. Indeed, precisely the same statement may have a radically, even antithetically different meaning given a change in context or (what amounts to the same thing) the addition of some major new element. A classic example of this appears in the Old Testament relative to the New Testament. The Old Testament is the sacred myth of Israel with whatever meaning the community of Israel finds imaged there. As a body of myth, that material has existed over time and shaped the Spirit of Israel in a remarkably consistent fashion.

However, if and when one adds the "person of Jesus" to that body of material, the meaning radically alters, even though the words do not change at all. Suddenly, the Law and the Prophets (Israel's denomination) becomes the Old Testament as distinct

135

from the New Testament, and what used to be the WHOLE story (from Israel's) point of view, now becomes only the prologue. Absent Jesus, and the Old Testament reverts to its former state as Law and Prophets. Forget about which version is "right," because right simply does not apply. The truth of the matter is that for 2000 years, two separate communities have perceived radically different meaning in identically the same material. This situation simply could not occur in history, but it makes absolute sense, indeed it is to be expected, in mythos.

Being aware of this phenomenon in mythos is critical to any understanding of meaning, for it will be the case that the same story will appear in two different situations. Because it is the same, we might assume that it has the same meaning, and then will be surprised when the separate groups hold radically different interpretations. A great deal of time would be wasted seeking to determine which interpretation is "right." In truth, both are right, and we must concentrate on the meaning in context as opposed to any abstract "correct" interpretation.

OBJECTIVITY In mythos, the separation between subject and object, observer and observed does not happen, at least not with the kind of nicety that apparently pertains in history. This means that objectivity in any normal sense of that word is precluded when working with mythos.

In history, objectivity is not only possible but essential. Under ideal circumstances 100 scientific historians may be assembled to review a given historical datum, and if all the historians adequately control for their individual subjective bias, the resulting interpretations should be equivalent. If this is not the case, one may suspect sloppy work.

The impossibility of true objectivity when working with mythos derives from the fact that mythos operates as a field and will change meaning given a change in the field. This means that when an individual enters that field to observe what is going on, the nature of the field changes as does its meaning. This change may be minor or great depending on the power represented by the observer, but the change will occur. For example, should I as a consultant enter an organization when it is known that I have some special, but undefined relationship to the leader, my very presence may have major effects upon the field of mythos, and the way that the story is told without my saying a word.

There are several corollaries to this. The first is that consistency of interpretation should be looked for, not so much between observers, but rather between observations of the same observer. Should two observers perceive different things, it may be the case that one is "right" and the other "wrong," but more likely (presuming equal skill and practice) it will be true that both are correct in their individual contexts.

A second important corollary relates to the usual distinction between data collection and intervention. From the point of view of history, one may presumably collect all of the appropriate facts, analyze them, and then intervene in some strategic or tactical way. Such a presumption is not valid when working with mythos, for it turns out that the "facts" themselves will change in the process of collecting them, which means that intervention and collection and analysis are part of the same thing. This obviously produces certain practical and methodological problems. On a practical level this means that intervention begins at the point of contact and not at some later time when all the facts have been collected and assessed. The methodological problem requires that the "facts" (stories gathered) be assessed not as some abstract "pure data," but rather in terms of how they appear under the conditions of collection. For "collection" and the "collector" will change the facts (see the first corollary above).

MEANING IS IN THE VOID Whereas history communicates meaning in direct statement, mythos communicates meaning in the Open Space or the void. If we take the "historical" statement cited above about Columbus and the ocean blue, such meaning as may be there is contained in the words uttered or written. Should that statement be less than clear, the way of history is to add data until the statement is literally dense. All possibilities are covered, and we know the size of the ship, shade of blueness, number of the crew, name of the patron, duration of the voyage, and so on. Such dense statement is very useful in the context of history, but it is absolutely antithetical to the way of mythos. Mythos communicates in the structured Open Space created by just enough detail to set the limitations of meaning, but with plenty of room for the imagination (Spirit) to grow.

On a practical level, the fact that mythos communicates in the void with a minimum of structuring detail suggests that this means of communication is tremendously efficient, and the apparent size of the mythic elements relatively small. It is the "little story" that counts.

MYTH MAY BECOME TRUTH The intention of history is to describe the truth. But the material found in any given body of myth may or may not be true in the sense that it is historically accurate. It is only necessary that this material be credible and familiar so that it could be true. Once basic credibility has been established, mythos moves beyond being accurate in order to structure the Open Space within which meaning (truth) appears. Put another way, mythos is the ground from which the truth appears, and the reference point from which the true is determined to be true. In this sense, mythos may become truth to the extent that truth is encountered there.

MYTH IS NOT SPACE/TIME DEPENDENT History is bound by time. It is structured on a time line which gives meaning to the idea of past, present and future. There is a distinct "before" and "after," and once something has slipped into the past, it is no longer present. History is concerned to talk about what is past, with the tacit understanding that the past is past, and therefore gone.

Mythos operates independent of time and space. Insofar as mythos manifests Spirit, it may do this from a distance without regard for years or miles. For contemporary organizations this means that the Spirit of the group may be communicated across national boundaries or time. For older organizations such as the Christian Church, mythos represents the Spirit of the leader, now dead some 2000 years, with such immediacy and self-validation that the believer may say, "I know Jesus Christ." If we are to believe the words used, the "knowledge" referred to is not to be understood as "facts about" (although that may also be true), but rather immediate personal encounter. Mythos, in short obviates 2000 years of history.

THE HABITAT OF MYTHOS

By habitat, I do not necessarily mean a place; mythos may be discovered in any and all parts of the organization. Rather I am thinking of those special conditions under which one may most likely catch mythos "in the act." These conditions are established by the functions of mythos, which may be boiled down to an essential four: Definition, Initiation, Support, and Challenge.

DEFINITION In the first instance, mythos defines the group or organization. That is to say, "It is our Story, and it makes us different from all others." To the extent that you know The Story and the story is your story, you are part of the group. More to the point, so is everybody else who shares in that story. In terms of "catching mythos," this boundary-setting function is important, because every time "our organization" is juxtaposed with any other organization, normal "turf protectiveness" will require staking out the territory. This will almost automatically mean that The Story will be told. The boundary-setting capacity of mythos becomes most apparent in situations of high risk (perceived or real). For example, when organizations merge (both before and during the process) one is quite apt to hear many accounts of "how it was in the old days before `they' came along."

INITIATION   Until a member participates in the mythos of an organization, he or she really isn't "there." Modern organizations seem to feel that they have completed the initiation process when the personnel forms have been filled out. Actually, the initiation is only begun at that point. The next, and most important activity occurs when the new employee hears the war stories. One strategy for capturing mythos is therefore to follow a new employee around and listen to what he or she gets told. Naturally, if nobody ever tells the tale, that would be a reasonable indication that all was not well in the organization.

SUPPORT   A major function of mythos is to sustain the group in times of trouble. When events outpace the time and energy available, the group members will respond on the basis of their organizational DNA, mythos, which will give standards and role models. For example, one would expect in some future time, should Chrysler Corporation get in trouble again, to hear stories of how Iacocca did it in '81. To catch mythos, one may usefully watch out for crisis; in the calm before the storm or in the sequelae, it is almost guaranteed that the tale will be told.

CHALLENGE   A final function of mythos is to challenge the group, for one will find in the tales and ritual activities not only the accounting of how it all got started, but also strong pointers as to where things should be headed. Thus, in reflective moments when the future is the issue, stories of the "founder's dream" are quite likely to surface. By the same token, when the organization demands "the very best," stories which elicit that "best" are very likely to be told, as for example the story of the SS Speer told in the Jonathan Corporation at the beginning of a new job.

    None of these "locations" of mythos are sure shots, but if attention is paid to them in addition to a more rigorous and orderly searching across the spectrum of the organization (described below), the shape of the culture will begin to emerge.

APPROACH TO FACILITATION

    My approach moves in four steps. In Step I, a general understanding of the organization is developed through a consideration of the history. Step II concentrates on the leader and his/her personal vision or understanding. In Steps III and IV, the or-

139

ganizational culture is studied and described, first in microcosm, and then more broadly.

ORGANIZATIONAL SCAN (Step I) One begins with all the facts and figures, and the mode of operation is pure working level historian. To the extent possible, it is imperative to determine in an "objective way" the "who," "what," "when" for this organization. The relevant questions would certainly include, but not be limited to: When did it all start, where, and under what conditions? Who are (or were) the major figures, the founder(s), associates, adversaries and present day leaders? What is the structure and shape? How many divisions, and who reports to whom? And if part of some larger organization — what is that organization, and where is the "fit"? How many people employed, products produced, services rendered. And where does this all take place — in one location or spread across the country or around the world? What about significant events, major breakthroughs, reorganizations, defeats? Is there a merger in the past or future? And what is going on right now; winning, losing, treading water?

Obviously there is work here to fill a lifetime, and the question quickly becomes, How much is enough? Unfortunately, there is no hard and fast answer, but as a general rule, it is useful to keep going until the "bounds of the organization" have been walked and there is reasonable confidence that no new major pieces of territory will suddenly come into view. Territory here is not only spatial, but also temporal, which is to say, one should be able to start from the early days, when the organization was just a light in the founder's eye and spin a reasonable and consistent story down to the present moment such that most old-timers in the organization would say, "Yes, that's our organization."

The organization must first be explored at the level of Data and Information and Language. What are the facts and figures on the one hand, and what are the peculiar (unique) words or names by which the organization holds everything together? The observer's intent is to achieve basic literacy.

WHICH DIRECTION? — THE LEADERS VIEW (Step II) The essential question here is, Where does the organization think it is going, or would like to go? The first-cut approach is preliminary only. It begins with the leader. The issue at hand: what is his or her understanding and vision of and for the organization. Starting with the leader is obviously a very "top down" approach, but one which acknowledges the power realities in most organizations, and also takes into account the central role of leadership in the process of transformation.

The conversation with the leader usually starts at the level of facts and figures, production goals, plans for expansion, recitation of the immediate problems and possibilities. But the objective is to move beyond that to a consideration of the essential logic which governs the leader's approach to the organization, and even further, to that personal vision of what things should be like and what success in the field would mean, if achieved.

The issue here is not "fact" but what the leader thinks the situation looks like, for the truth of the matter is that, regardless of the facts of the case, the leader's perception is important and powerful. This is the leader's personal myth as it relates to the organization, and the "eyeglasses" through which he or she views the organizational world. Judgment as to "right" or "wrong" are beside the point at the moment.

More crucial is the question, what would it feel like if success were achieved, which tries to get at the issue of the quality of Spirit desired. Taken out of context, the answers to the last question may appear vague and ill considered, for they are usually couched in phrases like, "I want this place to be electric with excitement" or,"What I want is a happy ship." One leader said, "I want to teach engineers to fly."

The initial scan of the organization, accomplished through a look at the "history" and at the leader's perceptions, provides a jumping off point for the major concern, which is to understand and assess the quality and direction of Spirit in the organization as a whole, and the ways in which that Spirit is (or is not) accomplishing the tasks at hand or the ones coming into view.

SYSTEMWIDE EXPLORATION (Steps III and IV) One story once told does not a myth make. For myth (or more properly mythos), is that common bond of story fabric which, under the best of circumstances, exists across the consciousness of an organization in order to give it unity, shape, and direction. The fact that some element of mythos appears in the mind of one person, or even in the front office, is interesting but not necessarily significant. In seeking to understand the culture, it is essential to range broadly across all aspects of the organization in a systematic fashion.

Step III begins at the conclusion of the interview with the leader, at which time, he or she is asked to identify a small group of individuals (10-12) who are "important" to the organization, and willing to be interviewed. "Importance" may be defined any way the leader chooses, but it would certainly include members of the senior staff, particular individuals with whom the leader regularly confers such as a secretary and or administrative assistant, and not to forget adversaries and opponents.

One cannot begin with the central question, "What is the mythos?" Indeed, even a more colloquial phrasing of the question such as "What is the story?" does not produce very much useful information. Hence, a more indirect approach is required which centers around three questions: 1) Who are you and how did you get here? 2) What is this place (organization)? and 3) What should it be?

The first question is designed to set the stage and allow the person to talk about something which is presumably quite comfortable — themselves. The information gained here also has the practical utility of placing them in the general scheme of things as developed in the initial "historical" exploration of the organization. It is important to know, for example, how long a person has been with the organization. An old-timer will undoubtedly have a different, and possibly richer version of the story, than a newcomer, although that does not make the old-timer's version more valid. Indeed it may well be that the newcomer version is of greater interest and significance, because it is likely to be presented in "its essence," stripped of all the little details.

The second two questions go to the heart of the matter, but they get there quite indirectly. These questions are designed to sound as if specific information is requested, but they function in a rather different way. In a typical interview, the subject will respond to the questions ("What is this place? What should it be?") in terms of the data and information of their experience; dollars expended, people employed, numbers produced, job descriptions and the like. But inevitably (at least that has been my experience), the person will turn from the recitation of facts to the telling of stories by way of example. The words will go something like, "You really can't understand this place . . . it's like . . . well, last week," and out comes the tale.

This change in mode from "fact reciter" to storyteller is almost always signaled in advance by a noticeable shift in body position. At the beginning of the interview, the person is either sitting stiffly in the chair, or may even be slumped over. But when the "story is about to begin," there is a distinct movement forward as if to engage the listener.

In listening to the interview responses, it is important to remember what you are looking for. The data and information is of interest only in that they establish the context. The real concern is the "little stories" that are told (so the subject thinks) just by way of example. Sometimes the telling of these tales is an extended performance. But just as often, the stories will pass by in very reduced form, just a few words, or even a single word. . . a Heavy Word.

142

In the early phases of the effort, much is going to be missed, but that is probably just as well, because what does come through are those central stories that "everybody" knows. My experience to date suggests that even though this initial group is quite small and has been designated by the leader, there is a very high probability that most, if not all of the major operative myth will put in an appearance. A not incidental point is that the actual number of major myths (not counting local variants) present in any organization is actually quite small, usually not exceeding five or six, and sometimes one or two. This generalization holds true even for organizations of considerable size.

PRELIMINARY ANALYSIS AND OBSERVATION Once the initial interviews are complete, they must be analyzed in terms of the stories present, and the ways in which these stories function together to image the organizational Spirit. All of that is then run against the first statements made by the leader concerning his or her vision for the organization and the directions that are to be pursued. The areas of consonance and dissonance with the leader's vision and in the material itself are identified, and a preliminary strategy developed. I will describe the process of analysis shortly, but for the moment, I want to finish outlining the interview and observation procedure.

Step III of the process comes to an end with a presentation of the preliminary information, interpretation and strategy to what might be called a focus group. Typically, this group is composed of the leader, those interviewed, and possibly a few additional individuals chosen by the leader. The membership of this group is crucial, and the leader should be advised that although others may eventually be chosen and added, it is very useful to have the "right" people in early on. The "right" people, not incidentally, should not be limited to those that may be expected to automatically agree with the leader.[64]

The purpose of the group is two-fold: to validate the stories and to assess the proposed interpretation and strategy. The process of validation is simple and direct. Basically the story is told, and if it has been told "correctly," that becomes immediately apparent in the smiles and other facial expressions of the group. On the otherhand, if it is off the mark, the group is quick to make corrections.

---

[64] At the time that I wrote this book Open Space Technology was hardly more than an interesting idea. That status has changed markedly. Open Space Technology is now a very appropriate choice for organizing these Focus Groups, and in fact that has been my practice for the last several years. For further information on the technology and its application please consult *Riding the Tiger* and *Open Space Technology: A User's Guide*, both published by ABBOTT PUBLISHING

The second task of the focus group is to consider the interpretation offered, and the strategy suggested. The interpretation and proposed strategy will have been built from the interviews conducted thus far, and hence are only preliminary. If the job has been done well, the interpretation and the proposed strategy will provide a common ground upon which the assembled group may work out a consensus as to how things are, and what should be done, even if the group diverges widely in terms of individual view points. What seems to make this possible is that by starting with their stories, which they have acknowledged as being present in the culture, there can be no argument about that, and even if they don't like the stories, they must recognize that significant portions of the organization see things "that way." The question then becomes, What to do about it? — which leads to discussion about strategy.

Caveat Emptor While it is quite clear that much exploration remains to be done in the organization as a whole before the results can be accepted or strategy embarked upon, it is also true that the very process of this exploration will effect change within the mythic structure of the organization. The fact that an occasion is provided for the story to be recalled will inevitably bring old issues and old feelings (shapes of Spirit) to the surface. As this occurs, there is the opportunity to subtly shape that story in "positive" directions just by the way one listens and gives feedback. Shaping this story is an essential part of Collective Storytelling, and as such constitutes a powerful tool. It is, therefore, tremendously important for all concerned to know that this tool is in use, that they trust and communicate with the user (in this case me, the consultant), and also be thinking carefully about the possible results. Thus, as noted above, the intervention begins at the point of contact, and for sure, it is well under way when Step III is initiated.

In Step IV, the story is sought in all levels and sectors of the organization. Specifically, this means interviewing a representative sample from the executive, middle management, and working levels of all major sectors (departments, divisions) of the organization. The actual numbers here can get quite large, but not unmanageably so. For example, in a professional organization of 2500 with offices located across the country, this was accomplished with 143 interviews. In a larger organization, the number of interviews will obviously increase, but not in direct proportion to the number of individuals involved.

The obvious question is, How do you know when enough is enough? Certainly there are statistical methods for the determination of sample size, but in my experience, there is both a simpler and more effective way. One simply proceeds in each level and sector until such time as the stories begin to repeat themselves, and then do one or two additional interviews in that place. It is possible that some story will be missed, but it is quite unlikely that it will be an important one. After all, the central concern is with the Spirit of the total organization and with the culture that has been, or is, shaping Spirit. Some additional story known only to a select few in a corner of the organization will probably have marginal impact.

There is a safety check which comes from the original exploration of the organizational history. As that exploration is done, it is useful to make note of such events and circumstances which are likely to have entered into the operative mythos and thereby may have some formative impact. Using a checklist, it is possible to turn up a few surprises, but in my experience, that is rare. It is well to remember, however, that just because something happened (major breakthrough, layoff, merger) does not mean that the organization will have seen that event as significant, and therefore included it in the story about itself.

Observation To this point, I have been discussing the process exclusively in terms of interview as a means of access to myth or verbal story. There is, of course, the whole other side of mythos, namely ritual, which may only be accessed through observation. Observing ritual in contemporary organizations however, is not without its difficulty if only because the idea of "having ritual" is so foreign that there is very little if any formal recognition of this side of life. The corporate calender, for example is not very likely to list "coming ritual events" although those events do occur and one may observe them by being in the right place at the right time. To be sure, there are such things as board meetings and annual sales meetings, graduations, award nights and the like. All of these are rituals, although unfortunately they are usually pretty threadbare and may hold little connection with the life of the organization. Perhaps the best and most vital example is in a sales organization after a banner year when the awards are given out, and the great stories are told.

Despite the avoidance, even abhorrence of ritual in many organizations (the military being a major exception), the ritual is there and must be observed if a full picture of mythos is to be developed. Obvious ritual acts are fairly easy to spot. In those situations some act is performed for no readily observable reason. For example it may turn out that a chair is often left vacant at a particular meeting table. There is no practical reason for this, although it turns out upon examination that an ancient president used to sit there, and it is held vacant in his honor. . .and thereby hangs a

145

tale. By noting apparently anomalous behavior, and following up to learn "the story," rituals may be identified, and their meaning ascertained.

In other situations, the process of observation becomes somewhat trickier, because the observed behavior still maintains some useful, practical function which may mask the import of the ritual activity. For example, surgeons and operating room personnel scrub their hands prior to an operation in order to get their hands clean. But there is also a heavy ritual overlay to this activity which will only become apparent through a critical observation which enables one to separate out the function performed from the meaning imparted. In other words, do not concentrate so much on what they do as on how they do it, and simultaneously, pay close attention to what else seems to be going on. In the case of the scrub room, even minimal observation will show that the hand washing routine is not only done with care, but usually with a sense of awe or concentration — which is quite appropriate for an act of ritual purification. In addition, the conversation will often reveal fragments of the story, tales of surgical daring do. To be sure, discussion of golf scores will also work their way in. But nobody said that rituals always had to be serious.

ANALYSIS OF MYTHOS — THE MYTHOGRAPH

Once the tales and ritual acts have been gathered, the problem is to make sense out of this collection by arranging the material in such a way as to perceive the quality and direction of Spirit within the organization and then develop strategy for its enhancement. The mythograph is the mechanism.

The mythograph is a formalized representation of the organization onto which may be plotted the elements of mythos. In the example which follows, I have utilized stories from a variety of nameless organizations; nameless to protect the innocent, and a variety in order to demonstrate a range of possibilities and situations. No single organization, or at least no organization of which I am aware, ever looked like this.

DELTA CORPORATION The organization is the Delta Corporation. Historical research has revealed that it is a small, relatively young high technology firm. It began operations seven years ago based upon the inventions of the founder Harry Smith. At the time, these inventions established the state of the art, and for a period, the growth of the corporation was meteoric in terms of sales, employees and public perception. Plant and facilities were outgrown before completion, and it appeared that there was a unending market for the product. At present there are 2000 employees, down from a peak of 3500, a new CEO, and frustration.

At the age of three years, things really couldn't have looked better. Bright and exciting people were attracted to Delta Corporation, the product was selling, and the future appeared to be without limit. There was, however, a small cloud on the horizon which appeared more as an opportunity than a problem. The product was selling so well that it was virtually impossible to keep supply anywhere close to demand, and since other corporations had brought out their own versions, Delta Corporation faced the choice of either a progressive diminution of market share or a massive expansion of plant and facilities. Appropriate financing, however, was a complicating factor in what otherwise seemed to be a clear choice to "go for the gold."

To that point, Delta Corporation was closely held, indeed, Harry Smith owned it all. While the expansion might have been funded through further lines of credit, Harry took the advice of financial friends and decided to go public. At the time it seemed a very intelligent thing to do, for the product was selling like crazy, public interest and confidence were high, and besides it looked like a golden opportunity for Harry to begin converting his hard work into increased net worth — while at the same time getting the funds for plant expansion. The public offering was a instant sellout. Best of all, the value of shares seemed to increase daily. But for all of that, there was trouble in River City, because Harry was a dreamer and an entrepreneur. Although he enjoyed his newfound status and wealth, he experienced the role of full time executive as not a little intimidating and frankly boring. Given a choice, he would infinitely prefer to be back in the garage where it all started, thinking up something new and wonderful. Indeed, that is where Harry was increasingly to be found, which was not exactly the place from which a major expansion might best be directed. In a nutshell, things began to slip.

For the next three years, all the overt signs looked up, but inside, there was a very different story. Had not the product been outstanding, the end would have come almost immediately; but with a good product and strong reputation, the dollars flowed in and covered the pain of management mayhem, which eventually translated into sloppy workmanship, late orders, dissatisfied customers, and ultimately angry stockholders. One gray day, Harry found himself on the street, a good deal wealthier, but no longer the president and chairman of Delta Corporation.

The new management swept in like a fresh broom. Cost reduction and quality control measures were instituted, old timers booted though a succession of reorganizations, plant and facility brought up to snuff. . . but it just wasn't working. To make matters worse, that outstanding product was now six years out of date. It still did what it used to do, but that was nothing compared to what was presently available. The whole market had changed and Delta Corporation was no longer an integral part of the picture. Worst of all, the Spirit inside just didn't seem to be there when it came to taking that inspired leap into new thought and new products. The corporation was a model of organizational efficiency, but that was about all.

The present CEO was quite clear as to what she wanted, but mystified as to how to get there. She knew that survival depended on outstanding new products, but the management tools available only seemed to stifle their development. Regardless of how many times she uttered the word "innovation" or how closely she followed the eight-fold way to excellence, nobody was ready to take the leap, and they all played it safe. In an off moment, she put the whole situation quite succinctly, "What I really need," she said, "is engineers who can fly." It seemed that the flesh was willing, but the Spirit was weak.

THE MYTHOGRAPH OF DELTA CORPORATION

CEO — "We need engineers who can fly"
History — Going down hill

Levels   Sectors

	Finance	R&D	Production
Exec	Killing of '82	Old Harry	Making the Quota
Mid	Cashflow kid	Golden Fleece	Reuben
Shop	In Praise of Wilbur	Serendipity Sam/Leper Colony	Zebra

FINANCE The finance sector was the total creation of the new management. Rumor had it that old Harry kept his accounts in a shoe box, if he kept them at all, and the new CEO introduced state-of-the-art financial management.

148

At the executive level, the story was "The Killing of '82." The story related how the new financial VP sold more tax losses under the new tax laws than anybody could possibly have dreamed of. The truth of the matter was that he had a lot to sell, given the profligacy of old Harry, but even so, he did an outstanding job. In fact, selling losses, he made a profit.

At the middle management level, the story surrounded a hero of sorts, "The Cashflow Kid." The Cashflow Kid had a marginal understanding of what the business was all about, and he cared even less. However, he was extraordinarily good at managing cashflow, and making an excellent return on short term deposits.

At the working level in finance, the story was, "In Praise of Wilbur." Wilbur was actually the inhouse computer, and the personnel at this level took genuine pride in the tricks they had taught the computer to play. The story of Wilbur was rather strange in that nobody ever spoke of what Wilbur did for the corporation, only how elegant he was in his performance.

RESEARCH AND DEVELOPMENT At the executive level in R&D, the story concerns Old Harry, the president. In fact, the VP for R&D was Harry's original collaborator, who now lives only in the past. His story is one of creativity gone sour. But for all of that he remembers (as do his colleagues) the sheer excitement of the old days when inventiveness and innovation were the coin of the realm, and old Harry was in the saddle.

Middle management had been installed by the new CEO, and charged with the responsibility of getting a handle on the R&D dollar. Fresh from business school, they had carefully established goals and objectives, and when the researchers failed to perform on schedule, the managers assumed that the fault lay with the "science boys." The story here was the "Golden Fleece" awarded monthly to the researcher who's project showed least potential for profit.

Down at the benches, in what had been the heart of the operation, a small but curiously dedicated group of researchers survived. There were two stories here, one surrounding a strange individual known as "Serendipity Sam." Sam was an extraordi-nary, bright individual who took perverse delight in having been awarded more Golden Fleeces than all of his fellows put together. He worked largely by himself or with one or two associates, and despite the environment, which could only be called deadening, he managed to generate an aura of excitement and a series of innovations.

The second story down at the benches was, "The Leper Colony." The Leper Colony was the self-chosen title adopted by the five older researchers, all of who had been rough contemporaries of old Harry. But when the new management layer was added, they found themselves excluded from all power and decision making. They passed their days waiting for their pensions and taking some strange solace in their name.

PRODUCTION In the last area, Production, the executive level story was, "Making the Quota." Here the numbers were more important than what they stood for. Indeed, those at the senior level seemed to have little concern and less knowledge about what it was they produced, they cared only for the numbers, and best of all, an increase in those numbers every month.

The Spirit of the middle-level production managers was captured by the story of "Reuben." Reuben, it turned out, was a manager of extreme political sensitivity. He was inevitably at the right place at the right time, with his backside covered . . . and apparently as a consequence, had enjoyed a meteoric rise from the level of supervisor.

Last but by no means least, down on the shop floor, the story was a strange one indeed. The Zebra was a local bar frequented by the workers. On one particular evening, a heavy snow covered the ground and was quickly increasing in depth. The workers, having stopped for a short one on the way home, found the street impassable when it came time to leave, or at least that was a plausible excuse. By the time the snow plows broke through, the party had reached new highs of conviviality, although the exact details were a closely guarded secret. Those who had participated drew close in a conspiracy of silence, while the remainder of the workforce awaited the next big snow in hopes that they too could be initiated.

ANALYSIS AND ASSESSMENT

In analyzing the mythograph, the key thing is to remember that each element (myth) represents, and in a sense contains, the Spirit of the place, and furthermore, provides indications of the quality, force and direction of that Spirit. Under ideal circumstances, in a truly high-performing organization, all cells (each level and sector) would show the same story, or at least the same story with minor variations appropriate to that level and sector. That sort of a picture would be indicative of a uniformity of Spirit with the potential for an unimpeded, powerful flow which may be focused on the tasks at hand, and those which may come to hand. Although the organization might be structured in a rigid hierarchical fashion, the commonality of the story (representing the Spirit) connects departmental boundaries and unites the organization in a common purpose. In this situation, the culture is coherent, and the Spirit is free and flexible.

Thus, the first aspect of analysis is to consider the mythograph as a whole and note the relative continuity or discontinuity (degree of focus) of Spirit as represented by the stories listed. The second aspect of analysis (which leads to strategy-building) considers the mythograph in terms of what is available within the extant organizational mythos which may lead directly, or with a little help, towards the desired organizational function. Remembering that each element of mythos represents a "quantum" of Spirit, the key question is, does the organization presently possess the kind and quality of Spirit necessary to achieve the desired goals? Even if that quantum of Spirit is weakened or distorted, it may become the basis or centerpiece for a new configuration of Spirit (a new Story).

WHAT TO SAY ABOUT DELTA CORPORATION? Considering the mythograph of Delta Corporation, it is obvious that there is no one story. Indeed, there appears to be a different story for every level and sector. The fact that the CEO experiences her environment as low on innovative Spirit is hardly surprising, for the capacity for Spirit to flow through her world in a focused and directed manner is virtually prohibited by the fact that nothing connects to anything else. Each little cell within the organization has its own story which shapes and forms their Spirit, and few of them show even a general relationship to any other. Were we to map the Spirit flow-patterns of the organization, the picture would appear as a series independent swirls feeding on themselves, and going nowhere as a whole.

Actually, the situation is somewhat more complex, and if anything more destructive. A closer look at the mythograph will tells us that, all appearances to the contrary, there are some connections, but not necessarily of a healthy sort. For example in Finance, all the stories center around money or more accurately, numbers, which is what "Wilbur" is good at. The focus of this complex of stories connects with a similar interest in Production (Making the Quota), at least at the executive level, and finds another parallel in Research at the mid level (The Golden Fleece). So we might visualize a rather contorted flow. Not exactly freeflowing and unimpeded, but there is a connection.

Another link appears to exist in Research between the executive level (Old Harry) and the technical level (The Leper Colony and Serendipity Sam). The stories are hardly inspiring, but they do seem to relate on some essential level around "exciting exploration," even if all of that is only a memory. The story of "Serendipity

Sam" is an exception to the otherwise unrelenting gloom, and in fact constitutes the one bright ray of hope.

If we take both constellations of stories, as weak and loosely associated as they may be, and lay them out on the mythograph, a most disturbing picture of Spirit emerges. Instead of simply being incoherent and dissociated (the original impression), it now appears as an unproductive conflict between the "new management" and the old "science boys," and the linchpin is the "golden fleece." This is a classic case of mythic dissonance in which the organization expends more Spirit in fighting itself than it does in productive work. Furthermore such free energy as is available (at the mid- and shop-floor levels of Production) spins off and out in a noncontributory fashion.

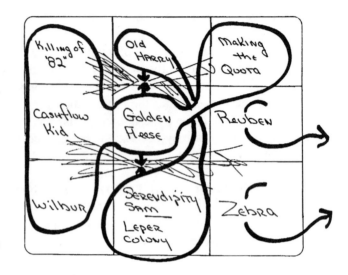

The picture of the Spirit of Delta Corporation developed to this point is not encouraging, but it certainly supports the CEO's perception that while the flesh may be willing, the Spirit is weak. Only now we are in a position to see graphically what some of the reasons might be. Ultimately this will be very useful in terms of developing a strategy for turning the situation around. First, however, there is an additional piece of analysis to be done. We must consider the elements of mythos in relationship to the desired way of being for the organization.

If the CEO has any hope of realizing her goal for the organization as being a place where "engineers fly," the issue and opportunity is, how to create that nutrient environment in which the imagination can take off to think some thoughts that have never been thought before — from which new exciting products might be developed, produced and marketed. Anything less than that, and she is basically out of business.

152

In order to realize her intention, she will require an organizational way of being which is certainly Pro-active, and ideally Inter-Active. With a Pro-active organization she might anticipate that orderly capacity for planning and problem-solving which at the very least would allow for the measured development of new products with some assurance that they will be produced and marketed in a cost effective and profitable way. That would represent an enormous improvement over the present situation.

On the other hand, if she really expects to storm the walls of innovation, and come out with something that once again establishes Delta Corporation as a state-of-the-art operation, moving quickly and easily in the ebb and flow of the high-tech market, the Inter-Active mode of being is clearly more appropriate. As Interactive, Delta Corporation would experience the breakdown of artificial barriers and boundaries so that research ideas flowed into product design, on to production and out to the market. Although procedures and departments would still exist, their presence would be more by way of convenience than necessity, and in any event, employees would think nothing of jumping over departmental walls if the nature of the work required it. Thus, research and researchers would no longer only be found in the lab, but out on the shop floor or even in the finance offices, seeing how their ideas really worked or arranging for financing for new efforts. And it wouldn't be a one way street either, for folks from the shop floor might be found in the lab pointing out potential production problems before the design was set in concrete.[65]

Confusing to an outsider for sure, but quite possible provided everybody knows what the business is, and keeps their eye firmly on the goal, with relatively less attachment to the forms and structures of organizational life. Inevitably, problems will arise, and procedures should be followed, but when the Vision (goal) is clear, so also is the direction, and that is a surefire way of insuring that only the relevant problems and procedures are dealt with, instead of allowing problems and procedures to become the business. Vision is uniquely communicated by mythos, but for all of that to take place, mythos must be adequate to the task and appropriate to the organizational situation. And therein lies the central task of leadership.

Put most sharply, the question is, how do you facilitate transformation in an organization slipping into Re-activity and verging on extinction, towards a way of

---

There really are organizations that function this way. The Jonathan Corporation was one of them at the time I did my study. In essence what I am describing here is a super skunkworks, to use Tom Peter's phrase.

being appropriate to the environmental demands. Dealing with this will mean re-configuring the existing Spirit so that it is truly focused on the task at hand.

DEVELOPING A STRATEGY

In creating a strategy it is important to remember what you are dealing with, and where you want to go. The "what" in this case is the Spirit of Delta Corporation as imaged by the operative myth. And the "where," at least as expressed by the CEO, is to move towards a condition of high performance in which "engineers can fly." This strategy must recognize the present conditions in which Spirit is largely cycling in on itself in small disconnected units. Or, to the extent that Spirit is connected and coherent, it is organized in two opposing forces centered around the "science boys" and "numbers." Under these circumstances, there is little "flow-through" which might energize and direct the prosecution of business, and in fact a tremendous amount of energy is simply spun off and wasted in useless conflict.

An effective strategy will smooth out the flow (avoid side eddies and bottlenecks) and direct that flow towards the achievement of the organizational goal. In simple graphic terms, the intent of the strategy would appear as follows.

Spirit ▸ *High Performance = "Where Engineers Fly"*

The elements of the Spirit flow are given by the previously identified content of mythos. It may appear that there is very little to work with, and that things are so confused and incoherent that the intelligent thing to do would be to scrap the whole thing and start again. There is one glimmer of hope; the story of "Serendipity Sam." Were it possible to free the Spirit contained in that story located in the depths of the R&D Sector, it is just conceivable that the CEO might realize her goal. Of all of the stories present, "Serendipity Sam" is the only one that represents the kind of excellence and innovation that in any way equates with the idea of "engineers flying." Thus an initial step in building a strategy would appear as follows:

Spirit ▸ *Serendipity Sam = High Performance*

There are no small problems attendant to "Serendipity Sam," hidden as it is in an obscure portion of the corporate culture. To the extent that the story does have currency (power), it is a negative sort, having become the object of scorn through the association with the tale of the "Golden Fleece." And the "Golden Fleece" is part of a larger story complex ("Taking Care of the Numbers"), which essentially controls the culture at the moment.

If the CEO is to be successful, it will be necessary to transfigure the culture so that the present dominant force is in some way neutralized, or realigned behind (in support of) the Spirit represented in "Serendipity Sam." Actually, one would scarcely want to neutralize the dominant force (the Numbers), for it is essential to the function of the organization. The problem, however, is that at the moment, "Taking Care of the Numbers" has become the dominant power, to the exclusion of everything else. A more suitable Spirit flow would appear as follows:

Taking Care
of the ► **Serendipity Sam = High Performance**
Numbers

There remains some considerable amount of negative and/or nonproductive Spirit present in the organization, which left to its own devices will continue to spin in on itself, and contribute little if anything to the corporate objectives. Specifically, there are the stories of "Old Harry" and the "Leper Colony." In their present form and position, these stories are "sour" and actually pollute the atmosphere. But it is worthwhile noting that, at their core they contain some essential elements for the productive life of the organization; each of these stories carries the sense from Out of the Depths along with a picture of the organizational Vision. In present form, the Spirit represented here is hardly useful, but if Delta Corporation is ever to get back on track, it must regain its Vision and reconnect to the Depths or that primal realization of what it is all about.

Making the stories positive, and aligning them with the creative (innovative) spirit represented by "Serendipity Sam," would create the sort of "depth connection" which could ground Delta in its past as a jump off point for the future. Given the successful accomplishment of this task, the flow pattern of the organization would appear as follows:

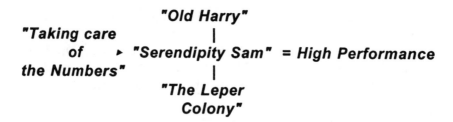

"Old Harry"
|
"Taking care
of ▸ "Serendipity Sam" = High Performance
the Numbers"
|
"The Leper
Colony"

There are two additional stories ("Reuben" and the "Zebra"), which although they may capture some genuine elements of Spirit, are nevertheless at some remove from the central thrust of the organization as the CEO envisioned it. These stories may therefore be left for the moment with the hope that, if the larger Spirit flow pattern can in fact be developed, the Spirit resident in those stories may be re-channeled into the mainstream.

At the strategic level, the task at hand is to conceptualize the re-channeling and redirection of the organizational Spirit to support organizational goals. In developing this strategy, we have obviously been operating at a high level of abstraction, but by using the elements of the organizational mythos as "counters," it becomes possible to visualize the major elements of the Spirit, while simultaneously imagining different configurations of that Spirit which are more conducive to productive work. At this juncture, we have an outline image of Spirit which is focused on the task at hand, and which flows in the direction that the CEO has in mind. Given effective facilitation of the process of transformation, one might hope to achieve an end-state in which the organizational culture operated as a coherent field, molding and shaping the Spirit over time, in a manner conducive to the performance of useful work. In other words, Delta Corporation could get on with the job. The End State might appear as follows:

FROM STRATEGY TO IMPLEMENTATION — TACTICS

In moving from strategy to implementation it is useful to remember that we are dealing with mythos, which requires special treatment. Therefore, a number of approaches which might work in other contexts, are simply precluded. Since it appears that innovation has become buried in the depths of the R&D Sector, for example, and that the place of burial has subsequently been covered over by a dominating concern for the numbers, it would be tempting for the CEO to haul the appropriate people into her office and tell them that they had the story all wrong, and that in the future, things were going to be different.

This direct approach might well work in a situation where the concern was some objective way of doing business, a specific procedure, for instance, which should be followed. However, in the case of mythos, this sort of telling, ordering, directing simply does not work, and in fact often becomes counter productive, for the reason

157

that mythos does not operate on the level of "talking about," but rather on the deeper level which provides the content and context for such conversation. "Telling" someone to have a different mythos, or to hold the same mythos in a different way, will usually not even be heard. Such statements literally fall outside of the frame of reference (paradigm) of the listener, and as a consequence make no sense. For mythos, after all, is the frame of reference.

A most likely outcome of directly telling someone that their mythos is wrong is that the objectionable mythos will actually be strengthened in the mind of the holder. As strange as this might seem, the logic is fairly straightforward: if it is true that mythos, as held by a particular group or individual, actually represents the self-understanding hence life — it is not surprising that direct challenge will be met with increased resistance. Since mythos represents the source of meaning, denial of mythos will subject the holder to meaninglessness, which is obviously not a condition that anybody would willingly enter into. Hence the typical response is to perceive the challenger as "crazy" or worse.

Another apparently more moderate, direct approach to the issue at hand, *explanation*, will also prove to be ineffective. Explanation depends upon a common base of logic and *a priori* belief, which allow one to move in sequential steps from one position to another (presumably better) way of looking at things. When the issue is the "common base" itself, explanation has nothing to move "from," which makes "getting to" more than difficult.

It is no wonder, then, that leaders find dealing with mythos difficult and frustrating, for essentially all of the major tools provided by their formal training (logic, explaining, taking charge and ordering) are either nonoperative, or counterproductive.

LEADERSHIP BY INDIRECTION The alternative is leadership by indirection, which orchestrates a new, positive story, created so far as possible out of the existing elements of mythos, which captures and excites the organizational Spirit, and focuses it in productive directions. By using existing mythos, the basic, conservative nature of culture is acknowledged, and the Spirit of the organization preserved. In the case of destructive mythos (bad stories), the approach must be to leave them alone, and to literally outflank and overpower their negativity with the positive nature of the new story.

Leadership by indirection is leadership appropriate to mythos. Such leadership understands mythos or culture to be its primary arena of activity, and therefore utilizes practical and theoretical tools relevant to the task. In actual operation, leadership by indirection may appear quite similar to, or the same as, other forms of leadership. But the difference lies in perspective and intention. Direct leadership views the artifacts of the organization (plant, facilities, products, balance sheets, bank statements, paychecks) as they are in themselves, and in terms of what they actually do. Indirect leadership considers instead their inherent capacity to "tell the story" and thereby shape the Spirit.

For example, a "paycheck" is just a paper through which funds are transferred from the organization to the employees as compensation for their work. But the paycheck also functions in a more powerful way. It is a unique symbol of the relationship of organization to employee, and may therefore constitute a central part of the story which shapes that organization. Obviously the amount of money appearing on the paycheck communicates essential information about the relative importance of the work performed. But it is also true that physical characteristics such as the color of the paycheck, and other apparently minor details in its appearance, may play significant roles in the way the artifact tells the tale, and indeed, what tale is told. For instance, if there are different colors for salaried and unsalaried employees, switching these colors, even if the amounts remained the same, would be likely to create confusion in the Spirit of the place. Salaried employees might suspect some diminution of status, and the unsalaried probably wouldn't understand.

For purposes of leadership by indirection, each and every piece of organizational life is, or is potentially a powerful mechanism for telling the tale. To the extent that the leader is concerned to shape the Spirit, the means lie readily at hand in all of the artifacts of that world. The task of the leader becomes one of orchestrating the artifacts and happenings of the organization in order to create new or enhanced mythos. Absolutely nothing is precluded, and virtually anything in the color, form, smell, sound, and movement "vocabulary" of the organization may be used powerfully to weave the tale.

NEW TOOLS FOR THE JOB Rendering the tale in a powerful and economical fashion will require different ways of thinking and the utilization of skills not normally found in the curriculum of business schools. In order to see and utilize the rich, variegated vocabulary of the organization, consisting of color, form, smell, sound and movement, it will be necessary to reach beyond the normal confines of organizational practice.

Color The use of color, as in the paycheck example above, necessitates a sensitivity to intensity and hue usually found only with the competent graphic artist. Yet if the leader is to function well in the world of mythos, he or she must see not only what everybody else sees, that colors are different, but must move on to the finer distinctions as to which colors are most appropriate to what situation. Red for passion, blue for inspiration, yellow and orange for warmth, green for growth, for sure, but what about the special colors of the organization — blue for the Navy and IBM, Army Green.

Most organizations just "get painted," a function left largely to Maintenance. Although Maintenance may end up with the physical job, orchestrating the event is too important to be left to individuals with no sense of what the mission is. Or then again, perhaps Maintenance has an exquisite sense, which is reflected in the color environment they create. If this is so, they are pulling one "lever of power" which is equal to or greater than any single element of the leader's "normal" arsenal of tricks.

Form (plastic) The physical form of an organization (not to be confused with its manner and style) is a powerful channel for Spirit and a means for telling the tale. Where a plant is located and how it is laid out (geometry) will permit (or deny) certain ways of being. Long (linear) buildings produce the "bowling alley effect." The ball starts at the front and rolls toward the back. A very good shape for simple production lines, but quite difficult when knowledge is the product. For knowledge emerges in nonlinear ways, a product of multiple interactions.

There are also those collective forms such as "our product" which represent physical expression of what we hope and dream about. The forms of our organizational life usually do something practical, but in addition they also "tell the Story" in important and powerful ways.

Smell is another grossly underrated player, for human sensitivities to smell (good ones and bad) are extreme, and the capacity of any particular smell to vector intention and galvanize response is truly remarkable. One whiff can conjure up memories and produce responses which a thousand words could barely suggest. This fact is understood well by the perfume industry and women. It is also "not for nothing" that most major religious organizations have historically utilized this sense to add breadth to the telling of their tale. If you thought that incense was burned at services of worship only to cover up a lack of bathing (although it may also do that), you have quite missed the point. Even today, a wisp of a particular incense I first experienced in an Easter Mass celebrated in a Russian Orthodox Church 20 years ago, will bring me right back into that powerful sacred space.

So what do our organizations smell like? Normally we make every effort to insure that they don't smell at all, which usually means that the air is filled with some powerful commercial antiseptic, which frankly smells just awful. Perhaps the "clean smell" is appropriate to the hospital operating room, but such sterile olfactory input is not likely to stimulate great flights of fancy and imagination in anybody other than a surgeon. While I was working with Jonathan Corporation I came to associate the pungent mixture of sea salt, tar and fresh paint common to all shipyards with the exhilarating experience of watching a high performance outfit really doing a job. Given that same smell, I am right back there again.

Sound, both verbal and nonverbal is another of the human world that communicates powerfully, and yet is largely unconsidered in the organizational world. While it may not be possible to orchestrate the sound of our corporations with the same exactitude and finesse of the conductor and the composer, it is certain that we can do a much better job than we do. Again, the tendency in modern organizations is towards the absence of sound, as if silence were somehow conducive to productive work. Yet we know from an enormous amount of experimental evidence that sensory deprivation (particularly absolute silence) is a marvelous and almost surefire way to drive people mad. To be sure, too much sound, or the wrong kind of sound (otherwise known as noise) is not very helpful, but that fact should not lead to the conclusion that no sound at all is the desired state. What we need is the right sound, the appropriate sound. For example, it was discovered in a clinical division of Dupont that playing Baroque music softly over quality speakers (instead of Musak) made a measurable difference in the quality and output of the "thinkers" resident there. Now baroque music is not every-body's sound, and indeed may be noise to a few, but some sound is the right sound, and determining how the organization should sound is a consequential part of leader-ship by indirection.

Motion Last, but by no means least, there is motion. Even in sleep we move, and there are patterns to that motion which will tell the skilled observer more or less what is going on. Awake, Homo sapiens is constantly on the move, and we tend to make a distinction between "productive" motion and "nonproductive" motion. The former is called "work" and the latter "play" or just moving around. While it may be true that not all motion accomplishes some particular task, it does seem to be true that very few, if any, motions occur without communicating something. How we move, apart from what ever might be accomplished, therefore becomes a potent means for saying who we are, how we feel, what we intend, in short, motion in all forms is a powerful means for telling the story, our own and the story of the organization.

Thinking about motion in the life of an organization seems largely limited to mapping traffic flows, and looking for the most efficient routes. Although such thought may have its uses, it totally overlooks the elemental communicative power present in the way we move. For the purposes of leadership by indirection, this represents a great loss. There are, of course, those who have made a lifetime work out of understanding human motion and have elevated its performance to a high level of art. The proper word here is dance, and the individuals are known as choreographers.

Typically dance is reserved for the stage, and is thought about as something different from (abstracted from) ordinary life. Dance is not different from life, but it is certainly an abstraction, suggesting that all of life is a dance, only sometimes we do it with greater intention and artistry. The thought is caught neatly in the title of one of Edward Hall's books, "The Dance of Life."

For purposes of leadership by indirection, the dance of life, or to put it the other way around, life as a dance, is an essential understanding, and represents a strong tool for the shaping of mythos. This is not to suggest that board meetings should be opened with pirouettes, or the assembly line started up each day with a few grande jettes. But that idea is not as farfetched as it may sound. The Japanese, have discovered that beginning the day with some coordinated nonproductive (as we would see it) movement, goes a long way towards "getting folks together," aligned and attuned for the work at hand. They have even imported this practice to the United States, and one will discover the workers at the Toyota plant in Tennessee out doing their exercises before the day's work begins. Actually, the "exercises," at least as they are performed in Japan, are much more than old fashioned calisthenics. In fact, they are some form of the age old martial arts which contain (and entrain) a whole philosophy of life in the motions performed.

THE PHASES OF IMPLEMENTATION

For any organization standing at the edge of open space with a full realization that the old way isn't working anymore, and the new way has yet to be found, the primary issue is the passage through that Open Space, and the articulation of a new Story, a New Covenant, a new way of being there. Facilitating that passage is the

162

concern of the moment. The elemental factors for this are found in the color, form, smell, sound, and motion "vocabulary" available to the organization, which may be orchestrated to create a fabric of meaning and direction to guide the way. Words and statements will be important, but in many ways superficial, for too often they lead to "talking about" the present situation and future possibility, when the real issue is the creation of the conditions under which Spirit may emerge in new form with new power.

It would not be stretching a point to understand the process at hand as a dramatic event or sequence of events, with the leader as director or conductor, and others filling in as stage hands, prompter, property managers and the like. The stage is the physical space of the organization in all of its dimensions. As a dramatic event, there are four essential elements: 1) Reaching the Depths and Perceiving the Vision; 2) Griefwork; 3) Collective Story telling; 4) Celebration. In listing these elements, it may appear that I am suggesting a strict linear process. That may be true in rough terms, but as often as not, the elements will overlap or occur simultaneously.

REACHING THE DEPTHS, PERCEIVING THE VISION "Reaching the Depths" is an intentional play on words. On the one hand, it means acknowledging all of the pain and frustration within the current life of the organization. This is a difficult task to be sure, and one that most leaders would choose to avoid. But, for the process of transformation to begin, and in order for it to be facilitated to successful conclusion, somebody has to face things just the way they are — with no fancy dressing or excuse. If ever there were a prime expression of what it means to know the "loneliness of command," surely that is to be found in the moment that the depths are reached. The view is not appealing, for it consists basically of the end and non-availability of further alternatives, given the present way of doing business. Reaching the depths occurs when it becomes inescapably clear that there are no more workable stratagems for survival. Things as they were aren't any more.

Reaching the Depths also has a remarkable clearing capacity, for at such a moment, all of the nonessentials, the "might have beens" and "if-onlies" move out of the way, and what's left are the basics. The central and only question is, "What's it all about?" It may turn out that the answer is "nothing," in which case that is the end: literally, figuratively and finally. Or the answer may be "something," perhaps not clear, precise and definitive, but something. That "something," whatever it may be, is sufficient to switch the polarities, change the valences, convert "end" to "beginning," and initiate the odyssey across the Open Space. Rounding the corner down in the depths is something that leadership must ultimately do alone, but it surely helps to have some friends around.

Leadership's new sense from the depths is where everything begins, but it is insufficient in itself, for others must participate if the journey is to start. More to the point, this participation becomes possible only when there is concrete awareness of how things might turn out — the function of Vision. The specifications of the Vision, as detailed before, are: 1) Big enough to include everybody (Serendipity Sam and the numbers folks); 2) Powerful enough to motivate and carry the crew through the hard places; 3) Doable in the sense that there seems to be a reasonable possibility the whole thing may successfully be accomplished.

Building the vision may be left to natural processes, as the leadership, in the normal course of events, interacts with associates and communicates in word and deed, the color and sound of the New Idea. There are, however, several techniques which can enhance and speed this process, one of which is guided imagery.

Guided imagery is a process which has been formally developed over the past several years, but it has its roots in the much older religious practice of guided meditation. The essence of guided imagery is for a leader[66] to describe a series of images in vivid but scant detail while the participating individuals are invited to "enter into" that image and explore the open space created while adding their own details and meanings. In a typical session, the participants will be led into a relaxed state through a series of controlled breathing exercises after which the image is presented. The content and sequencing of the images is critical to assisting the group to develop a new vision.

One form for guided imagery begins with a simple nonthreatening image of a "comfortable place."[67] In this image, the participants are asked to call up to their minds any place where they really feel at home. That could be a quiet beach, open meadow, a childhood "special place" or even their own bed. They should notice what it is like (smell, taste, texture, colors). After a while, the process is stopped, and the group shares the images produced and what it was "like" to be there.

---

[66] The "leader" here may be "THE LEADER", but typically this function might better be performed by someone else.

[67] The images and sequences presented here were originally developed by Robert Phileo and some associates.

164

The next exercise begins to go to the heart of the matter. The image here is that of a boundary — which might be a wall, side of a cliff, edge of the ocean. The group is asked to conjure up such an image, and then explore it. Can they get around it, over it, under it? What does it feel like physically, and most importantly, how do they feel in the presence of that boundary? Once again, the images are shared. The importance of this exercise is that boundaries can mean many different things to people (beginning, end, barrier, opportunity), and how we perceive boundaries is very critical to the way we deal with the future.

For a group just entering into the process of transformation, the information generated here may be the most important information they could have. It is important to note that there is no "right" perception of boundaries, and in any given group, there will be a wide difference of interpretation. But if it turns out that everybody sees boundaries only as end and barrier, it is reasonable to expect that the group will have a very difficult job in transversing the Open Space of transformation. Personally, I have never found such uniformity, which is fortunate, and it is useful for the group to know that some of its members will be facing the future with a great deal of fear, while others will take the "journey over the edge" as a real challenge. The fainthearted, however, are not to be scorned, for their caution will in fact be useful. By the same token, the real "chargers" will show their mettle when the going gets tough.

The last exercise deals with the future directly, and involves an imaginary trip to an unknown place. The "place" doesn't make much difference; one may "go out into space" or "down" into the high energy world beneath the atom. The point is not so much where you go, just so long as it is different from the present, and really allows the participants to throw off the present conceptions of time, space, furniture and the like. The next step is the RETURN to the organization at some indeterminate time in the "future." The participants are asked to try and figure out "when" that time is, but most of all to note "how things are." What are they doing, what is the business? How are people relating to one another? What do the customers look like? After a bit of this, the group stops again and shares, and from this sharing come the bits and pieces of the new Vision.

Guided imagery is not for everybody, but I have successfully used the approach with a wide variety of individuals and groups ranging from very conservative senior executives to military officers. In order for it to be workable with any group, it is essential that the procedure be introduced in such a way that it doesn't seem strange or outlandish. This is not too difficult, because in fact virtually everybody has had some prior experience with the phenomenon of imaging, whether that be in the form of daydreams, or as a child playing the great game of "let's pretend." In guided imagery this normal process is orchestrated, and directed towards a specific result, namely creating the new Vision for the organization. Even if it is not possible to utilize such a formal procedure, due to the temper of the group, or temperament of the leader, the essential steps and ideas are important. In facilitating the emergence of a new Vision, the group has to begin to see some pictures which they can share in common, and use to guide them along the way as they proceed through transformation. Without such powerful referents, it is all too easy to get lost and discouraged in the nuts and bolts of organizational life.

GRIEFWORK Griefwork is what any organization must go through as it lets go of the old and prepares for what is yet to be. Whether griefwork is pursued in the formal setting of an organizational wake, as in the case of Delta Force, or in some less formal environment makes little difference, and it is largely a matter of personal and organizational style and custom. Nevertheless, the essential steps must be experienced, and it is incumbent upon the leader and those who would assist him or her, to make sure that this becomes possible. In the first place, it is imperative that all the members of the organization understand that it is perfectly all right to talk about what happened before, and to acknowledge the sadness of it. Leaders in a hurry to get on with the new business may feel that time is being wasted, but in fact it is very well spent. It also may seem that this grieving will go on forever, but more often than not, given some strong sense of the Vision and the future, the process is self limiting. It will end when the work is done. More to the point, when the process is terminated prematurely, the grieving actually continues, but in a subterranean, invisible sort of way which only saps the organizational Spirit, and yields a depressing number of false starts toward renewal.

Griefwork carried to some reasonable termination is an essential pre-condition for getting on with the business. But griefwork is only truly effective in assisting people let go when they have some glimmer of what they can eventually hold on to. Griefwork, therefore, is best conducted in the context of Vision.

COLLECTIVE STORYTELLING Weaving the new tale is the essence of leadership and lies at the heart of assisting with the process of transformation. In constructing this tale, it is necessary to consciously "link back" to the organizational potential as represented by the Depths, Vision, and understanding, and the ways this potential may have been actualized in the life of the organization. Whatever the new tale may turn out to be, it cannot jettison all that went before, but, must make a place for all that has been done, and for the heroes and rebels of the past. This becomes the basis and connecting point for what will occur in the future. By now it should be clear that this new tale is not just a revised business plan, new financial projections and the like, although these and many other elements from the everyday life of the organization must be woven together to create that fabric of meaning that gives shape and form to the Spirit of the place.

At this juncture, my previous comments about the color, sound, motion, and smell modes of communication available to the organization become particularly useful, for the intent is not just to say a new story, but also to give it a depth of reality in time and space that can occur only when the full spectrum of human communication is brought into play. The leader may start with a "story line," to use some words from the world of drama, but that is just the framework around which may be orchestrated all of the other elements. Well done, it should be possible to smell the story, move with the story, touch the story and so forth. Each part should contribute in its own way, and none should be allowed to dominate. But most of all, the new story must be fabricated with sufficient Open Space to allow all members of the organization to join in its creation with their own imaginations, so that the story truly becomes their story — or more accurately, "our" story. How all this might be done may become clearer when I tell the end of the Delta Corporation tale. But I would emphasize that there is no "one right way," or putting it slightly facetiously, this is not a matter of painting by the numbers. Telling a good four-dimensional story is a real art. Indeed, it may be the highest form of art.

CELEBRATION There is one last aspect to this orchestrated drama of transformation, and that is celebration. Somewhere in the folklore of American (perhaps Western) organizations it seems to have been written that work, by definition, cannot be fun. I would take serious issue with that idea under any circumstances, but especially when the subject is transformation. It is quite true that the process of transformation is difficult, and indeed may be tedious and painful, but it is also true that transformation brought to culmination is a moment of high triumph. Fun may be too light a word, and joy may be more appropriate, but frankly the two run together in my mind and experience, and either one will do. When an organization has successfully negotiated the Open Space, the moment is contagious and explosive. People tend to smile a lot, which leads to snickers, laughter, and downright roars. Something in the nature of corporate decorum and sense of propriety tends to put a damper on this, and while some limits are clearly in order, celebration is not only natural, but essential. The point is not just to have a good time, although that is important, but to definitively mark a turning point in the history of the organization. Later on, and down the road, when once again the environment turns, it will be more than incidental to have this point of reference locked securely in the corporate memory. Celebration after transformation is every bit a critical as griefwork before it really gets underway. There are no standard operating procedures here, although it would be well to salute the past, honor the heroes and welcome the future. How all that gets done is a matter of time, place, resources and imagination. If it feels good — do it.

DELTA CORPORATION REVISITED

When last we considered Delta Corporation, a strategy had been born which suggested a new configuration of Spirit appropriate to the emerging environment as well as the history and resources of the corporation. Let us suppose that the necessary visioning and griefwork have taken place, and it is now time to orchestrate the conditions within which the new Story may be told collectively. Before beginning, I would hasten to add that the forthcoming description will scarcely demonstrate all the possibilities or even most of them, but it should provide a reasonable example of how the whole business might be approached. Other examples will appear in the case studies to follow, but neither they nor Delta Corporation can possibly represent the last word in terms of the tools or approaches available.

Orchestrating the process of collective storytelling and creating liturgy will ordinarily take place over an extended period, but it must focus in some particular location and time. In the case of Delta Corporation, the commencement occurred in the context of an off-site retreat described as an "Organizational Self-Assessment." This form was chosen in part because it related to the task at hand, but mostly because it had been part of the regular strategic planning cycle instituted by the new management. Even though the objective was something new and different, "Collective Storytelling," the form related clearly to the past of the organization.

On the appointed day, 35 individuals from all levels and sectors of Delta Corporation assembled at a nearby conference center. The CEO was in charge, but her approach appeared somewhat strange to the participants. They had anticipated that she would open up the meeting with a series of "lay-ons," dictating the corporate results she desired, and requesting the group to assess past performance and present capacity with a view to establishing a sequenced approach to the achievement of her objectives.

In fact, the CEO behaved in a very different way. She opened with some stories of the early days describing the excitement and intensity of Old Harry and the Garage Gang (presently known as the Leper Colony). She even had one of the early models of Harry's machine out on a table. Most people had never seen one. It looked rather primitive, but during the coffee break, members of the Leper Colony surrounded the ancient artifact, and began swapping tales of the blind alleys, the late nights, and the breakthroughs. That dusty old machine became a magnet. Young shop floor folks went up and touched it, sort of snickering as they compared this prototype with the sleek creations they were manufacturing now. But even as they snickered, they stopped to listen as the Leper Colony recounted tales of accomplishment. It may have been just a "prototype," but that is where it all began.

As the coffee break was coming to a close, the CEO asked the participants to divide up into small groups, and to spend the next several hours sharing with each other what they individually hoped for Delta Corporation. She emphasized that anything was fair game, and that the groups should make sure that everybody's hopes and dreams were on the table, even if they appeared contradictory. The point here was to see how rich the new story could become, and not attempt to achieve closure early on.

While the small groups were out in their sessions, the seating arrangement in the main meeting room was rearranged. What had once been the standard lecture hall configuration was reshaped to become a circle, thereby creating an open space. In the center was the old "prototype," still covered with dust, sitting on a low table. It seemed rather silly and out of place, but it definitely created a presence. When the group reassembled, they found their seating arrangement somewhat discomforting, for instead of facing the CEO as the source of power, they faced each other. In addition, the old prototype formed the foreground from every point of view. Sort of seeing the present through the past.

The CEO didn't lead the meeting so much as orchestrate it. True, she called on the various groups for their reports, but beyond that, her most notable contribution was to link the emerging story of one group to those of the other groups. Usually this was done with an absolute minimum of words. She merely turned from the speaker and said something like, "Isn't that rather like what Reuben was talking about?" All the while she was looking at Reuben. With such permission, Reuben (or whoever) would take the lead. Things became fairly confusing at times with hopes and dreams flying all over the room, but somehow with a nod or a gesture, the CEO would quiet the tumult, and the story became richer and bigger.

The real show stopper occurred when Serendipity Sam got up to talk. True to his reputation, he didn't report with the rest of his group, but chimed in later with a cascade of ideas, dreams, visions, all clothed in a thick veil of technical jargon. But there was no escaping the excitement. Whatever he saw was clearly bigger and more powerful than anything they were into at the moment. It not only reached the state of the art, but defined it. You could see the Leper Colony prick up their ears. They hadn't heard such excitement and innovation since Old Harry left the corporation. To be sure, elements of the new management found Sam's performance not a little strange, for it simply didn't follow the rules of orderly development they had carefully created.

Regardless of the rules, the excitement was real. In short order the sour old Leper Colony jumped right into the middle of Sam's description, asking for technical details, and suggesting some of their own. At moments, it looked as if the whole meeting would dissolve, for the R&D folk were in a feeding frenzy, and the rest of the participants had a very hard time keeping up. but nobody could doubt the Spirit. . . it was just palpable.

Acting on her intuition, the CEO quietly stood up and went over to Sam, who by now was standing in the back of the room completely surrounded by the Leper Colony. The noise level was fierce, but the rest of the group was being left out. Taking Sam by the hand, the CEO led him to the center of the circle right next to the old prototype. There it was, the old and the new — the past, present and potential. She whispered into Sam's ear that he ought to take a deep breath, and start over in words of one syllable. He did so, and in ways less than elegant, the concept emerged. He guessed about applications, competitors, market share, and before long, even the old VP for finance was drawn in. No longer was he fixated on selling losses, but rather thinking out loud about how he was going to develop the capital to support the new project. The guys from the shop floor forgot about The Zebra, and began to spin a likely tale as to how they might transition the assembly lines in order to make Sam's new machine. Even the Golden Fleece crowd became excited, telling each other how they always knew that Serendipity Sam would pull it off. They conveniently forgot that Sam had been the recipient of a record number their awards, to say nothing of the fact that this new idea had emerged despite all of their rules.

Well, by 5:00 o'clock, the place was a mess, but the cocktail hour and dinner were transformed from the usual exercise in collective anesthesia into a real celebration. To be sure, nobody had made one of Sam's things yet, but the dream was there, and a new story was born.

WHAT HAPPENED?   The first thing is that the CEO trusted her sense of the flow of Spirit, while simultaneously using the developed strategy as a means of keeping score and suggesting the "next moves" in her effort to orchestrate the story. She understood that the main order of business was to create an appropriate environment in which the old story might be examined and renovated. The organizational assessment format was, at least in part, a "cover." It looked sufficiently "standard" so that even the most conservative might feel at home. At the same time, this format provided sufficient open space to permit innovation.

The CEO rightly started with the history or Depths of the organization and acknowledged what the original dream consisted of. It wasn't a heavy treatment, but sufficient to ground the group in a sense of where they had been.

The use of the "prototype" was brilliant, providing a physical point of grounding, appealing to the senses. You could touch it, play with it, and in the nonverbal vocabulary of the organization, the roots and depths were called forth in a way that words could never quite accomplish. In the same vein, the change of the seating pattern after the opening session from straight lecture hall to circle, evidenced a real appreciation for "Spirit space." The physical change alone would not have created the results intended, but it architected the right space for the drama that would eventually take place.

As for the drama itself, that was outstanding . . . improvisational theater at its best. With a basic script suggested by the strategy, the CEO orchestrated a series of movements that gave powerful expression to the quality and direction of Spirit she hoped to encourage. The move from straight line chairs to circle indicated the break and change in form that occurs in transformation. And the circle itself is the symbol for open space, which she worked with artistry. By leading Sam from the periphery to the center, and placing him in conjunction with the prototype and herself, she represented and instigated the process in the consciousness of the group. Over and above whatever words may have been spoken, the basic geometry of the occasion and the symbolic movement within that geometry, articulated the hoped for direction and shape of Spirit.

Allowing the group to engage in a little brain storming was a rather timid way to open up the process of story-building, but a stronger technology such as guided imagery would probably have been too much. So she gets "A" for sensitivity.

The role she played was also exemplary. By orchestrating rather than directing, she encouraged Spirit to express itself in suitable form rather than coercing its appearance and shape.

171

It is true that the CEO could have more carefully programed the appearance of her storytellers. For example, she could have scheduled formal presentations by Serendipity Sam, but had she done so, the effect would have appeared contrived. The fact that she "let it happen" radically increased the impact, but not without some risk. However, the risk was minimized by the strategic plan for the Spirit flow in her head, which suggested that there were several ways to bring Sam on center stage. The most powerful way was the one she tried, but there were backups. For example, given the linkages between Sam's story and the story of Old Harry she could have engineered a different sequence with the same final result, but without the same degree of finesse.

The actions of the CEO towards Sam were really good. She followed her intuition (tracked Spirit) by taking Sam's hand, and established the linkage between formal power (her own), and the emergent natural power (Sam's). Collectively they symbolized (ritualized) the new story. The actual movement of Sam into the center of the circle literally created a new story, which because it was not spoken, had a subtle power of communication that words alone simply could not approach.

Also worthy of note is what the CEO did not do. She carefully avoided any challenge, direct or implied, to the elements of mythos which did not fit with the strategy and objectives she held for the corporation, such as the story of the Golden Fleece, Zebra or Reuben. The strategy was to essentially "outflank" these stories with a new, positive, and powerful story which basically "sucked" the less desirable stories into its area of influence and overwhelmed them.

IMPACT OF THE OFF SITE

Once the meeting had been concluded, it is reasonable to ask what the real difference might be, both immediately and in the long run. The answer is ambiguous, for essentially nothing has changed, but everything is different. The organization exists basically as it did before, with the same structure, reporting mechanism, liabilities and assets. As the world would see Delta Corporation, and indeed as many employees would see it, nothing has changed. The difference lies in the reorientation of Spirit, and the fact that the CEO has managed, if only for a short time, to align that Spirit in a way appropriate to the opportunities of Delta Corporation as she has come to understand them. Instead of a number of disconnected centers of Spirit all feeding upon themselves (or loosely organized into two conflicting camps) and contributing little to the overall flow of the organization, there was, for a short moment at least, a new sense of continuity and purpose. That was different and will stand in the corporate memory as a standard, for better or worse. At best, the experience of continuity will allow the members to build on that experience in order to create, in structure and form, viable way of being there. At worst, the experience will stand as a hollow mockery and painful reminder of what might have been making the present way of being all that much more intolerable.

The passage through Open Space (transformation) does not guarantee a permanent change. But that does not mean the passage was not real, that the difference does not exist. All of which brings up an interesting question: How long does transformation take? On the one hand, it would appear that transformation is virtually instantaneous, for, Spirit may alter its direction and intensity with little, if any consideration of time. It changes with the rapidity of the passage of a mood, which after all is but an expression of Spirit.

The question is rather like the one about how long it takes to fall in love, and the answer may equally be a life time, or no time at all. A profound change in Spirit really occurs out of time, and indeed time is measured in terms of "before and after" the moment of change. That is the difference between kairos and chronos. In terms of understanding the occurrence of transformation, the essential timelessness of Spirit change is crucial, for there is a natural tendency to equate importance with "a long time." Something that happens very quickly, in an instant as it were, can't be very important. All of that is to confuse what went before, and what came after the "moment"[68] of transformation. There is a difference, but whether or not the potential resident in that difference can be actualized and maintained over time will depend on a number of actions yet to be taken.

MAKING IT REAL, MAKING IT LAST — THE CREATION OF LITURGY

The process begun must be continued and nurtured, for a story once told will quickly be eroded unless it is retold and embedded in the organizational consciousness in a variety of ways. It must become real and an ongoing part of life, which is to say, it must become Liturgy, or what the people do.

Basic to the creation of Liturgy is a strategic view of the organization as this may have been developed in the process of research and modified (shaped) during the Off Site.

---

[68] The word "moment" is a special one, and as used here comes from the work of Soren Kierkegaard see "Philosophical Fragments". op cit.

It will be noted that this strategic view is very close to what I previously described as the potential "endstate" when we were talking about the strategy of facilitation. There is, however a significant addition — the Off Site itself, which has now been introduced to the collective self-understanding of the organization at least in a limited way. The net effect of the new configuration of Spirit represented by this graphic is to create the conditions under which it is at least possible that the CEO might realize her goal of an innovative organization in which "engineers may fly." The Off Site provided an initial experience of just such a phenomenon, but making this more than an epi-phenomenon will require moving the whole business into the continuing mainstream of organizational life, which is the function of Liturgy.

In Liturgy, time and space in general are claimed and made specific to a particular organization. Less abstractly, Delta Corporation must now realize the benefits of the Off Site in the "here and now."

LITURGY AND SPACE

Space is not just physical space (the distance between here and there), but also what I might call Spirit Space, as defined by the structure of an organization. Organizational structure dictates within general limits how business gets done and by whom. Organizations that structure themselves in hierarchical stovepipes understand that the business is run from the top down, with the chief taking all authority and the rest exercising their responsibilities as well as they are able. In such Spirit Space, work can get done, but the limitations set upon aberrance (read innovation) are extreme. There is no question, though, that the shape and flow of Spirit is controlled over time, and what the people do is described (circumscribed) by the space they are allotted.

For Delta Corporation, the stovepipe hierarchy will not be conducive to the flow of Spirit as they have come to experience it. A more appropriate structure is suggested by the shape and flow of the Off Site meeting itself — the circle. Although the details may be a little vague (good liturgy is not invented overnight, and indeed it evolves with use),[69] the central idea would be to place all significant organizational elements around the circumference of the circle with the leadership function located at the center.

Understood as a circle, Delta Corporation, in all of its several components may enjoy a high level of interaction made possible by the basic geometry, for there are no "corners to go around," nor are there any bottlenecks. Each division will experience direct "line of sight" communication, so that there may be easy passage between Production, R&D and Finance. As an environment for innovation, this understanding of Spirit Space is very important, for it means that ideas originated in any place may quickly be passed to all others, allowing for a rich mix of ideas, resources and personalities, with few if any restrictions in terms of organizational boundaries.

---

[69] The idea of the circular organization has been advanced by Russell Ackoff. What I have to say here owes something to his thinking, but the similarity is more in terms of name than details.

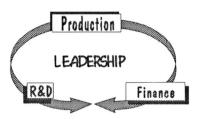

There is, however, a basic difficulty with the circular configuration, given by the fact that some aspects of Delta's operation require a much more linear approach; because Delta also produces a product, which necessitates a sequential flow with boundaries. Indeed, the old structure of Delta was very conducive to production, once a product had been developed. The problem lay in the fact that all of Delta was configured for production, which took a heavy toll on innovation.

What appears as a potential conflict and contradiction is actually an opportunity for leadership to exercise some newfound skills in managing Spirit. By understanding that form follows Spirit, it becomes clear that there is "no one right way" but rather "appropriate ways." Thus for production, where linear sequencing is very important, it is appropriate to structure that way, whereas innovation, requiring much greater openness, might be given just that. Perhaps even more important is the realization that not only is there no right way — but over time (and even very short space of time) there will be many "right ways" which may rapidly come and go.

The possibility for managing this potentially confusing situation is given when leadership is exercised at the level of Spirit. From this vantage point, structure is understood to be an important, but only temporary expression of Spirit. The fact that given structures may change, perhaps so fast that they can hardly be perceived as discrete entities, will come as no surprise, but rather will be the anticipated experience. What used to be understood as abnormal, aberrant and disastrous (the breakdown of structure) is now understood to be the natural order of the day.

Leadership itself becomes a rather different thing than it had been, which is why leadership is placed at the center of the circle, and called leadership as opposed to the leader. To the extent that the story told is collective, leadership must be shared, which means it is a function to be participated in by a number of individuals whose role is to monitor and shape the culture of the corporation in order to focus the Spirit on the tasks at hand. Given the complexity of the culture and the challenges confronted, no one person can possibly have the resources to do it all, all the time.

Does this mean that the CEO is now out of a job? Not at all, but the job has certainly transformed. No longer is it the CEO's primary function to direct the operation of the corporation, but rather to take responsibility for the orchestration of the new Story in all of its forms (tuning the field), and to insure that this story is embedded in the life of the organization as an effective Liturgy. What may appear as a loss or diminution of power is in fact the reverse; instead of operating at the superficial level of "orders" and "memos," the CEO has understanding of, and access to the most primal elements of human life. The responsibility is immense, and her values are crucial. Should she choose to use this power for the narrow control of those within the world of the Corporation, she may, for a period, dominate and constrict the Spirit. That would be self-defeating and result in the ultimate destruction of Delta Corporation. The alternative is to use this same understanding and power to strengthen and liberate the Spirit. The choice will be hers.

PHYSICAL SPACE Bringing the New Story of Delta Corporation into the here and now is not just a question of organizational structure (defining Spirit space) but, equally, of claiming the physical space of the corporation and making it expressive of, and responsive to the Spirit of the corporation. This may be as simple as choosing the corporate colors so that the paint on the walls creates an ambience in which the Spirit may grow, or as complex as aligning the assembly line so that it not only moves product from start to finish, but also creates an environment in which those who work there perceive meaning. Attention must be paid to the sounds, smells, color and shape of the place so that space becomes uniquely Delta's, conforming to and confirming the story they tell and the Spirit they are.

TIME Just as space must be claimed and shaped to support the Spirit of Delta Corporation, so also time. While the calendar and clocks may roll in conformity with everybody else in the world, there must also be a special time for the corporation. Accounting firms have "tax time" and agricultural firms have "harvest time," and Delta must have "Delta time."

Initiation The special time of an organization begins with initiation, some constellation of events which marks the beginning of an employee's or member's presence in the time (and space) of the organization. Such initiation may begin with the health forms, contracts, telephone numbers, and job descriptions, typical for the commencement of employment. All of these things are important in themselves, and constitute a first step in defining the dimensions of the Spirit of the organization of the newcomer. The initial elements of employment, however, may become infinitely more powerful to the extent that they are consciously woven together to form a fabric of meaning which places the new member in Delta time. The basic intention is to bring folks "up to speed." Not just any "speed" mind you, but the peculiar or special speed of the organization, which means passing through time in congruence with the unique rhythms or cadences of this organization.

Creating such a process of initiation is no idle task, for it essentially establishes the pattern of Spirit which may then continue throughout life in the organization. Done well, it will establish a "liturgical sense" (an awareness of what the people do), which creates a solid basis for future action. Done poorly or not at all, the new member is set adrift with little if any guidance as to "how things are done around here".

Central to the whole process is the hearing and becoming part of the Story, which uniquely communicates how we function in time, or what time means to us. After all, it is the story or mythos which contains the past, present and potential (future) of the organization. It will be important not only for the major storytellers to tell the tale, and for the artifacts of the organization to be seen and touched, but there must be some "rite of passage" so to speak, through which the newcomer is enabled to relive the story and thereby experience directly the unique sense of time for that organization.

This "rite of passage" may actually be built right into the ongoing work schedule (on the job training as it were), but there should be a definite ending point, at which time clear recognition is given to the individual as a bona fide member of the community. Organizations usually have "probationary periods" during which skills and attitudes are tested out. Such periods may have infinitely more impact and effect if, in addition to determining typing speed or decision making skills, mythos is represented emphatically, and at the end there is a formal ceremony of acceptance with appropriate awards and symbols. For the Delta Corporation, this might be a lapel pin of the old prototype or even, if carefully done, a Golden Fleece, now given in recognition of quality and contribution. Parenthetically, transvaluing previously negative symbols into positive ones can be a very powerful technique, serving to remind the organization and its members of the transformation it has gone through, and the way in which the Spirit has been reformed to pursue new directions.

Celebration The claiming of time — unique, special Delta time, begins with the liturgy of initiation, but unless that claim is extended and constantly strengthened, time will loose the special qualities which distinguishes the organization. Extending the claim on time may be accomplished in part through a series of special celebrations.

Celebration, as we have noted, is not a normal part of organizational life, which represents a distinct loss. But when it comes to stamping "Delta" on time in general, celebrations have a powerful contribution to make. The celebrations must not be trivial, but they should be fun (however fun may be defined in the organizational culture), and most important they should represent the primal elements of mythos which give shape to the Spirit of the organization. For Delta Corporation, this might require a Founder's Day in memory of Old Harry, for even though he is no longer part of the organization physically, the continuation of his Spirit of innovation is essential. Other possibilities would include, Serendipity Week, a weeklong recognition of innovative contributions made to the organization, or Making the Quota Awards, given periodically to those who do just that. One might even think of a revival of The Zebra, a monster party for those who have contributed well on the shop floor.

Isolated celebrations may be useful, but they become more effective to the extent that they are programed and linked together over the course or a year, which then provides a liturgical expression of the Spirit of the organization throughout the basic time period, and an opportunity for the renewal of that Spirit on an ongoing basis. The year becomes not just "some year" or any old year — but uniquely and specially the organization's year. Such a year might begin with the ceremony of acceptance for new hires, thereby clearly bringing them in at the "start of things," but also providing all other members of the organization an opportunity to reconsider their own membership and what it means. At appropriate points, other celebrations might be added, not just on a random basis but in such a way as to retell the story of the organization. The model for this is the liturgical year of the church and synagogue which takes the believers through a reexperiencing of their mythos on an annual basis.

An even more powerful way of claiming the year occurs when the various celebrations are not only linked by some general logic, but actually embedded into an ongoing, recognized and necessary process for the organization as a whole. The process chosen will vary with the organization. In the automobile industry, it might be the "model year," or that process by which the new models are designed, and brought into production. This is liturgy at its best — truly an expression of what the people do.

The annual planning/budget cycle for the organization is a most likely candidate. Viewed from the perspective of mythos, the planning cycle is the quintes-sential telling of the tale, or at least it should be. On a practical level, numbers are crunched, budgets are prepared, and resources allocated, all of which are very impor-tant to the life of an organization. Real planning is telling the story of where you have been and where you hope to go. Numbers are just the form.

If planning is storytelling, which occurs over the course of the fiscal year, what better mechanism exists through which that year may be claimed and made the special time for the organization? Planning therefore may provide the appropriate context or setting for celebration of those moments of meaning (kairos) when the Spirit of the organization achieved some decisive new shape or direction. For Delta Corporation, one such moment occurred at the Off Site, which could easily and logically become an annual event, to recognize a moment of passage and simulta-neously to perform a very practical function as the beginning or end of the planning cycle. As such, it offers the opportunity not only to discuss budget, products and personnel, but also the chance to re-member (put back together again) that marvelous moment when Serendipity Sam cut loose, the Leper Colony went into a "feeding frenzy," and even the old VP for Finance got excited. Rather than a dry meeting buried in the trivia of organizational life, it could become a high moment of celebra-tion commemorating the time when Open Space had been crossed.

Chapter IX

THE INTERNAL REVENUE SERVICE
APPEALS DIVISION

The following case studies come from my client experience. I chose them as reasonable examples of working with Spirit. In as much as a number of years have passed since this work was done and it has not been possible to follow up on what has happened since, I can make no claim as to present state. However, at the time of writing, I asked the principals involved to read the documents, and they indicated that my representation was in accord with their recollection.

The Appeals Division is part of the Internal Revenue Service, the great and powerful IRS. Although Appeals is perhaps the smallest of major IRS units, its function is unique and critical both to the health of the parent organization and to the integrity of the American tax system. It is the purpose of Appeals to provide fair and impartial review and settlement of contested tax cases without subjecting either party (the taxpayer or the government) to the hazard and expense of formal litigation. In recent years, the division had been subject to major changes due to the radically altered world in which the IRS exists. The present issue was the transformation of what once was a small, elite group of technicians into an efficient, quality-conscious, and much larger organization.

My work with Appeals is complete, but sufficient time has not elapsed in order to speak of anything approaching long term results (or the lack of same), Nevertheless, the case will demonstrate the development of an intervention and the thought underlying that process.

HISTORY

In its present form, Appeals is a relatively modern creation, but the appeals function goes back to the 1920s as an offshoot of the tax court. By 1939, this function had been split off and located with what became known as the Technical Staff. The Technical Staff was a very small, select group of IRS personnel who were called upon to render technical opinions regarding the interpretation and application of the laws and regulations. This put them directly in the "gray area" between where the words of law stopped and complex situations arose. In those days the case load was quite small, presumably due to the relative simplicity of the law and the temper of the American taxpayer, who seemed largely agreeable to abide by the rules as they were stated. Following World War II, the tempo of the times changed radically as America moved out of the wartime period into the enormous economic and social development of the late '40s and early '50s. Under these conditions, it was no longer possible for the Technical Staff to handle the business, and so in 1951 it was expanded and given a new name, the Appellate Division. The staff members were known as Appellate Conferees.

By present-day standards, the Appellate Division was still quite small, having no more than 200 members. It was based in Washington, and for a time, all those who would appeal a case had to journey to the capital city, although eventually a circuit-riding procedure was instituted which took the Appellate Conferees out into the hinterland.

The most significant fact about the Appellate Division was that it was indisputably the elite corps of the IRS. The Appellate Conferees were chosen because of their experience and knowledge, and it was commonly recognized that one could not even be considered for "membership" before at least 15 years of service in the IRS. The use of the word "membership" may appear strange, but in fact the Appellate Division was a closely held club in which only the elite were to be found. Positively, the Appellate Division represented an enormous resource to the IRS, and to the American taxpayer. The collective wisdom and experience of the Appellate Conferees was truly impressive. A recent Deputy Chief Counsel said that when he joined the Service as a young lawyer fresh out of school, he held the conferees in awe, for "they were the teachers." The basis of their respect came not only from the years of experience, but also from the fact that their daily fare was the truly difficult cases, filled with ambiguity. By definition, few cases came to Appeals unless nobody knew the answer, due to unclear, conflicting, or nonexistent laws or regulations.

To insure that only such difficult cases arrived on the doorstep of Appeals, there was a two-step review procedure, which was designed to separate out the malcontents and misunderstandings, which the Appellate Conferees called the simpler, or sometimes the "garbage cases." If it got to the Appellate Division, it was heavy business indeed, and would be considered with the utmost care, with virtually no thought given to the time or resources expended. Thus the taxpayer was assured that once in Appeals, they were going to deal with extraordinarily competent and experienced personnel who would brook no interference until the case had been heard and settled to the conferees' satisfaction. The review would be fair, impartial and independent, for the Appellate conferees answered to nobody but their colleagues and their own conscience. If it was felt that a prior decision was without merit, it was reversed. Once a decision had been made, it was then justified with elaborate supporting statements, which appeared more as an academic treatise than bureaucratic statement.

The independence and authority of the Appellate Conferees was imposing and generally well deserved, given the quality of those who exercised it, but there were also liabilities. Not the least of which was a genuine distancing and separation from the rest of the Service. The Appellate Conferees were virtually a law unto themselves. This meant that few, except for the initiated, had any clear idea of what the Conferees actually did. That in itself would have been no particular problem, except that more often than not, a decision from the Appellate Division meant the reversal of a prior decision, and that could only mean somebody else was wrong and therefore potentially subject to censure.

To fully understand this situation, it is useful to know where the Appeals function sits in the IRS world. Essentially, there are four major elements organized as a chain. At the front end are the Service Centers, which receive the tax returns as they come in and enter them into the system. Next comes Examination, and the function here is to audit the returns with the expectation of raising the actual tax. Exam, as it is called, is the bane of many taxpayers, for when the phone rings, or the letter arrives bearing the message that the IRS wants to talk, that is Exam. Given the purpose of Examination, it is not surprising that the revenue agents who work there find their greatest professional rewards from "setting up the tax" — that is discovering the mistakes (or worse) of a taxpayer and going for an "adjustment" (read "more tax"). More often than not, the process will end here, for either the taxpayer will agree and pay up, or possibly convince the examining agent that the tax paid was justified. However, if agreement does not take place, the taxpayer has the right to go on to Appeals. The last step, is litigation in the tax court.

It may occur that Appeals will agree with Exam, but in more cases than not, there will be some difference. The basis of this difference may reside in the fact that Appeals was "right" and Exam was "wrong," but it is equally possible that it will occur because of a difference in intent and point of view of the two components. Whereas Exam is intent upon getting the greatest tax dollar, it is the purpose of Appeals to conduct a fair and impartial review with an eye to a settlement, which takes into account the "hazards of litigation." In other words, the Appellate Conferee must not only reconsider all the facts and figures in the light of the appropriate statutes, but also make a judgment as to what would happen if the case were taken to court. Supposing that it seemed there were a 50-50 possibility of winning, it is not unlikely that the settlement offer would be in the 50-50 range. It is important to note that this settlement is a negotiated settlement, which means in effect that both parties must give a little bit, and that the final position cannot, by definition, be fully support- ed by any extant law or regulation, usually because such law or regulation does not exist.

Seen from the point of view of Exam, settlements reached in Appeals not only reverse all their hard work, but also (and this is perhaps the truly maddening part) seem to do so in disregard to the "rule book." In short, there is a built in structural conflict between Exam and Appeals which is essential for the effective function of the total system, but the basis of misunderstanding and, occasionally, animosity between the elements. Thus in Exam, Appeals is jokingly referred to as the "gift shop" or "Santa Claus," for they give it all away. Sometimes that joke is pretty thin.

In a word, the Appellate Division was not only separate, aloof and elite, but it also appeared to operate "outside of the rules." Such an aberrant phenomenon does not rest easy in any large bureaucracy, and it is predictable that sooner or later the system will attempt to bring the "rogue organization" into line. For 20 years (1951 through the early '70s) the Appellate Division maintained its useful but uneasy position, however, as the '70s moved along, some major new forces appeared in the environment and the situation changed quite radically.

These new forces were essentially four. First of all, the tax law itself had grown increasingly complex, which meant, if nothing else, there were infinitely more opportunities for misunderstanding and disagreement. Secondly, the tax rate had consistently gone up so that J. Q. Public, individually or corporately, found their dues to Uncle Sam consuming a major portion of their income. Thirdly, the inclination to protest became almost a reflex action. Whether this last factor arose from the protests of the '60s and '70s or from the enormous increase of available lawyers seeking work is probably unanswerable, but the net effect was quite clear. Folks just weren't going to sit still if they even suspected that their rights had been violated. Last, there were just more people filing more returns. If you add in some amount of fraud and abuse, you have a situation by the end of the '70s, for which the tax system was never designed, and which yielded a crisis of increasing proportions.

The system response was fairly predictable and quite inadequate, people kept doing what they had always done. Exam continued to "set up the tax," and the Appellate conferees considered the cases that came before them with the same care and judicious pace they had always used. The effect was an enormous backlog. Cases piled up on the doorstep of Appeals until there was scarcely room to work, and when the taxpayers became frustrated with the slow pace, they headed for the tax court, which quickly became overloaded. The system had reached "tilt", and decisive action was required.

Over a relatively short period of time at the end of the 1970s, several things occurred which dramatically changed the nature and composition of Appeals. The so-called two levels of appeal were consolidated into one, and no longer were the Appellate Conferees insulated from the relatively less complex cases. Furthermore, those individuals who had handled the simpler cases under the old system were physically moved into the appeals structure, and they, along with the older Appellate Conferees were now called Appeals Officers. Outside of dramatically increasing the size of Appeals, which had grown slowly from the original select 200, this consolidation introduced a whole new body of individuals who possessed far less experience and stature. The old elite club was ended, and almost anybody could be an Appeals Officer.

Next, Appeals was shifted from a relatively autonomous position within the IRS structure to become a division of Counsel, the litigating arm of the Service. The fact that this move might have the effect of diminishing the public perception of independent review by making it seem that Appeals had now become the equivalent of a pretrial hearing was apparently outweighed by a gain in administrative effectiveness. The move, however, had deeper symbolic implications, for it essentially reversed the previous status order. Whereas the Appellate Conferees had once been the "teachers" of the lawyers, particularly the newer ones, they were now placed in a diminished position. As one senior member of Counsel put it, "We used to be in their bag, now they are in our bag."

Then the managers arrived. In an effort to bring order out of the impending chaos, it was determined that the whole operation had to be brought under much tighter management reign. Historically, management had never been a major concern of the Appellate Conferees who operated in their domain rather like an academic department. While it is true that a senior member had the responsibility for assigning the work, and reviewing the disposition of cases as represented by the impressive supporting statements which justified the proposed settlements, little concern was given to how fast the cases were moved or how many were brought to settlement in any given period. The primary emphasis rested upon the quality of the work regardless of how long it may have taken. In short, "modern management" as a special skill was marginally present and little regarded.

Given the enormous backlog, to say nothing of the radical increase in the size of Appeals with the arrival of those individuals who had previously conducted the first level of review, managers, almost any kind of managers, were critical. Since that skill was not to be found among the old Appellate Conferees, it had to come from elsewhere, and in fact the new managers for the Appeals Division were recruited from all over the Service, and especially from Exam.

By definition, these new managers had not been part of the old club, and therefore had little idea of precisely what it was that Appeals did. Indeed, one might suspect that they carried with them some of their previous dubious opinions of Appeals as the "gift shop" run by Santa Claus. However, the new managers did understand moving cases, and in relatively short order, instituted a number of procedures to control inventory (the number of cases "in house"), increase the agreement rate and lower the time spent on individual cases. But not without considerable cost and friction.

From the point of view of the older Appeals Officers, it seemed that the barbarians had arrived. Indeed, their whole world had been turned upside down. Whereas they had once been the undisputed elite corps, they now found themselves close to the bottom of the totem pole, resident in a foreign land (Counsel) and under the supervision of individuals who lacked (as the conferees saw it) even a marginal understanding of what the whole process was about, and perhaps more important, what quality meant. Perhaps most galling was the fact that the managers, who now occupied the senior positions in the several offices, held the authority and responsibility for reviewing and approving all settlements. While this clearly made sense as an administrative procedure, it meant that individuals who had never settled a case in their lives were now passing judgment on the work of those who had made a professional career of doing just that.

The situation from the managers' point of view was doubtless no less confusing and perplexing. Their mission, as they understood it, was to "move cases," and the means available included time accounting and other statistical controls, in addition to new, more efficient office procedures and technology. Although these approaches seemed quite rational and essential, they were greeted by many of the older Appeals Officers with something less than enthusiasm. As seen by the managers, the major problem was not so much the work as the workers, at least some of them, who became known as "The Curmudgeons."

One incident, which might be called the "Dictaphone Wars" gives some of the flavor. In one region, the managers had determined that in order to increase efficiency, the use of Dictaphones would be a great advantage. The Dictaphones were ordered and placed with the Appeals Officers, who were told that from hence forward that dictating and not longhand was the expected procedure. Compliance was slow but visible, except in the case of the old curmudgeons.

In one instance, a very senior, and very competent Appeals Officer positively refused to go along. He agreed to have the Dictaphone in his office, but insisted that it be kept in the farthest corner. As for using it, that was out of the question. Finally, management decreed that no supporting statements would be typed unless they were dictated, but still no movement. In the last stages the Appeals Officer apparently gave in, but as it turned out, he was writing his statements out longhand, and then dictating them into the machine.

It is an extraordinary tribute to the professionalism, dedication and competence of the managers and the Appeals Officers that the whole thing did not just blow up. In fact, over the next several years following the reorganization, measurable progress has been made in terms of controlling inventory and speeding the process. But not without some real losses. The old Appellate Division, for all its faults, was a remarkable institution, which in its time contributed greatly to the integrity of the tax system. But it must also be recognized that the world for which the Appellate Division was made no longer exists. The Appeals Division stood at the Open Space — there was no going back, only forward towards a new way of being.

INTERVENTION AND THE FUTURE

My association with the Appeals Division began in 1983 when the director, Howard Martin, asked me to address his national managers meeting on the subject of Organization Culture in Transformation. Apparently my thoughts struck a responsive

Organization Culture in Transformation. Apparently my thoughts struck a responsive chord because after some additional conversation, we entered into an agreement to ". . . develop an innovative approach to improve individual and organizational performance in times of extensive change, utilizing the concept of organizational transformation with particular emphasis to be placed on Appeals' organizational culture."

That piece of language actually appears in the formal US Government Request for a proposal. I quote it in part to indicate where we were to start, but also to demonstrate that, public perception to the contrary, there are some federal administrators who are willing and able to take risks in order to improve the effectiveness of their organizations. The fact that this is a formal public document emanating from the Internal Revenue Service is perhaps even more remarkable.

The situation in Appeals, as I began my work, represented a marked improvement from what I came to understand to be the immediately prior history described above. In the first place, it had been rapidly expanded to handle the increased workload, and now possessed some 2400 employees operating coast to coast. But more important, some of the trauma associated with the changeover from the Appellate Division to Appeals Division had begun to fade if only with the passage of time. Some of the older Appellate Conferees had retired, but not nearly as many as one might have anticipated. Those who remained seemed to be making a reasonable adjustment to the new conditions. At the same time, the new managers had become increasingly knowledgeable about the appeals function and what it was they were supposed to manage.

Nevertheless, there were still some rough edges, to say the least, and Howard Martin felt that the organization had by no means reached its full potential. Part of the problem was that the workload, at least in some parts of the country, was absolutely fierce, occasioned in large measure by the appearance of the tax shelter cases. At one point, there were in excess of 400,000 disputed cases waiting in Examination. Without going into the technicalities, it may be said that number, added to the "normal" workload, would simply bury Appeals. Or worse, if Appeals were bypassed, and all those cases were to head for the tax court, the system would close down. But workload aside, it appeared to the director that the available resources of human spirit and energy were not being utilized most efficiently. In a word, there was turmoil in the system which resulted in a net energy loss.

My task was threefold. First, to take a look at the organizational culture as represented by the operative mythos, in order to provide the Director with a strategic to serve in a consultative capacity during implementation. The methodology employed was essentially that described in the preceding chapter. All told, I conducted 122 interviews in all seven regions, all major offices and a selected number of smaller offices. The interviews spanned the organization from senior personnel down the latest hires and lowest levels. I also interviewed a smaller number of individuals from the world surrounding the Appeals Division, including senior IRS officials and "practitioners" (CPAs and lawyers who ordinarily do business with Appeals).

Before going further, I wish to make clear that although some of the material which I will describe may appear negative and problematical, I discovered Appeals to be an incredible organization, with the vast majority of those I came in contact with taking genuine pride in the work that they do, and feeling it essential that not only must the work get done, but be done well. To be sure, certain criticisms were offered on all sides, but almost without exception, those criticisms were presented in a positive fashion. All of which meant to me that despite the trauma of the past and the difficulties of the present, the basic spirit of Appeals is impressively strong.

THE SPIRIT OF APPEALS

Russell Ackoff has said, "To understand a system, you must first see it in the context of the next larger system." I have found this to be very good advice, and so the first cut effort is to see Appeals within the world it inhabits, as imaged by the stories told about it. Viewed in this light, Appeals' world is hardly appealing. Graphically, this world might be represented by a series of layers as follows.

BAD BUREAUCRAT
INFERNAL REVENUE SERVICE
SANTA CLAUS
APPEALS

The first layer is the world of the general public, which for the past several years has seemingly come to believe that many or perhaps most of the problems of their existence may be traced to the heavy hand of government and more specifically to the "swollen bureaucracy." The fact that two successive administrations (Carter and Reagan) have run on a platform which excoriated the bureaucracy, has served to underline, and perhaps enhance the perception that lift any rock, and there you will find the "Bad Bureaucrat." This is not to suggest that federal service, like any other large organization, is without fault, but the issue is not the truth of the situation, but rather the perception, which creates its own kind of truth.

Within the federal service, there can be little question that the least favored element is the Internal Revenue Service. I can't support this with a large number survey, but then again, I am not sure that I need to. The reasons why the IRS ends up in this position are not hard to fathom. Nobody likes to pay taxes, and everybody has to. So if you are negatively disposed toward the federal service, the most obvious target confronts all citizens every April 15. Not surprisingly the IRS comes to stand for the "Infernal Revenue Service."

Within the IRS (the next layer down), the story about Appeals is "Santa Claus" (discussed earlier). Told as a joke, or with real seriousness, the idea is that Appeals is giving away the store.

This picture may be somewhat of an overstatement, but I do not believe it is far from the truth. To the extent that Appeals has a legitimate and essential task to perform, it should be clear that regardless of any problems internal to the organization, the surrounding environment represents a significant difficulty.

THE STORY OF APPEALS — FIRST TAKE

Following an initial series of interviews (with the 12 "important" people chosen by the director), I presented the story as I had come to understand it to a small focus group consisting of the director and his immediate staff. The purpose of the presentation was to get a preliminary reaction and also to check out the rudiments of an overall strategy that was beginning to emerge in my mind. All of this had to be done prior to going out to the field, because as I indicated previously, once in the field, the intervention is already started, and it is essential that all key players (in this case the director and his staff) clearly understand what is going on.

The primal story of Appeals is "Black Hats and Blue Ribbons." It seems that in the early days, the Appeals Officers (then known as the Appellate Conferees) considered themselves so separate that they would not have their work typed with the usual black ribbon, but rather chose blue so that nobody could possibly mistake their work for the work of another. In addition, they tended to dress alike in dark suits, and when they went out for lunch, they went together. The senior man would lead the way, with the others following along in rank order. On the head of each was to be found a black hat. The restaurant of choice was the same each day, and no mere mortal in the service would be expected to join them.

The second story I called "Trauma Days." Basically, it related all the pain and confusion which occurred with the end of two levels of appeal, the shift over to Counsel, and the arrival of the "managers." But in the way of organizations, these details tended to drop out, and the whole constellation of events was simply referred to as "those days." If pushed, the officers would give the details, but it was quite clear, particularly when talking to older Appeals Officers, that the memory was so unpleasant that they would prefer not to be reminded. Contained in the "Trauma Days" stories was a sense of fateful wistfulness. The element of fate appeared because all would acknowledge that the ways of the old Appellate conferees were no longer adequate for the needs of the IRS as it faced a quite different world. It was inevitable that things were going to change. But the acknowledgement of the necessity for change was made with wistfulness, for the old days, for all of their irrelevance, spoke of rigor and quality which now seemed to have become lost in the rush to move cases.

The next story I called the "Battle of Aces." ACES, is an acronym for Appellate Conferee Executive Study. This study was initiated in the early '70's by the then Director Klotz. It represented a self-study by the Appellate Conferees through which they were supposed to carefully consider their changed environment and develop ways to work more efficiently, while still maintaining the quality they held so essential. In retrospect, the recommendations generated appear quite legitimate and normal. For example, the report recommended that Appeals Officers be treated as professionals, and be given both the freedom and responsibility of that status. However, when the report was finally finished, and sent "up" to the level of the commissioner, it was rejected.

The rejection of ACES occurred for a variety of reasons, not the least of which was that just as the study was concluding, the Employees Union (NAIRE) was forming and actively recruiting. It seems that the union adopted many of the ACES's recommendations as part of their negotiating position, with the net effect that what began as a cooperative study became an adversarial position. In any event, ACES was killed. Regardless of the actual reason for its demise, that demise was perceived by managers and Appellate Conferees alike as the end of the old way of doing business, and the appearance of the new order. Things were going to go a different way — and that way was the "way of management."

Even though the ACES report had been dispensed with over 10 years ago, it continued to represent a perceived threat on the part senior management to the point that when this present intervention was begun, one senior official commented, "Oh, we are not going to do ACES all over again!" The power of that emotion was frankly surprising to me particularly on the part of the managers, for they, after all had apparently won the battle. My sense is that in addition to whatever logical justification there may have been for the move from the "old way of doing business" to the new "management oriented approach," the overplus of emotion (as I saw it) derived from the fact that Appeals as it had existed, represented an aberrant phenomenon in the life of the IRS. The joke was no joke: Appeals was separate, aloof, elite, the Santa Claus, and didn't play by the rules. When the opportunity came to bring this element in line, it was done with a vengeance.

In any event, it seemed the battle of ACES continued to be fought even though the war had long since ended. On the one hand, there were the Appeals Officers, who sincerely believed that they had a special mission to carry out and possessed special qualifications to perform that task. On the other hand, there were the managers, who were apparently less concerned with quality and professional competence than with agreement rates, the statistics of cases moved. Of course in individual cases, particular managers or individual Appeals Officers could "see the other side," but that was the story, the myth, and it seemed to shape much of the present conscious of the organization.

In fact, the Battle of ACES was not a single myth, but two myths in conflict, and as such represented a prime case of what I have called mythic dissonance. On one side there were the old Appellate Conferees, the subject and authors of ACES, representing, as they saw it, the high standards of quality, rigor and excellence, all of which were perceived to be threatened by a blind thrust towards quantity. On the other side of what appeared as a real donnybrook, were the managers who understood themselves as the saviors of Appeals, riding in at the moment of destruction to preserve the appeals function from the arcane and antiquated practices of the old "curmudgeons." The sad truth of the matter is that both were right, both were wrong, and neither could function without the other. In addition, a great deal of energy was being dissipated in the conflict that might better have been utilized in the processing of appeals.

The last story is "Circle the Wagons." According to this story, Appeals is caught between the forces of Counsel and Exam, with Counsel seeking to integrate Appeals into their structure and process, while Exam excoriates Appeals for giving away cases (Santa Claus) and not moving them fast enough.

If all of these stories are understood as the elements of the Mythos of Appeals, constituting the culture and determining the shape and function of Spirit, it is not surprising that life was perceived as somewhat less than smooth.

When I first laid out the stories as I found them, I was rather surprised that Appeals functioned as well as it did. Indeed, the fact that Appeals functioned at all I attributed to a basic, continuing, but weakening belief that the appeals function was essential, that the Appeals Officers were still the elite, and therefore, regardless of the immediate difficulties, the job was going to get done. In a word, the story of "Black Hats and Blue Ribbons," for all of the hard knocks received, was still present, and in many ways dominant.

When it came to developing a strategy (albeit preliminary), it seemed to me that the critical move must be to release the Spirit represented by "Black Hats," and allow it to appear in new form. There was no question that the old ways were no longer appropriate, but it was absolutely clear that, for the Appeals function to be effectively carried out, the sense of excellence and eliteness must be present in more effective form. If the objective was an effective, high-performing Appeals, the place to start was with old "Black Hat and Blue Ribbon" story, and use that as the centerpiece. To the extent that story could be aligned with, and supported by, the managers' story, a positive outcome might be expected. This would mean unlocking the managers' story from its presently unproductive and conflicted relationship with the "Heros of Aces," and reversing the present relationship in which it appeared that the managers were dominating the Appeals Officers, to a new situation where the Appeals Officers were "out front," with the managers creating the appropriate supporting environment. The key lay in building the story of the Appeals Officer as a responsible, competent professional without attacking or diminishing the story of the managers.

In presenting this material to the focus group, I made it very clear that the strategy suggested was only preliminary, and would require a great deal more investigation before being acted upon. At the same time, however, it was important for all to understand roughly what my thoughts were if only because in the next phase of the intervention, as I moved out through the organization, my presence alone, and the way that I shaped my questions would inevitably affect the outcome. At the time of presentation, it appeared that general agreement existed both in terms of the validity of the story as told and the essential outlines of the proposed strategy.

Given this agreement, I began the next phase which involved visiting all seven regions, most major offices, and a number of the smaller units. Over the course of a four month period, I had the opportunity to interview a representative sample of all

Appeals personnel from senior managers and Appeals Officers down to the lowest levels of secretarial and support staff. In addition to asking my standard two questions, (What is this place, and what should it be?) in order to gain further insights to the operative mythos by way of expanding and/or validating my previous findings, I also had the opportunity to test out the logic and feasibility of the proposed strategy. This was done by "playing back" to the interviewee, towards the end of the interview, the Story as I was coming to understand it. On one level I was concerned to see the reaction to what I had to say, but at the same time, I was aware that just by virtue of retelling this story in a significant number of times and places, it begins to assume a reality in and of itself. To the extent that the story aligns with and reflects real, but previously unspoken aspirations, it not only assumes reality in the sense of currency, but also power as a container or vehicle for the organizational spirit expressed in a new way.

One way of looking at what I was doing would be to see the emerging story, as I was telling and retelling it, as a musical instrument which was being tuned and shaped by trial and error. In essence what I was looking for was a form or version of the Story which resonated with the collective self-understanding and simultaneously gave expression to a new way of being (new covenant) for the organization as a whole. Thus, an important part of my journey through "Appeals land" was to act as a surrogate for the director in the process of collective storytelling. It is for that reason that the director and I had to be absolutely clear as to what I was doing and what the potential outcome might be. While it might look as if I was only listening to stories and telling a few of my own, in fact this activity, if done with sensitivity and skill, would represent a most critical part of the whole undertaking. There is no such thing as "just a story."

THE STORY OF APPEALS — FINAL TAKE

Shortly after I started on my journey through the "land of Appeals" several things occurred which affected what I was doing, and the way I was seeing things. The first was a request from Howard Martin that I look specifically for hero stories concerning the "managers." He perceived correctly that while my exclusive emphasis on the Appeals Officers themselves as they might represent a new version of "Black Hats and Blue Ribbons" was quite understandable in terms of the tradition of the Appeals Division, that emphasis could end up being very destructive if it were not balanced with a more powerful and positive version of the "Managers' Story." Hence he asked me specifically, "What are the hero stories for the managers?" or, as I came to understand it, how would you tell the managers' story in a positive way.

The second thing which occurred was Howard Martin's decision to do a little storytelling on his own. The particular story line which he chose was the independence of Appeals. This was a central part of the old "Black Hats and Blue Ribbons" tale which emphasized the uniqueness of the Division and its function. In a very skillful and low-keyed way, Mr. Martin began to use several opportunities that came his way in speeches before meetings of the "practitioners" (CPAs), magazine interviews, and in senior IRS staff meetings, to embed the idea that Appeals could only perform its essential function to the extent that it truly operated as an impartial, independent body, no matter what the administrative arrangements might be (i.e. the connection with Counsel). As a way of positioning and contexting Appeals, I felt his strategy to be superb. It was quite clear to me that on a practical level (actually getting agreements with the taxpayer) the perception of independence was essential in order to encourage the taxpayer to negotiate, and also to provide the Appeals Officers with a sufficient sense of their own professional self-worth so that they might be effective negotiators. Despite my sense of the "rightness" of Howard Martin's approach, I also felt that there was something missing which I couldn't quite put my finger on.

During the next four months, as I crisscrossed the country interviewing the Appeals' staff, I saw the major findings of my preliminary interviews largely con-firmed, but there were a variety of additional details which served to complicate and confuse the picture. For example, when I talked to secretaries and records clerks, two major stories appeared which stood in stark contrast and conflict. The first story, which I might call "The Garden Spot of IRS" depicted Appeals as THE place to work. The second one, which I called "Nobody Loves Us," described the life of the secretary or clerk as being at the forgotten end of the totem pole where only the drudge work was performed. It seemed that nobody cared what they did, just so long as they ground out the cases. The surprising part about these stories was not that they existed, for in all likelihood similar tales will exist in any organization, but rather that both tales would, more often than not, be told by the same person. To the extent that these two stories described the parameters within which the self-understanding of the people involved might be worked out, the resulting image could only be ambiguous and conflicted, as indeed it seemed to be in actual day to day working situations.

The secretaries and clerks were not the only examples of such ambiguity and conflict, indeed I found a whole series of conflicted pairs at all levels of the operation. For example, among the Appeals Officers, one story — "We Handle the Tough Ones," described how only the very complicated and difficult cases came to Appeals, those cases for which there was no clear cut answer. At the same time, the same officers would tell a story which I called "Buried in Garbage," which related how they had become buried with trivia, simple cases which presented no real challenge except for the sheer numbers involved.

Further examples of this ambiguity included "Appeals Independent," which ran against "The Orphan of the IRS." The first story echoed a theme from the "Black Hats and Blue Ribbons," and was in fact the very theme that Howard Martin was trying to bring into focal attention. However, the second story described how Appeals was simply left to its own devices and largely misunderstood.

Another pair was "The Elite" and "Some Aren't." The "Elite" was in part another flashback to the days of Black Hats, but it was more than that, for it also represented a present feeling that the Appeals Officer was an outstanding example of the best of the Internal Revenue Service. At the same time, the contrasting story ("Some Aren't") reflected the belief that the quality of officers had radically slipped since the old days.

The last conflicted pair was "Independent Professional" and "No Settlement Authority." The story line of "Independent Professional" described how the individual Officers would "go up" by themselves against a phalanx of corporate CPAs and tax attorneys in order to convince them of the wisdom of settlement. The opposing story highlighted the painful fact that although the officers were seen to be sufficiently competent to enter the fray, in the final analysis they were treated like neophytes who had to have their work checked out by higher authority. Put another way, the officers were given the responsibility for reaching settlement without the authority to conclude the deal.

Each of these stories by themselves was not necessarily disruptive, although if only the purely "negative ones" had existed, the overall self-image described would have been pretty bleak. However, the more positive stories seemed to balance that, so that the general spirit was more "up" than "down." Of course, there is always some degree of ambiguity in organizational life, and it might appear that the conflicting stories only reflected that "normal" situation. But it appeared to me that something more was going on, and that in fact the cognitive dissonance produced by the conflicting images was having a very adverse effect. In some ways it would almost have been better had the Appeals Officers and the other staff been able to see themselves as universally bad. At least that would be a consistent picture, and one could come to terms with that in whatever way seemed useful. However, just as some sort of equilibrium seemed to get established, the "opposite" story would surface and the working environment would once more be perturbed.

As I examined the emerging image of the spirit of Appeals as represented by the stories told, it became apparent to me that the strategy I had previously proposed in terms of heightening the image of professionalism on the part of the Appeals Officers was heading in the right direction, but that it was insufficient for the task, primarily because it did not deal with the "other side of the house," the managers. Howard Martin's question, "What are the hero stories of the managers?" remained to be answered. More to the point, it became apparent that smoothing and focusing the energy flow within the Appeals organization could only be accomplished from a position of advantage that essentially included BOTH the managers AND the Appeals Officers.

I knew that one could not eliminate negative myth by denying it. In short the shadow side, conflicting stories would remain disruptive forces until or unless some new, powerful and more positive story might be introduced which might "outframe" them (place them in a larger context) and effectively neutralize their negativity by focusing the intention of the organization on some higher, yet nevertheless attainable goal.

At this point, I asked myself, "What is the business?" What is it they are really trying to do?" And of equal importance, do they understand what that business is, and is that understanding reflected in some powerful way in the stories told? The theory was; given some positive and powerful sense (Vision) of the business, Spirit might be vectored according to that Vision, thereby jumping over, if not neutralizing the negative, disruptive aspects of the present mythic structure.

The key to the business or, more exactly, a new way of describing the business which might "outframe" the existing stories and give them a more positive impact, began to appear as I sought to answer Howard Martin's question: "What are the managers' hero stories?" In the first place, when I asked my interview question, "What is this place," the almost universal initial response was to quote for me a portion of the mission statement as contained in the manual, to the effect that Appeals was in business to, "achieve fair and impartial settlements considering the hazards of litigation." In the case of the managers interviewed, this initial statement was most usually followed by some stories about how many cases were moved, and what the rate of agreement really was. It became clear to me that the true management heroes were those who effectively achieved high rates of agreement with a low level of what were known as "overage cases" — cases which had hung around for a long time. The

197

"score card" for the managers was readily available in the statistics routinely gathered from each office that measured these elements.

The difficulty with this way of defining heroes lay simply in the fact that the Appeals Officers could look at precisely the same data and see not heroes, but insensitive individuals who cared more for the numbers than for the quality of output. If ever there was a clear indication of culture in conflict and turmoil within an organization, this was it, for the "hero story" of one significant component was in fact the "devil story" of another major part. Furthermore, given the fact that the business had been defined as it was (achieving high levels of agreement), there would seem to be no way to alter the situation, for the managers were clearly doing what the business demanded, and further, were collecting statistics that could prove that they were doing a good job. Doubtless, no manager would say that they were opposed to quality work, but the truth of the matter was that there was no readily available way to measure quality, and as a consequence it appeared (certainly to the Appeals Officers) that the quality of the agreement was given only lip service. Push come to shove, the critical statistics related to high levels of agreement and low numbers of overage cases.

Given the fact that most contemporary organizations, and certainly the Appeals managers, have extreme difficulty in taking seriously (for any lengthy period of time) anything that cannot be measured and reduced to numbers; the statistics are the story. It became clear to me that a new story — giving equal time to "quality" and a number of other things held dear to the Appeals Officers could not be told until or unless the business was defined in a different and broader way and some new numbers were gathered to represent that new understanding of the business. A clue to the development of the new story was given through some chance comments made by several Appeals Officers who noted that while Appeals officially held the agency's responsibility for negotiating agreements with taxpayers, in fact cases were settled through agreement by other elements of the IRS, specifically Exam and Counsel.

In the case of Exam, such negotiated agreements were done quite unofficially, but the truth of the matter was that a revenue agent could often bring a case to closure (get the taxpayer to pay up) by using his judgment not to apply the law and regulations in the strictest possible way. Counsel on the other hand had explicit authority to negotiate a settlement, even on the courthouse steps if the terms seemed fair or advantageous. The alternative was to proceed to trial, which would consume a great deal of time, effort, to say nothing of money. Since both Exam and Counsel seemed to be doing the business of Appeals, it might be reasonable to expect that some smart senior level administrator would see the possibility of real savings. Simply close

198

Appeals down, transfer both the function and the personnel to Exam and Counsel, and eliminate the overhead. Surely, if the only business of Appeals were to achieve a high level of agreement rates, that might be more efficiently accomplished by consolidating the effort, and at the same time getting rid of an aberrant, troublesome component of the system. Excellent idea, unless there were some other useful function that Appeals were performing that was presently unacknowledged.

The "other" thing that Appeals might be doing was suggested by the mission statement for the whole Internal Revenue service, which went as follows:

> The Mission of the Internal Revenue Service is to
> encourage and achieve the highest possible degree of
> **voluntary** [emphasis mine] compliance with the tax
> laws and regulations and to maintain the highest degree
> of public confidence in the integrity and efficiency of
> the Service. (IRS Manual, Sec. 8134.2)

With a little reflection, it became obvious that "voluntary compliance" was an essential, if for no other reason than that no matter what the general taxpayer might think, there is no force available to the IRS which might, by any stretch of the imagination, broadly coerce payment. The simple truth of the matter is that if taxpayers in large numbers (perhaps as little as 10-15%) were to refuse to cooperate, the system as it currently exists would cease to function. It turns out that the American taxpayer, unlike his or her brothers and sisters around the world, generally complies with Uncle Sam's annual fund drive. Key to this willing compliance is a general consensus that the system is fair, and confidence that it will remain so. If for any reason that confidence is shattered, things just won't work. This suggests that no matter what else the IRS may do or not do, maintaining public confidence is critical.

What does this have to do with Appeals? Everything, because it seemed to me that of all the elements of the IRS, Appeals held the key slot when it came to taxpayer confidence. The reasoning here may be a little obscure, but it boils down to the following: If you leave out strange tax laws with large loopholes (which certainly do not contribute to taxpayer confidence, but which are also the exclusive domain of Congress, and therefore beyond the control of the IRS), the major threats to taxpayer confidence lie in two areas, misunderstanding of, and lack of clarity in the law and regulations. If the taxpayer does not understand the law, which is more than possible given its complexity, there is little likelihood that he or she will have confidence in the administration of that law. But lack of understanding is only part of the problem, because in point of fact, the law and regulations are often ambiguous and sometimes intentionally so. This may seem strange, but if the law were sufficiently detailed so as to be clear on every possible point, there wouldn't be room in all the libraries of the world to hold it. Viewed from the point of view of voluntary compliance and taxpayer confidence, it is incumbent upon the IRS to insure that taxpayers understand the law, even if they do not agree with it. And even more important, that in those situations where the law is intentionally or happenstantially vague, some mechanism be made available to "work out the differences." The tax court is the final arbiter when it comes to working out implications of the law which are not apparent in the direct statement. But if all areas of dispute had to be submitted to the tax court, nobody would win except possibly the lawyers.

In any event, when you look at the overall structure of the IRS, and the place of Appeals in that structure, it may be argued that Appeals is in the critical place to maintain confidence. While it is true that all parts of the IRS should have this concern, it is also true that Appeals has a special role. Thus, for example, Examination doubtless should be fair in the conduct of its audit, but the truth is that there is built into the Exam-taxpayer dynamic a basic adversarial relationship, which certainly might be controlled, but probably can't be avoided. In Counsel, the adversarial relationship is quite overt, for when a taxpayer deals with Counsel the concern is litigation.

In between is to be found Appeals, and by definition, any taxpayer who comes to Appeals is unhappy, which means there is but a short distance to loss of confidence. If, however, while in contact with Appeals, taxpayers is brought to understand the law or regulations or made to feel that their cases have had a fair and impartial hearing with an appropriate resolution, confidence in the "integrity of the service" will be maintained. This is not to suggest that all taxpayers will "like" the outcome, for truth to tell, nobody ever likes paying taxes. But for sure they can respect the outcome and be made to feel that it was fair.

There is an additional aspect to the importance of the Appeals' clientele, for it turns out that most taxpayers who appear in appeals (certainly in the more complex cases) are represented by a CPA and/or lawyer. So even though Appeals may see less that 1% of all taxpayers, those that they do see come represented by some of the finest professional talent in the country. While a particular taxpayer will usually only appear in Appeals once, the practitioner will appear again and again. What the practitioner thinks about the quality of treatment is critical, for if they perceive a lack of fairness or a lack of competence, they will be sorely tempted to take full advantage of what they can only see as weakness. Of equal importance, they will communicate their feelings (particularly negative feelings) to their colleagues and customers. Thus, one senior practitioner who looses confidence in the system is very likely to spread this disaffection in a rather large circle.

So what is the business of Appeals — the possible New Story? Succinctly put, it is "to maintain taxpayer confidence through impartial consideration of the facts of the case, in the light of the hazards of litigation, leading to a fair agreement." Obviously this sounds rather like what Appeals said before, but there is that significant difference, the addition of taxpayer confidence. And why couldn't other elements of the IRS do just as well? The answer is that both the other major elements (Exam and Counsel) are by intent and in practice, adversarial in nature. To do their job, they need to be, but given an unhappy taxpayer with a legitimate grievance with the system, neither Counsel nor Exam are very likely to improve the situation. So it now may be said to that smart senior administrator: You may get rid of Appeals only with high risk, for even though you may continue to get agreements out of court — what you will miss is that extra special treatment which allows for the maintenance of taxpayer confidence. If this really is the New Story for Appeals, there are some implications for Appeals itself and the way it thinks and talks about itself. I noted previously that the statistics gathered by the Appeals managers related only to the number of agreements reached and the speed with which they were arrived at. The good manager is one who does both with dispatch. But it should be noted that it is quite possible to achieve many agreements at high speed, and totally miss the whole element of taxpayer confidence. To do that one need only to "give away the store." The taxpayer will quickly agree and doubtless be happy with the result, although that same taxpayer will have an eroded sense of confidence in the system. Indeed, he will know for a fact that the system is essentially unfair, needing only to be pushed in order to cave in.

How to tell this "new story" in terms appropriate to the culture? To do that we clearly need a new number and the number proposed is "The Taxpayer Confidence Index." Essentially, this would mean surveying all taxpayers, post agreement, as to their feelings about the system and their treatment. The key questions would relate to whether or not the taxpayers felt they had a fair hearing, were treated with respect and in a professional manner. The results could be expressed on a scale, 0-5 or 0-10, with the high number being the most positive. From there on out, one would simply tally the score by taxpayer, Appeals Officer, and office. The taxpayer confidence number would then stand, along with the agreement rate, as a measure of effectiveness by which managers and Appeals Officers might be evaluated.

Without going any further with the details and mechanics of this particular proposal, I wish to back up in order to summarize the nature of this strategy and the desired impact. You will remember that Appeals, at the point where I became associated with the organization, had essentially passed through a major series of traumatic events which had shaken the old organization of Appellate Conferees to the roots, and forced it into a very new direction. The mechanism for this switch was the advent of the managers who were able to gain control of a situation of massive confusion and vast overload, but not without a large cost. With the introduction of management control, the Appeals Officers were reduced in stature and prestige, at least in their own eyes. So as one problem was solved, another was created. It is true that the work flow of the organization with the advent of the managers was rationalized and speeded. But it is also true that those who were responsible for the production of that work felt, to some major degree, compromised and devalued.

Effectively, what had happened was that the process of transformation had been initiated, and apparently stalled half way. It was quite clear to all (managers and Appeals Officers) that there was no possibility of returning to the golden days of "Black Hats and Blue Ribbons," nor did anybody really want to. But by the same token, the situation as it had evolved was not fully productive either. Indeed both managers and Appeals Officers were spending some considerable amount of energy on conflict which might better have been turned to the job at hand. The problem was that the major story line of Appeals was quite adequate for the managers, given their self-understanding, but the same could not be said for the Appeals Officers. With that same major story (getting agreements as fast as you can) the Appeals Officers often felt as cogs in a machine that cared little about their professional status.

Assisting the organization across the Open Space required among other things, creating a story of sufficient magnitude that all parties (managers and Appeals officers) might find the room and space for the collective spirit to grow. And that story related to taxpayer confidence. To the extent that this new story might be embedded in the collective consciousness of Appeals (and of equal importance, in the larger IRS world), not only would the managers have an understandable place in the sun, but so would the Appeals Officers. For taxpayer confidence clearly cannot be maintained when those who are directly responsible for the interface operate with any less than the highest professional standards. For Appeals Officers this would provide both reason and impetus to maintain and upgrade their own standards of excellence. For the managers, the New Story implies, indeed requires, a rather different way of managing. No longer is it simply a question of pushing the largest number of cases through in the shortest possible time, but now it becomes absolutely essential to play a supportive, nurturing role relative to the Appeals Officers which creates a positive working environment in which the work is not only done, but done with distinction. The managers must learn to manage by indirection, and not by telling in fine detail just what to do.

The actual tactics in this case may appear so simple as to be hardly of consequence. In essence, there were three points. First, Howard Martin continued to spread the idea (story) of the independence of Appeals, thus providing the necessary space for some freedom of movement and development. Second, in order to provide the rationale and justification for that independence, the whole concept of taxpayer confidence and Appeals' central role in relationship to that, was articulated at all possible points. And third, as a concrete means of telling (ritualizing) the New Story, the creation of a Taxpayer Confidence Index was introduced as a central objective for the coming fiscal year with the understanding that once created, it would then be used as a critical part of the evaluation of specific offices.

Given this "meta strategy" which revolves around the creation and embedding of a New Story, a new vision of what the business is, a number of other more concrete activities may be entered upon within the newly created context. These might include management training programs to impart the idea of "management by indirection," task forces to upgrade and strengthen the self perception of the secretaries and clerks, making them more effectively part of the team, the creation of the Institute of Certified Appeals Officers, and a number of others. It should be noted, however, that none of these more "practical" innovations could be really effective in and of themselves. They all become meaningful and powerful only within the larger context as concrete expressions of the New Story. Thus, these innovations make the Story real, but at the same time, they become possible only in the context of that story.

As I indicated at the beginning, the time elapsed from the point of intervention until now is not sufficient to permit long term assessment. However, Howard Martin's (the director) perception of what has happened and the likely results follows:

> "Though many of your specific ideas have not been
> implemented, the principal one has been implemented.
> You assisted us to identify the actual role of Appeals in
> the Internal Revenue Service. We learned from this that
> we could establish our identity by telling our story as
> we believed it should be, i.e., an independent profes-

sional body to thoroughly and impartially consider tax disputes. After we started defining our role as an independent quasi-judicial body, the Tax Division of the AICPA (American Institute of Certified Public Accountants) and the Tax Section of the ABA (American Bar Association) also adopted this, as well as many officials within the IRS. All of this storytelling has defined our role now and in the future, and a much healthier organization has resulted. With your assistance, we were able to take the initiative and design our future rather than reacting to others. . .Finally, the approach was so very effective that the organization seems to be demanding change, at least not resisting it, and is open to improvements."

Chapter X

THE EASTERN VIRGINIA MEDICAL AUTHORITY

The central issue addressed in this case study is how to effectively integrate a large medical care complex into the fabric of the community in which it exists when both the community and the institution are in the process of transformation.

HISTORY

The Eastern Virginia Medical Authority is a strange institution by almost any standard. In most respects, it appears functionally as a health science center with a medical school and associated hospitals, but organizationally it is a very different sort of creature. In fact it is an "authority" as in a bridge and tunnel "authority," chartered under the laws of the state of Virginia, and is effectively under the direction of seven city councils. To understand how such a creation came into being it is necessary to consider its context historically and geographically.

The Eastern Virginia Medical Authority, EVMA, is to be found in the lower southeastern corner of the State of Virginia in the area surrounding the largest deepwater harbor in the nation, the port of Hampton Roads. While the shipping companies of the world know the place well, it seems that most of the rest of the world has been largely unaware of its existence. Known vaguely as "Tidewater Virginia," the region has existed for 300 years as a disparate collection of cities who have largely sought to go their own way with little regard for each other or the world beyond. Except for the attractions of Virginia Beach and the presence of a large Navy base, few people either came or went, and the natives seem to have prefered it that way.[70]

---

[70] This is scarcely an adequate description of the area, but it is sufficient to set the stage for the case study. I will offer much more detail by the way of background for the next case study which will deal with the region as a whole.

Twenty-five years ago, the region could conservatively be described as a medically underserved area. Although there were somewhat less than a million people living there, few sophisticated medical care facilities existed in the area, and the quality and quantity of such care as did exist left much to be desired. For those individuals with serious problems and sufficient money, treatment was sought 100 miles to the north in Richmond or an equal distance to the south in the Raleigh-Durham area. Those without the necessary funds simply made do with what was available.

The medical renaissance began as the dream of one man, or at least that is the local myth. The man was Mason Andrews who combined an amazing set of talents with incredible determination. Mason was a doctor, an obstetrician to be exact, who was well known in the area, and had overseen the birthing of many of the local citizens. At the same time, Mason was a politician and the community activist. When it came time for Mason to run for the city council of Norfolk, which he did successfully many times over, he ran on the campaign slogan "Mason Delivers," and deliver he did.

As a physician, Dr. Andrews was profoundly aware of the lack of quality and medical sophistication in the region. And as a politician he could see the adverse effects upon the population. He was also keenly aware of the difficulty involved in doing anything substantive about the problems. Significantly raising the level of medical care for the region would require an enormous amount of money, but even more than that it would require the cooperative effort of many diverse elements. Given the later (cooperation), the money might be gathered together — but cooperation, particularly on a regionwide basis was virtually unheard of. In truth, the seven cities of the region had existed as independent warring fiefdoms for longer than anybody cared to remember.[71]

In the context of this situation, Mason Andrews dared to dream what most people would have considered an impossible thought, that there should be a medical school in the region. The reasoning was quite straightforward. If there were a medical school, it could serve as a center of excellence which might attract more competent physicians to the area, train local people, and last but by no means least, provide the faculty which could serve as a care resource. Thus health care in the region might improve.

---

[71] To be accurate, it should be said that only the cities of Norfolk, Portsmouth, Hampton and Newport News had been engaged in the 300 year war. The balance of the cities (Virgina Beach, Chesapeake and Suffolk) had only come into existence as cities a few years before.

Few people could argue directly with the logic of this dream, but many argued anyway for a variety of reasons. First of all, there were two other medical schools in the state which worried that, should another school be created, their exclusive access to state funds would be curtailed. It was bad enough that the schools should have to share the largesse of the state, and even though they agreed on little else, they found it in their self-interest to conclude that a third school was not needed. Then there were the local practitioners who worried publicly that the advent of the school would bring about "socialized medicine," which meant that they would have to compete. When questioned, the local Docs all indicated that of course they were competitive — but privately they were not so sure.

In an effort to garner support for the idea, Mason Andrews and some other co-conspirators arranged for nationally known medical consultants to come to the region and offer their recommendations. They, along with the State Council of Higher Education, officially concluded in 1963 that the region was a logical place to establish a medical school. Private conventional wisdom, however, suggested that "no way" would the region ever be able to generate the cooperative spirit necessary to raise the essential funds. While I can't prove it with anything like historical certainty, I think it may well be the case that these "private negative thoughts" of the national experts (and not a few local residents) ended up being the decisive factor which caused the community to turn to and create the necessary funding. It was one thing to have fellow Virginians turn thumbs down (the other medical schools and their friends in Richmond, the state capital), that was to be expected, and considered to be a normal part of the annual game of state appropriations. By the same token, having the local physicians also object was also reasonable, if only because they were doctors, and should know what they were talking about. But, having some outsiders view the region in negative terms was simply out of the question. In fact, it played directly into the hands of a small but remarkable local leadership.

In the late '50s Tidewater in general and Norfolk in particular could not, by any stretch of the imagination, be viewed as an elegant cosmopolitan setting. The truth of the matter was that the city was in a deplorable state. The turn started to come through the efforts of one Charles Kaufman, a local attorney of major standing, who along with a small band of colleagues began to use the federal urban renewal funds and local resources for the rebuilding of Norfolk. In fact they totally redid the city, but I think more significant than the actual physical reconstruction was the renewal of spirit. That effort provided the occasion for the welding together of a group of men who needed only a major challenge to set them on a course of positive action. And

207

having some outsiders suggesting that Tidewater could not respond to their own needs was like waving a red flag. In a word, the folks charged.

At the time, it seemed like things took forever to get going, but in retrospect it appears that the pieces fell together in rapid order, and in a style which I came to recognize as "pure" Tidewater. The legal entity for the undertaking, which was originally known as the Norfolk Area Medical Center Authority[72] was created in 1964 as a mechanism to support the development of the emerging Norfolk hospital complex. Even though talk of a medical school was clearly in the air, opposition to such an institution was quite intense, coming from the sources described above. With what I now recognize as a typical byzantine Tidewater tactic, special legislation was pushed through the state legislature authorizing the creation of, not a "medical school," but a medical "authority," with a charter so broad as to almost numb the mind. This charter specified that the authority should:

> ". . .plan, design, remove, enlarge, construct, equip,
> maintain and operate medical education institutions,
> medical and paramedical facilities together with related
> and supporting facilities and to do all things necessary
> and convenient to carry out any of its purposes."

I was told by those who were intimately involved, that the legislation got through primarily because none of the opponents thought anything would ever come of it. More to the point, it did not mention a medical school, and most of all, no state funds were committed.

The next issue was to raise the money, a not inconsequential task since there was a general agreement that something on the order of $15 million in the kitty would be required before anything could even get started. Given that large sum and the fact that no state funds would be available, it is not surprising that conventional wisdom felt confirmed in its opinion that nothing would ever happen. But conventional wisdom was wrong. How the initial funds were raised is a marvelous story in and of itself, but more than that, the

---

[72] The name was eventually changed to the Eastern Virginia Medical Authority in order to reflect the regional nature of the enterprise, and with the name change came the addition of representatives of the seven local cities to the governing Board.

story has become an essential part of the mythos of the region, and for that reason I relate the tale in some detail. This version comes from my notes following an interview with Porter Hardy, the chairman of the fund-raising committee. By way of introduction, I should explain that Porter Hardy was a congressman who knew virtually everybody in the region, and even though he was from the city of Portsmith, he was well known and well liked throughout.

Porter Hardy was one of the originals, and our conversation was nothing short of delightful. It was by no means an interview. I never did find out what he really thought EVMA was (my first standard question, "What is this place?"), but I did learn an awful lot about the kind of early machinations which produced the fund-raising effort that eventuated in EVMA.

It seems that over a period of years, Mason Andrews had gone to see him in Washington while he was in Congress about some kind of a medical school. It was no surprise then, when Mason Andrews set up an appointment one day to see Mr. Hardy in the company of three other well known gentlemen from the area by the names of Cox, Welton and Wood, just to talk about the general idea of the creation and structuring of a medical school. Nothing specific mind you, just a general conversation.

For a variety of reasons, the meeting could not be held at any time except Saturday morning when, it turned out, Porter Hardy had a dentist appointment. The time for the meeting came and went, and Hardy was still in the dentist's chair. So Dick Wood came down and extracted him from the chair, and the meeting began. Nothing particularly was settled and that really wasn't the point. The meeting was basically exploratory to discover whether Porter Hardy felt that something like a medical school might be feasible in the Tidewater area. That was all.

Several years later (1969), Mason Andrews called up and asked Porter Hardy if he would care to go to lunch at the Harbor Club (the business luncheon spot located on the top of the Virginia National Bank). Now mind you at this point, Hardy had absolutely no idea what the luncheon meeting was about or who else might be invited. When he got to the private dining room, there were in his words, "the 25 people who really ran Norfolk" all sitting around the table. Still nobody clued him in as to what it was all about, and the mystery remained until the meal had concluded.

At that point, Harry Price (a local retailer) stood up as the spokesman. According to Porter Hardy, "You will not find a stronger super-salesman than that Harry Price," and the issue was, Would he, Porter Hardy, head up the fund-raising drive for the new medical school? All he had to do, said Mr. Price, was raise $15 million. Porter's immediate response was, "You all are crazy." Nevertheless, he was not unaware of the fact that the power of the city of Norfolk, and as a matter of fact many of the surrounding cities was sitting at the table, so if it was possible that anything like this was ever going to take place, these were clearly the people who could get it done. Porter Hardy didn't say no, he agreed to "consider." "Considering" meant going downstairs to talk to Charlie Kaufman, who had not been able to attend the meeting. Hardy wanted to know if it was possible, and Kaufman, while admitting to being skeptical, guaranteed that enough money would be raised so that he (Hardy) "would not be embarrassed." Porter Hardy agreed, and the next act was convened several weeks later when the same group of 25 were gathered together for another luncheon. This time, Hardy was in charge.

Before the meeting, each of the participants was asked to bring a list of people who would be able to make gifts of $30,000 or more. The business of the meeting consisted in determining who among the assembled leaders could most effectively make the pitch to the various prospective donors. Those decisions were made with dispatch, and everybody headed for the door. At which point Porter Hardy called out, "Wait a minute, we haven't quite finished yet . . . you all haven't made your contributions." And they all came back in and sat down while Hardy called the roll. The first bid came in at $60,000, and it went from there. The last contribution was offered by a very senior patrician sort, who indicated that he was good for $100,000. Just as the assembled group was about to leave again, somebody suggested that they ought to visit Charlie Kaufman to see if he might persuade the Virginia National Bank to contribute $500,000. And so a small delegation was assembled, and off they went.

Included within this delegation was the senior patrician who had offered $100,000. When the possibility of the half-million dollar contribution was raised to Charlie Kaufman, Mr. Kaufman turned to the patrician and said "What did you give?," and the answer came back, $100,000. Kaufman's eyebrows went up, accompanied by something like, "You're a piker." At that point, the ante was raised to $250,000 if the Bank would go for half a million, and the deal was closed at a quarter of a million each.

Well, that is apparently the way it went. In the course of a one hour luncheon meeting and a little time at the bank, something over $1 million was raised. Whatever else this tribal event was, it was clearly a very high-stakes poker game, and it set the tone for all that was to follow.

From the time of that meeting with Porter Hardy and the central group until 1973, when the first class of students was admitted, the activity was fast and furious. On the fund raising front, the leaders developed a region wide infra-structure from scratch. Although major fund raising had been done within each of the several cities, nobody had ever tried to do such a thing across municipal lines. Even as the fund raising was going on, plans were being made for the medical school itself — everything from building design and construction to planning the curriculum. In 1971, the first dean of the medical school arrived, and by 1973, five years after the Harbor Club Luncheon, they were open for business.

From its inception, the school (indeed the whole authority) was an odd assemblage of pieces, unlike anything else in the country. So when it came to models, there weren't any. Normally[73] a medical school is either part of a private institution for higher education or of some state education system. It will possess its own "teaching hospital" which is necessary both to provide the clinical environment necessary for education and research and also a significant portion of the funding for the school generated from patient fees. Furthermore, a majority of its faculty will be on staff as full time paid employees. These "normal" conditions end up being very useful in order to create a relatively stable environment within which the school, with a single source of administrative direction, may operate in terms of control over their facilities and funding.

The situation with EVMA was radically different, and some would say impossibly so. In the first place the vast majority of the faculty, at least initially, were not on staff, but rather came from the community as unpaid volunteers or they were only partially funded. At the present time, for example, there are in excess of 600 "adjunct" (read not-full-time faculty) as opposed to somewhere around 150 full-time faculty. Second, the medical school had no hospital, although it was closely associated with the largest hospital in

---

[73] I am not quite sure that there is any such thing as a "normal" medical school, but they do seem to fall into a general pattern which I have characterized. And for sure, EVMA lay far outside that pattern.

211

Norfolk and 20 plus others around the region. Finally EVMA was not part of anything (in an institutional sense) which might provide it some support and protection. On the contrary, EVMA was on her own with governance supplied by a board of commissioners composed of representatives from the surrounding cities.

At its best, EVMA and the medical school which fell under its aegis was a radical new model of community-based medical education. At its worst, it was an administrative nightmare. In fact, the institution was a carefully crafted structure which arose out of, and in response to the peculiar needs and conditions of the region. For example; the matter of volunteer staff as opposed to full-time. Even though it is quite true that the sheer number of volunteers introduced enormous problems in terms of continuity and quality control, the presence of these community physicians within the medical school structure effectively brought one of the chief critics into the tent.

The same may also be said for the strange (and sometimes strained) mode of governance. The mere thought that one could bring the representatives of seven, often hostile municipalities into a single board and expect that board to exercise effective governance over an institution was viewed by some to be complete madness. But it worked. Indeed, this strategy spread ownership and responsibility around the region. Effectively what occurred was the creation of what we would now call a "parallel organization," which outframed the existing political organizations in order to create something totally new. It may be argued that over and above whatever health-care benefits accrued to the region through the creation of the medical authority, its function as a parallel organization in a divided region was (is) its most important function.

To say that EVMA is and was a unique, anomalous, bold venture is a fair statement. The central question, however, was, Would it work? With the advent of the first students, the experiment began.

The history of the early years of the institution reads like the "Perils of Pauline." There were soaring, and sometimes conflicting dreams emanating from a variety of places — and coming to earth in the midst of near fiscal oblivion and administrative chaos. Without going into the details, I believe any impartial observer would have to admit that the fact that the school happened at all, and continues to this present day, is nothing short of a miracle. At times it seemed that the life of the school hung by the slenderest (but perhaps strongest) of threads, the simple belief, held by a few, that it must work.

After five years of operation, there was good news and bad news. The good news was that the school existed, had graduated two classes of students and perhaps most remarkable, had begun to prove Mason Andrews' original premise correct, that the mere presence of a medical school would have a positive impact on the overall delivery of health care for the region. The fact of the matter was that with the arrival of the school, there also came individuals who introduced new sophisticated medical and surgical procedures. No longer was it necessary for the residents of the area to journey north to Richmond or south to North Carolina. In most cases, the appropriate skills and the necessary technology were now to be found in Tidewater.

But the first five years had also taken its toll. The first president left under a cloud, followed by the second dean. After their departure, an interim president was brought in from the outside who viewed himself solely in the role of a caretaker. With no clear direction from the top, the possibility for conflict and crisis was endless, and endlessly realized. To make matters worse EVMA and the Medical School, which had begun life as a community-based institution with little other support (financial or otherwise) had lost, or was in the process of loosing the confidence of the community. If ever there was a situation where an old covenant had ended, and a new one was needed, EVMA was a perfect example. The overt signs were painful and easy to spot; low morale, endless bickering and blame-fixing, with finances verging on the point of catastrophe.

Such was the situation when William Mayer, the new president, arrived on the scene to assume his duties. I appeared there shortly thereafter to act as his consultant.[74] The immediate issues were fairly clear. In order to avoid outright collapse, or what might have been worse, a slow agonizing death, morale had to be brought up, the community re-engaged, and the financial and administrative chaos brought under control. But most of all, it was a question of leadership and direction — telling a New Story if you will. Without this latter essential ingredient, most, if not all of the overt institutional problems would remain insoluble.

---

[74] In relating what happened, it may appear that all thought and activity was initiated by Bill Mayer or myself. That is far from the case, and indeed there was a marvelous cast of characters for this particular drama. In particular I would mention Joe Greathouse, the Vice President for Planning and Program Development. Little, if anything occurred which was not vastly strengthened and improved through Joe's careful and methodical input.

My area of concentration was to be on the interface between EVMA and the community at large, with the thought that if we could create a relatively stable and supportive environment for the institution, then it might be possible to deal effectively with the very serious internal problems. Failing that supportive environment, there would continue to be one brush fire after another. To quote the language from the letter of understanding which framed my consultancy:

> Our task is ultimately to create a coherent, formalized
> support environment for EVMA. This environment
> should do for EVMA what a university structure would
> do for any other health science center.

It was decided early on that some form of a strategic planning exercise would be very much in order, but how that might be put together, and what the final results might be were left for further development. My immediate task was to develop a reasonable picture of the culture surrounding EVMA as represented by the operative mythos. This took me on a journey throughout the region during which I conducted something in excess of 170 formal interviews. About one quarter of these were with EVMA staff and faculty, and the rest spanned the social and political structure of the region.

A surprisingly simple, but very devastating picture emerged. Essentially, there were two powerful and opposed stories. The first one I called "EVMA the Unifier." This story appeared in a number of forms with many details, but fundamentally it was a story of how EVMA had become the first and only enterprise that had ever united the region in a positive endeavor. The story was told with pride and no small amount of wonder, for to most of my interviewees, the thought that the region could ever be unified was almost beyond belief. One very potent version of this story told the tale of the High Stakes Civic Poker Game which I have already related. Few people knew or cared who was actually present during that remarkable luncheon, for in the way of myth, the historical details tended to get dropped. Indeed, to hear the story one might assume that more than a thousand had been in attendance. In a way, that judgment was correct, for as the myth gained currency and represented the spirit of the people who were or had become involved, it could legitimately be said that everybody was present. In fact, initiating a larger number of people to that story was an annual occurrence. To what extent this was conscious, I am not quite sure, but it happened, and it was effective. Specifically, each year as the annual fund raising drive for EVMA got under way, the story was told again as a way of connecting into the depths of the organization, and also as a challenge to the fund raisers, old and newcomers alike. The story, and participating in the story through the annual fund drive, had become a mechanism of bonding, a rite of passage. And at the center of it was EVMA. On a very crass level, if you wanted to determine the social pecking order for the region, you could do worse than look at who was on the central committee, and then who was sent out to talk to whom.

So it was not true that EVMA had no community support. If anything the support was almost overpowering and occasioned expectations regarding the institution that were in part quite unrealistic. The central dynamic at the heart of this story had almost nothing to do with a medical school *per se,* but rather it related to a deep longing for some effective kind of regional unity. Of course it was all disguised as a supportive effort to promote good health care, which, like motherhood, was virtually unassailable. Even though regional cooperation might be verboten, getting together for the better health of all, was quite legitimate. And the story about all that was "EVMA the Unifier."

The second story, which I called "EVMA the Omnivore," was quite different. It doubtless had its roots in the early days when the local physician community was less than enthusiastic about the advent of the new medical institution, but no matter how it started, it was very real and very destructive. The central story line here was that EVMA was in business to put everybody else out of business. In short, EVMA was to become the centralized medical/health-care colossus. Precisely how this was to be accomplished or what hard evidence might be cited in support of the idea remained vague and unstated, as is typically the way with myth. The point is that the story was there, and for those under its power, that story colored each and every act that EVMA took. New faculty and new facilities were seen to be *prima facie* evidence that the grand design was moving forward according to the plans and intentions of an un-named and unseen "power group."

The simple fact was that EVMA, at the time of my interviews, was in such complete disarray that massive takeover was not only out of the question, it was positively ridiculous. But this in no way lessened the power of the myth to stir the waters, and make an already difficult situation worse.

215

It became obvious to me why EVMA was as deeply troubled as it was, for the culture was essentially the product of opposing myths which slammed into each other with a power and intensity which left everything else in ribbons. Not only were these myths antithetical, they also essentially fed on each other. To the extent that EVMA the Unifier gained any adherents, that represented a further threat to those who perceived the world through the eyes of EVMA the Omnivore. And as long as this cycle of feeding and conflict was allowed to continue, it could only worsen until there was nothing left.

In conversations with Bill Mayer, I indicated that the situation was frighteningly simple. The two myths were powerful and conflicted, and to the extent that they represented the Spirit of the organization, it was frankly amazing that things were going as well as they were — and absolutely predictable that the situation would get worse. Given that mythic structure, little if anything done on the level of organizational practicality, was going to have any real or lasting effect. Even something apparently as objective as improving the fiscal situation would run into severe difficulty, and more than that would be perceived by those of the EVMA the Omnivore school as but another example of the great beast strengthening its talons.

The strategy evolved was extraordinarily simple, and might be summarized in the words of the old song — "accentuate the positive and eliminate the negative." But eliminating the negative could not be taken on in a direct fashion. What had to be done was to build upon the positive aspects of the myth of EVMA the Unifier, and make that so attractive and compelling that it basically outframed and outran the negative myth. I took some pains to caution Dr. Mayer that no matter what else he might do, he should in no wise challenge the myth of EVMA the Omnivore, for the only result would be to strengthen it in the minds of those who owned it. His reaction, like most other activist leaders, was to question my wisdom (or worse). As he said, "We have neither the intention nor the ability to take over the region. Why not just say that?"

When I explained along the lines that should now be familiar, how a myth literally created the perceptual world of the "holders," and to challenge that myth directly would be taken as a challenge to that world, and therefore would be met with resistance, he obviously understood conceptually but was still not quite convinced. However, some little time later, he told me of an incident which occurred when he had been invited to speak to one of the local

216

medical societies. While he did not challenge the myth of "EVMA the Omni-vore" directly, he apparently had come pretty close and as he was walking out of the room following his speech, he happened to overhear several of the doctors talking together in front of him. One doctor said to the other, "See, it is just like I told you, EVMA is going to take over everything, because Dr. Mayer just said they weren't interested. That's the way they always work. Soften you up and then go for it."

In order to build upon the myth of EVMA the Unifier, we could not simply take out a page ad in the local newspaper and proclaim that as our intention. We had to create a condition in which EVMA appeared in a power-ful and positive way as the unifier. It was less a question of saying than doing. More accurately, my intention was to create a liturgical environment in which the story and the action blended to express this aspect of the mythos of EVMA — in a way that words alone could never match.

The mechanism was at hand in the proposed strategic planning activity which Bill Mayer had previously felt to be essential. I was in agreement with the need for such planning and only suggested that in addition to whatever formal output there might be (a "Mission and Goals" statement or the like), the critical factor would be the process by which it was achieved. My intent was that we utilize the form of strategic planning as the occasion and op-portunity for collective Storytelling. There were several immediate implica-tions. First, we could not follow the rather standard approach of bringing in an external consulting team to perform a study and make recommendations, for that would result in the story being told by people who had no real stake in it. While such a consulting group might come up with outstanding recommenda-tions, they would not be the parties at interest.

Identifying the parties at interest was the critical chore. Certainly the senior officials in the Authority were to be included, but again, what has often become standard practice had to be rejected. Instead of a small group at the top heading the effort, with "paper" communication with the balance of the organization, we needed a different way to go. Our solution was to identify some 15 individuals from within the Authority representing all levels and areas including students at the medial school. To this we added a larger number from the community at large to bring the total to about 50.

Since our intent was not only to generate substantive recommendations but also to allow all that emerge out of the group as a new common Story, we had to allow sufficient time for growth; therefore, we consciously spread the whole process over what might seem like a very long time (six months), meeting for a whole day once each month, and we added some elements which might appear frivolous, namely cocktails and dinner each time we met.

The rules of the game were very simple. Each person was expected to contribute their version of what the New Story might look like. If that version was at variance with other or larger bodies of opinion, the right and duty of expression still existed. The only "lay-on" was that EVMA existed in order to serve the health-care needs of the region. Beyond that, the field lay open, at least as that field was pre-defined by the president.

In order to lend some structure to the effort, we moved in four phases each one of which addressed a separate question: 1) What are the health care needs of the region now and as they may appear over the next five years. 2) What institutions or mechanisms currently exist which are, or should be, addressing those needs (not counting EVMA)? 3) Which needs are currently unaddressed? and 4) Considering these unmet needs, what are the peculiar roles that EVMA should be playing?

By starting with a question dealing with the health-care needs of the region as a whole, two things were accomplished. First, we deliberately took the attention away from EVMA and the role that institution might or might not play in the future. The point here was to defuse to the extent possible the negative residue of the Omnivore myth. The first cut was not EVMA and what it should do, but the region in its entirety. The second accomplishment was rather more mundane but essential. By asking the group to give their best professional judgments as to the present and future needs, we allowed each person to operate from their own position of expertise. While they might know little if anything about EVMA, they knew what their own views were, and were more than willing to share them.

This sharing was itself important, for although most of the group present knew each other by name and reputation, many had never worked closely together before. As they shared their understanding of the problems and opportunities facing the region, they grew to know and respect each other better and, interestingly enough, found that they had more in common than difference.

Hence, the first question was intended to establish a matrix of under-standing, so that the emerging New Story of EVMA, no matter what it might turn out to be, would be grounded in a common view (Vision) of how things were, and where they needed to go. Had our intention only been the gathering and sorting of information, we could have accomplished the first part of the agenda in one session; but as I have indicated, there was much more at stake, so we took the time to allow each participant plenty of "air time" and opportunity to interact with colleagues during the formal sessions, and even more important — afterwards around the bar and over dinner.

During the six-month process, each of the questions was dealt with in turn, and eventually there emerged a sense of what EVMA should be in the context of the needs and resources of the region as a whole. This had the positive effect of making the EVMA story emerge as an answer to community need rather than a proclamation of EVMA intent. This is scarcely an innovative approach, but it was very powerful and fitted our needs exactly, for EVMA now appeared as the unifying element which completed, and in some sense rationalized, the regional picture.

A very central part of this "liturgical drama" was Bill Mayer himself. Given his position, this is not surprising, but his role had to be carefully thought through and orchestrated to achieve the desired results. As a strong and powerful personality, Bill Mayer was quite capable of a "Take Charge" kind of leadership. However, if the story of EVMA were to emerge as we hoped, and if Bill Mayer were to be connected with it, as was inevitable since he was president, a subtler approach was essential. This approach had to honor the openness of the whole process, and yet create a meaningful place for the president. A complicating element was the fact that Dr. Mayer was new to the region. This permitted a degree of latitude (the "honeymoon factor"), but it also meant that he was an unknown in a region where being known is critical. How he would be known was even more critical, for his personal success and that of the institution of which he was president. Bill Mayer had to become part of the story, and in some real sense, the embodiment of the myth of EVMA the Unifier. To do this it was essential that he practice the art of collective story-telling with a vengeance and epitomize leadership by indirection.

It might appear from what I have just said that my role was to instruct Dr. Mayer. Nothing could be farther from the truth, but it would be fair to say that I was able to provide some perspective and suggestions as we went along.

The appropriate word I suppose is "coach," but there was no question that Dr. Mayer was on the field, and had to play the game.

Despite the openness of the process which was critical, it would be totally inaccurate to assume that the Dr. Mayer had no version of the story he wanted to tell. Indeed, he had come to the position of president after a long and outstanding career in health-care administration at virtually all levels. In the past he had been the head of a medical school department, the dean of a medical school, and most recently, the individual in charge of all affairs between the medical schools of the country and the Veterans Administration. Based on this experience he had developed some very strong ideas as to what should be done, and how to go about doing it. Just to raise the ante, I believe that Bill Mayer also looked at this present assignment as his last major administrative post prior to becoming an elder statesman or retirement. He certainly had his story, and a moment's conversation with him would confirm that he held that story with a high degree of passion. He also understood that his story could not be The story, for The story must become richer and more broadly owned.

As the process moved along, Bill Mayer's role was by no means passive, but he absolutely avoided taking the floor in an official position to proclaim how things ought to be done. His style was an outstanding example of leadership by indirection. He paid exquisite attention to context and process. When it became apparent that somebody (and most especially an unpopular somebody) was having difficulty getting their thought out or understood, Bill Mayer was almost inevitably the first person to lend a hand and pave the way. Of course, Bill expressed his opinions, his version of the story, but he scrupulously did it in the same way as everybody else did, in the context of the small groups, from the floor in general sessions. But never from the podium as president.

There was one point in the whole process when I felt that Bill Mayer absolutely outdid himself in demonstrating how a collective storyteller should work. The issue came up as to whether EVMA itself should be a provider of healthcare, and if so to what extent. The importance of this issue derived from the fact that many individuals in the larger health care community were more than a little afraid of the competitive advantage which the Authority might have if it chose to enter the lists as a direct provider of health care. Bill's feelings on the issue were very strong; he believed it essential that EVMA provide health care in part to enrich the educational experience of the medical students and, of equal importance, as a means of generating income for the institution. Privately, Bill was practically beside himself, but to his undying credit, he never used his position as president to force his version through. In fact, a compromise emerged which allowed all parties sufficient room. But most important, the process of Vision-building and collective storytelling was held inviolate.

At the conclusion of the six-month process, it was very clear that a New Story had emerged which constituted solid ground for a New Covenant. Substantively, this New Covenant appeared between two covers as the "Mission and Goals Statement," but that was just a pale reflection of what had transpired. A comment from one of the participants is to the point. This individual had a general reputation of not being a friend of EVMA. Indeed, his voice had been loudly heard among those on the "outside" who didn't want EVMA in the first place, and who took no little pleasure in the seeming near demise of the Authority. In any event, at the conclusion of the process, this individual took me to one side and said, "You know, when we started all of this I came with the impression that we were supposed to plan for EVMA, and my thoughts were largely in the direction of a quiet funeral. It has now become clear to me that EVMA is us, and that we have been planning for ourselves."

The process described concluded in December of 1980. Now several years later, it is reasonable to ask, What were the results? While it would be foolhardy to suggest that all positive occurrences since (which have been many) are directly attributable to the intervention, it would seem fair to say that the intervention marked a decisive turning point which has since been capitalized on in spades. The New Story, or more exactly, the strengthened old story of EVMA the Unifier has now come to dominate the field. This is not to say that the tale of the Omnivore has totally disappeared, but it no longer exerts a destructive influence. This may be seen in quite tangible ways. For example, the budget has doubled in the intervening years as a result of a lot of hard work, but also, and perhaps mostly, due to the combined efforts of the community supporting something they now take almost universally as a positive good, which brings them together. Although it seems to be in the nature of such public educational institutions never to have sufficient funds, it is also a far cry from the period of only several years ago when projected deficits were running on the million-dollar-a-year level, off a much smaller base; and making the payroll was, more than occasionally, a real issue.

Further manifestation of this unified community support has been the raising of some $8 million for the construction of a new clinical sciences center. The import of this particular achievement is doubly impressive when it is remembered that the presence of a large clinical faculty was taken to be an enormous threat by those who saw the world through the eyeglasses of EVMA the Omnivore. Had that myth persisted, the clinical sciences center would have been all but unthinkable, and certainly not supportable to the level of 8 million, largely private-sector dollars.[75] In the intervening years, the Eastern Virginia Medical Authority has also emerged from its position as a little known local school of doubtful quality to a visible position of national leadership. Through the creation of the Howard and Georgeanna Jones Institute for Reproductive Medicine, the organization has become a leader in the new field of *in vitro* fertilization, which bore fruit on December 28, 1981, with the birth of Elizabeth Jordan Carr, the first in-vitro baby born in the United States. The essential difference between "then" and "now" is the product of a lot of hard work and no small amount of luck. But it is also the product of a clear Vision and a powerful Story which have effectively united the institution with its community to realize a dream that many thought impossible. In the words of Bill Mayer:

> The major difference, between then and now is that in
> 1979 the challenge and excitement was focused on
> whether or not this exciting organization, carefully and
> laboriously developed by so many was going to live or
> die. Five years later that is no longer the question, but

---

[75] For those unfamiliar with the world of academic medicine, the clinical faculty are those physicians who teach and practice the clinical arts, such as cardiology, internal medicine, surgery and the like. The clinical faculty is distinguished from the Basic Science Faculty which is concerned with such things as anatomy, physiology, and biochemistry. The point is that the clinical faculty are "treating doctors", who deal with real patients and charge money for their efforts.

rather: "Will we achieve in the future the level of excellence of which we are now capable? [76]

CONCLUDING THOUGHTS AND TRANSITION

As I was concluding my work with the Eastern Virginia Medical Authority, it occurred to me that the very mythology which had proven to be the source of strength for EVMA (EVMA the Unifier) could well turn out to be its undoing. In that myth, EVMA is perceived to be the focal point for union, which had brought a disparate region together for the first time, at least in any major way. Given this perception, EVMA was worthy of support, and that support was forthcoming. However, if the spirit of regionalism were ever to turn totally sour and negative, as in fact it had been during the majority of the area's history, EMVA would be in a very exposed position as the outstanding representation of that way of thinking. As I had gotten to know the region, it was by no means clear that something like that could not happen. Indeed, there was much evidence that the spirit of parochialism and municipal self-interest was not only alive and well — but perhaps even growing a "tad" (Virginian for "small bit"). So for a regional institution to survive, it would be well if it were set in a geographical environment which was positively disposed towards regional thinking. Otherwise, the institution could have a very short life. At the time, the regional spirit in Tidewater was far from healthy.

Then there was William Mayer, president of EVMA. He was a complete newcomer, with no independent power base other than the institution he headed, which itself was in some jeopardy. Furthermore, by dint of some considerable effort he had emerged as a teller of the tale of union. Were that tale to become unpopular, his fate would be predictable. More than that, it was apparent to me that in order for him to effectively lead his institution through the various snares and thickets of the charming, but often byzantine Eastern Virginia folkways, it was essential that he have some alternative "place to stand" which was at once respected, connected to the institution, supportive of regional thinking, and linked in a positive way to the community at large. In

---

[76] Mayer, William, "A Five Year Report to the Board of Commssioners of the Eastern Virginia Medical Authority" September 1984, pg 33.

223

order to serve his institution well, he needed a vantage point from which he could go beyond the recognized self-interest of EVMA, and speak with broader authority.

The problem was that regional thinking in general was by no means acceptable or popular in the Tidewater area, and no organizational structure presented itself as a meaningful place to stand for the current president of EVMA. Since these things did not exist, and to the extent that they were necessary for the future of the medical Authority, the only available option would be to create them *de novo*. To do that would necessitate altering the basic mythic structure (culture) within which 1,200,000 people, organized in nine cities and four counties, had found the ground and field for their individual and collective self-understanding for the better part of 300 years. Needed was an essential perceptual shift from isolation and parochialism, as the accepted view, towards a view of the world which took commonality and regionalism as it point of departure. Basically, one would have to do for a whole region what seemed to have been successfully accomplished for a single institution — create a New Story.

Chapter XI

A TALE OF NINE CITIES

The beginning of the story, at least so far as I was concerned, occurred on a beautiful fall evening (1980) as I stood on an apartment balcony overlooking the water dividing Norfolk and Portsmouth. The water way was filled with ships, everything from small harbor tugs to large naval vessels with a sprinkling of passenger liners and cargo ships. Across the way, the reflected lights of Portsmouth sparkled in the water, and to my left, I could see the enormous hulk of the United States, which had just been hauled out of the water in the largest floating dry dock in the world. One thousand feet long and almost 20 stories tall from the bottom of her keel to the top of her stacks, she stood like an instant sky scraper bathed in the strange orange radiance of sodium vapor lights while little men scraped her hull and applied new paint. Further to my left, I could clearly see the new buildings which made up downtown Norfolk. I can remember thinking to myself, "My God, what a fantastic place." It was vibrant and alive 24 hours a day with the coming and going of the ships of the world. Yet for all its business, it maintained an intimacy and human scale which is simply lost in harbors like New York. And all around, from virtually any point of view, there was water.

The only jarring note came from the headlines of daily paper I had just finished reading, which described in lurid detail the raging "Water Wars" which had begun the previous summer. It seems that the region was suffering a drought, and available fresh water in the city of Norfolk and elsewhere was approaching a critical shortage. Rationing had been instituted to the point of curtailing lawn watering and other non-essential uses, and unless the rain fell or other sources of supply were to be found, the situation would move from being inconvenient to downright serious. Actually, there was no immediate lack of water in the region, only certain parts of it, and the Water Wars chronicled in the paper resulted from the inability of the neighboring cities to share a resource that some of them were literally swimming in. It was but another chapter of the continuing saga of municipal jealousies which had been playing out for the better part of 300 years.

Water, both salt and fresh, was equally the bane and blessing of the region. It connected everything and divided everything. The local cities stood in close physical proximity, and their future development depended upon their capacity to share and work together. Yet between the cities (or at least most of them) stood the water of Hampton Roads and its tributaries, separating them like the moats of medieval castles. Were it possible to convert this powerful symbol-reality from "boundary" to "opportunity," from "separation" to "connection" the unity of the region might be effected. This conversion did not need to be physical, but perceptual, for the cities were linked by a reasonably adequate system of bridges and tunnels. Yet perceptually, the distance between cities might be measured in light years. Everything was "across the water," the "other side of the Roads" — as if the harbor were some impenetrable barrier. Changing that perception would involve creating a New Story, a new mythic structure in which water was the means of union. Given such a new story built upon the open space of the harbor, it was at least thinkable that the spirit of the region might be assisted in transforming from petty pockets of isolation and jealousy into something approaching connection and wholeness.

That was the idea, and it obviously connected in meaningful ways with my concerns for EVMA. To the extent that the spirit of regionalism was strengthened, EVMA's future might be secured. And by the same token, were it possible to develop regional organization to both support and reflect the telling of the "New Story," that organization could become the "alternate place to stand" for Dr. Mayer. Before going on to describe how this strategy evolved, it would probably be useful to back up a little and provide some further details on the history of the area.

The region as defined at the time of the meeting (1985), begins in the north with the city of Williamsburg and proceeds south to the North Carolina border, a distance of about 60 miles. It is bounded on the east by the Chesapeake Bay and the Atlantic Ocean and consists of nine cities and four counties (including Norfolk, Portsmouth, Newport News, Williamsburg, Virginia Beach, Hampton, Chesapeake, Suffolk, and Poquoson), all contiguous with each other and/or bordering on the Hampton Roads. At the present time, it is home for 1,208,400 people with an effective annual buying income of $10.5 billion. In aggregate, the region ranks in the top 50 market areas in the United States, although because of local divisions it had not been displayed that way. This has now changed, which is part of the story, but in the old days, the largest market area to appear on the charts ranked 143.

European settlers appeared in 1607 (Jamestown), and the older cities of the region date from that period (Norfolk, 1683). In short, there is a long history, much of which is critical to the history of the whole country. In 1776, George Mason's Declaration of Rights, written in Williamsburg, lay the ground work for the Bill of Rights which appears in the Constitution. And of course it was in this same region that the Revolutionary War ended with the surrender of Cornwallis at Yorktown in 1781.

World War II brought enormous activity to the area, for the Harbor was the home of a major naval installation in Norfolk and, across the water in Newport, the Newport Ship Building and Dry Dock turned out vessel after vessel. At the end of the war — there was an attempt to return to the somnolent days of a sleepy southern community, but unfortunately for that effort, the new people who had been attracted during the war days did not go home. The Navy continued to be a major presence, although relationships there may best be described by the signs that appeared in many yards saying "Sailors and Dogs Keep Off the Grass." On the positive side, the region was blessed with some of the finest natural living conditions on the East Coast.

It would not be stretching a point to say that for most of that time relations between the several cities ranged from nonexistent to conflicted. Rarely, if ever, was there any degree of mutual cooperation and support. For much of the history, the quality of these relationships made little difference, for the cities could afford to exist largely by themselves. In fact the presence of inter-municipal conflict was actually used to advantage by the various political establishments who argued to their respective constituencies that "such and such action" ought to be taken lest X city get the better of us.

In the 1960s, relationships became especially strained, particularly as concerned the city of Norfolk. Norfolk had always been the commercial center, and as it grew, it began to extend out into the surrounding farmlands (what is now Virginia Beach). According to Virginia law, a city may annex county territory, but the reverse is not true. As the cities' need for space grew, it was feared that "urban problems" would soon spill over the countryside. That provided the impetus, and overnight (literally) the cities of Virginia Beach and Chesapeake were created. The lines had been set, not only by history, but now by law.

Beginning in the late '50s, the private sector leadership in Norfolk began what eventually became a major renaissance though which the downtown portion of the city was literally redone. As that effort progressed, it became clear to these leaders just how enormous the potential of the areas really was and simultaneously, how far they were from realizing that potential. What stood in the way were the age old conflicts which in another day might have been considered amusing or even useful. That was no

227

longer the case, for the constant act of positive non-cooperation drained energy that could well be used in another way.

Thereupon began some efforts towards regional cooperation. It was assumed that everything could not be done at once; the considered approach dictated a "one piece at a time" strategy. Thus, it was suggested that the area develop shared police service (or fire, water, and so forth). It quickly became apparent, however, that the police chiefs (or fire chiefs) were just as infected with the old parochialism as everybody else, and these efforts towards cooperation ended in failure. Indeed, the failure of regional cooperation had become such a repetitive pattern that few believed it could ever be broken, and many doubted that it was even worthwhile trying. The single exception to this bleak pattern had been the creation of EVMA. That was the situation as I stood on the balcony that night. I wrote at the time;

> ". . . it appears that Tidewater is approaching or has
> arrived at a very interesting point. There is the obvious
> potential for the creation of a truly elegant human
> community of wealth, diversity, sophistication and
> position. Such a creation would represent the culmina-
> tion of the vision and effort of a dedicated leadership
> and an energetic population. To sacrifice such poten-
> tial, particularly when it is so close to realization,
> would represent major loss." *(Dreams and Leadership
> in Tidewater - Some thoughts*, unpublished)

I went on to suggest that whereas previous efforts to enhance regionalization had been based on a step by step approach in which attempts had been made to link various service elements of the region, all of which had failed, perhaps it was now time to try something different. I proposed that the solution might lie in creating a sufficiently large vision to include all components within the region that no one would feel constrained for turf. In short, do away with the turf battles by simply imagining an arena with room for all.

The dream I suggested was to develop the Tidewater area as "a major place from which the exploitation of the oceans may take place."[77] Conceiving and elaborat-

---

[77] *ibid* pg 8

ing such a dream could not happen just by saying the words. It would involve a lot of hard work, and a heavy dose of "future think" — which might sound a little bit like 2001 and Jules Verne, but the capacity to dream an un-imagined future provides precisely the material from which the future is made. Obviously, not all futuristic dreams come true (nor should they) but it is a fact in the human sphere that little if anything comes to pass which was not first dreamed. The lines from "South Pacific" are to the point: "You got to have a dream or how you going to have a dream come true?"

In practical terms, I suggested that the regional leadership might look to the seas as their point of union and basis for their future development. Given this perspective, the appropriate questions would be: What opportunities do the oceans hold for us? What present regional resources do we have that could give us a solid base for starting? And, What else do we need to develop in order to realize those opportunities? To get from "here to there," I acknowledged the normal practice of employing an external consulting group but recommended against it, in part because I was not sure that such a group existed, but mostly because it was inconceivable that they could dream Tidewater's dream. Dreaming after all is something you do for yourself. To give the whole enterprise a frame and an end-point, I suggested that these questions be dealt with preparatory to, and then in the context of, a major, international Symposium of the Seas.

The paper outlined a strategy which I thought might work for the whole region, while simultaneously meeting the needs of my erstwhile client, EVMA. I therefore took the paper to William Mayer with the suggestion that if he agreed, I might "float it about" in a limited way to see what the response might be. He concurred, and we chose a small group of six all of whom connected with the central power structure of the region, but were not the obvious leaders.

When seeding a story, it is well to place it in more than three and less than seven places at the edges of power. The reason for more than three is that the story cannot appear as the product (baby) of only one or two, because it is then too easy to stop. By the same token, the places of "seeding" should be limited (less than seven) or the whole thing loses its subtlety and it capacity as an Open Space to allow those further down the chain to buy in. Positioning it at the edge of power is critical, for it must be close enough to the center of things in order to be credible (if retold), and yet not right at the center of things at which point it may appear too heavy handed. The objective is basically to stimulate the mythos field in a limited number of places, and then, if that stimulation meets with a resonant response, allow the field itself to do the work. In short, no press releases early on.

The initial response was positive, but cautious. Positive in the sense that those who read the paper clearly resonated to the central theme both in terms of the need for unity and the idea of the sea providing the basis. Their caution, however, was obvious and came from many years experience in the region. The reaction might best be summed up in the words of Perry Morgan, the executive editor of the *Virginia Pilot* and *Ledger Star*, who said:

> "My question, Harrison, is whether you could or
> should do something to harden to some degree a beau-
> tifully proportioned but highly theoretical proposition."

Perry Morgan had placed his finger right at the nub of the central tactical question. The story had to be sufficiently open (vague) to allow for the imagination of others to move in and make it their own. But there must be sufficient specificity and detail to give it texture and structure, that is to say, make it credible. Morgan obviously felt that I should harden the case, and given where he was coming from, and indeed where most of the others came from, that was a very legitimate point. For the people who were hearing this story, and those who would have to join in later of if anything were going to happen, viewed themselves as "hard, realistic, businessmen" as indeed they were. While they might admit that previous efforts toward regionalism had failed, and acknowledge that there was some real virtue in having a dream and sharing a vision, they were quickly moved to the level of nuts and bolts, dollars and cents, hard plans. My sense, however, told me that the story, as presented, was good for openers, and that any more detail would slow the process of assimilation. The real danger was that the story become perfect, and perfectly mine. It would never become theirs.

It is worthwhile noting that the decision regarding detail versus openness made at that time had constantly to be remade and readjusted through out the whole project. Ultimately, if the regional spirit were ever going to cohere, the individuals involved had to experience a large degree of vagueness, which might positively become the space they needed in order to create a form for their collective spirit that went beyond its present parochial forms. But it could never be forgotten that Open Space is, by definition, without the old familiar limits, and therefore it may become downright frightening. Fear, of course, leads to withdrawal, and that can be the end of it all.

Under ideal circumstances, the hardness, details, and specificity should come as the product of the collective endeavor, but it remains true that some structure must be provided. There are no clear-cut rules here, though in practice I find it useful to give just as little structure as possible and always less than many might find desirable.

The story was out in paper and verbal form, and after the turn of the year (1981) a series of meetings occurred which involved a progressively larger and larger segment of the leadership of the region. Bill Mayer undoubtedly instigated some or all of them, but never did he appear in the central leadership role. That was left to those to whom the tradition of the area had accorded that status. For a period of several months, it appeared that the project would take flight, and indeed the discussions of the meetings were quickly getting down to the details — who, where, when, and how.

In the spring, a meeting was called to take place in Portsmouth with carefully selected attendees representative of the region as a whole. Going into that meeting, I thought that this would be the point of lift off, and indeed the discussion was positive, intense and enthusiastic. The meeting was chaired by Frank Batten, the chairman of the board of Landmark Communications, and those present represented a virtual who's who of the area, on all sides of the Hampton Roads.

Much of the discussion revolved around how to get an accurate tally of pertinent present resources in the region. It was clear to me that the group was beginning to come to grips with the enormity of the task that lay ahead, at the same time, I was more than a little concerned that they would get bogged down in the details and lose the larger picture. I tried to suggest as quietly as I could that determining pertinent resources depended in large part on having a clear sense of what they might be needed for, which meant that vision had to precede inventory. Or put quite simply, you had to know where you were going before you figured out how to get there.

As things turned out, my comments were appropriate, but my tactics were terrible. By raising the issue of vision, I had effectively taken the group out further than comfort would allow, and in response, they settled even more determinedly into how to create the necessary regional inventory, and who was going to do it. It was quickly determined that nobody in the room had the necessary time and expertise, and just as it appeared that everything would fall apart, Frank Batten indicated that he thought the "inventory" might be developed through the efforts of several of his investigative reporters. The feeling of relief was obvious, and the meeting adjourned.

My feelings were rather mixed. I was pleased that things hadn't fallen apart, but I wasn't entirely sure that they were really together. More to the point, I was

231

concerned that should the reporters really do a job, they would create just one more report that would sit on people's desks. Some mechanism was needed to bring a much larger segment of the regional leadership into the process, so that they not only unearthed facts but in the process began to experience the reality of regional cooperation. The story could not be built from facts alone, it had to become liturgy. Even though I could imagine such a mechanism, I hadn't a clue as to how to make it acceptable to the assembled group. As "businessmen" they perceived they had a "problem" (to gather some facts), which they were addressing in what they took to be the most expeditious way — send some folks out after the facts, and then have them report back.

What needed saying, and what I couldn't articulate, was that they didn't have a "problem" nor were "facts" the issue. They had an opportunity which might only be addressed if they (and a whole mess more like them) became personally involved in visioning the outcome and assembling the resources. At that point, they would no longer need to talk about becoming unified, they would be one, or at least a lot closer to being one than the region had seen before. Instead of telling a story or talking about how to tell the story, they would *be* the Story.

The reporters (for whatever reason) were unable to develop the inventory to everybody's satisfaction, but it took more than a year for all of this to become clear. In the interim, it seemed that things just "sat," and in terms of any overt signs of progress, there were none. I would have concluded that the whole enterprise was dead except for some persistent conversations which occurred during that year whenever I came to the area. People who had never been part of any of the meetings or received any of the material so far as I knew, seemed to know an awful lot about what was going on — and were more than a little curious as to what would happen next. Most curious was the fact that they were "sure" that something was going to happen "next."

In retrospect, I saw that the idea had by no means died, it was simply germinating. The truth of the matter was that we had gone too far out to the edges, and people just needed some time to catch up. One practical issue, which had never been really addressed was who was going to lead this venture should it really be undertaken. But the question of leadership was un-resolvable until there was a firm consensus that the whole thing was beyond the level of make believe and at least worthy of a damn good try.

Standing in the way of such a consensus was a larger issue which could not be dealt with directly, but just had to be "mulled." This issue was simply that if, by some wildest stretch of the imagination, the whole scheme actually worked — things really would be different. While there had been a lot of conversation and verbal agreement relating to the need for that difference if the region was to progress, I believe there was a slowly dawning awareness that once over the divide, things would never be the same again. While much of what might happen could appear positive, most of what lay ahead was simply unknown. Just to take one, but very crucial area, should the region actually unite, it was quite clear that the forms and probably the personalities of leadership would inevitably change. For a Southern conservative community (indeed any community), such change is not be entered into lightly. With the wisdom of hindsight (but very little hard evidence), I am now convinced that the major impediment was not, as I had supposed, that people were afraid that the idea would NOT work — but rather that it might, and what then?

If my surmise was correct, then the only antidote was time. People had to be given the space to imagine what it might be like, come to terms with the fact that they couldn't quite imagine it, and then reach the conclusion that given the alternatives (more of the same local bickering) and the opportunities (however they might appear), it was worth a try.

One major piece of learning from all this for me was the level of courage required. In a way, I had approached all this as an interesting problem or opportunity to utilize some "technology" in a very unique and complex environment. But the simple fact was, I could go home. It wasn't my region. This distancing was certainly useful when it came to plotting strategy and tactics, but it also makes it easy to forget that real lives are involved, and that the stakes, no matter how things turn-out, are very high. Transformation, as I have come to understand, is never free from pain and anxiety, and for good reason, it is fearsome and most often hurts. Life, death and resurrection are not just words.

In the spring of 1982, things began to move. The observable impetus came from Frank Batten, who had come to the conclusion that the reporters were not going to be able to do the job, and since he still felt that the "job," no matter how that might get defined needed to be done, he offered $15,000 for somebody to get on with the business. Mr. Batten's gift was clearly a turning point, but it in itself was not sufficient to explain what happened next, for after waiting better than a year since the last meeting, the pace picked up remarkably. Why or how this should have occurred, I have never been quite sure, but clearly the time (in the sense of kairos) was right.

With cash on the barrelhead, the question was what to do next. I found myself concentrating on the details of a process, but others were much more concerned about who would lead. This was but one of several examples of how I, as an outsider, failed to pick up on some essential in the culture of Tidewater. It turns out that what you do is actually of less importance that who does it, and the most important thing is to have the proper person at the head.

In retrospect the leader of choice was startling obvious, but how the decision was made is instructive. The truth of the matter is that there were less than a dozen individuals in the whole region who might fall within the zone of consideration. Whoever was chosen had to be sufficiently well known that his name would command instant attention. In addition, this person must be sufficiently senior and successful so as to be above any questions as to motive. And lastly, this leader had to have the positive regard of most, if not all of the power points in the region. I say he, because there were no women in the acknowledged leadership ranks of the region.

The first thought was that Frank Batten himself should be that person, and in many ways he qualified superbly, but for a number reasons, including the fact that he had been recently ill and was extremely busy, this would not work. Thereupon began a process of consultation among the power elite of the area. This consultation never took the form of a single meeting, but occurred over lunch and on the phone. In essence, each of the members of the consultative group were considered with a degree of affectionate dispassion that I found amazing. I say "affectionate dispassion" because everybody knew and respected everybody else, and all had been involved in one way or another over a long period of time with a multitude of projects. But the question here was who was precisely the right person. No votes were ever taken, but eventually one name emerged, Henry Clay Hofheimer II. In the way of the region, a small delegation was assembled to pay a call on Henry Clay, as he is known by virtually everybody. For obvious reasons, I was not a part of the delegation, so precisely what happened, I cannot say, but the outcome was that he signed on.

Henry Clay was the perfect choice from all points of view. At 76, he was the very image of the vital patrician. It was said that nothing of major social benefit had taken place in recent history without the substantial input of this gentleman. He was a major figure in the creation and funding of EVMA, and his involvements went from the opera to the zoo. His office and home were in Norfolk, but he summered in Virginia Beach, and was well known and respected throughout the region.

Those were the practicalities, but symbolically the choice was perhaps even better, for Henry Clay epitomized the bridge between the old and the new. His conservative demeanor gave comfort to those who might think that the whole enterprise was just "too far out," while his personal vision and love for the region drove him to consider the future, and in so doing, he freed others to do the same. Having told his own story over a lifetime, he possessed that inner security which accorded each participant the similar right and obligation. Most of all, he was committed. When I met him again after he had accepted the lead role he said, "This is the most important thing I have ever done." I heard him repeat this phrase on a number of occasions, sometimes with an extra bite, as in, "This is the most important thing I've ever done, and don't you people let me down." Nobody did.

Having a leader, we could now get on with the business of developing the process. Although the money had theoretically been given to conduct the inventory of regional resources there were in fact no stringent restrictions on its use. I thought this might be the opportunity to get back to what I perceived to be the necessary way to go; namely, start with vision, and then proceed to the nuts and bolts of what was available and what needed to be created. Consequently, I proposed that we use the funds to put on what I euphemistically called a "training session" in which leadership from the region might come to better understand what was involved and how they might go about getting it done. I was convinced that when it came to the actual planning for the future, and the collection of information, the participants themselves had to do the work. The essential rationale came from the thought that the whole project was basically aimed at creating the environment within which regional cooperation might become a reality. From this point of view, planning for the future and collecting data was only the mechanism and excuse for getting everybody together while simultaneously providing a concrete experience of doing something significant regionwide.

In more specific terms, I suggested a three-phase "training program" which would deal with: 1) A Vision of the Future; 2) Probable concrete outcomes of that Vision (dollars and cents, jobs); and 3) Creation of a plan of action to pursue all of the above with commitment gained from the participants to do just that. I further recommended that there be few if any outside experts talking to the group, but rather that the bulk of the activity and conversation be conducted by those immediately involved.

When I presented this plan to a small working group that Henry Clay had assembled, I was surprised to find acceptance, considering the fact that the plan represented a 180-degree turn from what they had previously been talking about. This acceptance may have been due to my eloquence or to the fact that nobody had a better plan, but I think what really turned the tide was my insistence that the participants themselves had the necessary expertise to do the job, and for sure, they alone had the self-interest to see it through. Hence no external experts. If nothing else, this appealed to an inherent spirit of "can do individualism" which is characteristic of the region.

235

The training session was scheduled for the fall of 1982, on three separate days over a six-week period. The reason for this spacing was in part a practical consideration that given who we hoped might come, there was little likelihood such busy people would be free for three consecutive days, except possibly over a weekend; but considering the social life of the area, that too would be difficult. The major reason for the separation of the meetings, however, was to make it possible to hold each session in a different place in the region.

Before the sessions began, there were several other pieces of important business, not the least of which was the selection of the participants. It was agreed that whoever was invited must be well known in their own area, close to the center of power if not actually part of it, and open to new ideas. The actual guest list was put together by Henry Clay with infinite care and many conversations. All told there were 42, and taken as a group, they were quite literally those people who made the region run or who would clearly do that in the future. Each participant was personally invited by Henry Clay.

The second piece of business was to secure the involvement of a gentleman who was well known in the region, though he could not be counted as a member of the "old guard." This was Harry Train, the four-star admiral who commanded the Atlantic Fleet, and was Supreme Allied NATO Commander. I had heard that he was about ready to retire, and furthermore that he had every intention of staying in the region. I knew that if we ever got the whole show on the road, we would absolutely need somebody to function as executive director. And what better choice than a four-star admiral especially if you were going to center your attention on the sea? Beyond the symbolic importance, which was real, Harry Train was perfect for the job, even though no job existed at the time I went to see him. He clearly had the "presence of command," but of equal importance, he possessed a sense of self that could put almost anybody at ease. In addition, he was open for new adventures. It is not insignificant that upon his retirement from the Navy and before assuming his duties as the executive vice president of the organization we had yet to create, he took three months to walk the 2138 mile Appalachian Trail by himself.

The first session took place in October. The site took no little time to find, but it was perfect. We used a restaurant situated right on the edge of Hampton Roads which was all glass and facing the water. If I had ordered the day, I couldn't have done better. There wasn't a cloud in the sky, and you could see the enormous harbor from one end to the other. The ships of the world passed in review, and while we were concerned to vision the future of the region and the sea, the sea and its abundance lay at our feet.

We started slowly with coffee and conversation in order to give all the participants time to meet each other and become imbued with the environment. Although most of those who came had heard of each other, many of them had never met. No matter what else happened, the gathering itself was a "first" for the region.

During the morning, my intent was to set the stage, and to do so in a way that all would find comfortable and informative. The subject was Vision, having a vision, and the process of visioning. To do this, we had three presentations which were the first and last in the three day program. The first presentation was made by David Belle Isle, then involved with strategic planning at Martin Marietta. He told what he called the "Bill and Mary Story," relating the then current takeover battle. His point was that Martin Marietta had no vision, which essentially set them up, and left them defenseless when confronting those who did. The next piece came from Colonel Frank Burns of the US Army, who related the story of Delta Force and how the Army used that mechanism to create a vision for itself. The last offering came from Judy Ellison who had been in charge of the Congressional Office of the Future and the Colorado state planning effort under Governor Lamb.[78]

The point of all this was not to specify how the region should move, but to make the whole idea of visioning the future a little less strange, and a little more possible. In the afternoon we got down to business. The format was an extended guided imagery. I must confess that I used this approach with trepidation, for the participants were by no means "New Age Folks." However, I felt we needed an experience which was clearly different and departed from the norm sufficiently to create the necessary Open Space in which everybody could work together. Of course it also had to relate to the task at hand.

The actual process and images used were essentially those described in the previous chapter, beginning with "A Comfortable Place," and including "Boundaries" and a "Journey to the Future." While some of the older participants evidenced a degree of discomforture, I was absolutely amazed to see how willingly and deeply each person became involved, and even more remarkable, how openly they shared the content of their own exploration.

---

[78] Frank Burns and Judy Ellison were actually part of the team that I had assembled to put the program together. They worked closely with me for the duration and contributed an enormous amount.

The first image (comfortable place) did little more than what it was intended to do, make people feel at ease with the process. But with the second one, things really began to work. When people shared their image of a "boundary" it became clear that some were quite frightened by the edges of things, while others felt mostly challenge. Most significant was the fact that they shared and really supported each other. In the long term, I think this particular exercise may have been one of the most important things we did, for it created a bonding experience that lasted throughout the sessions and into the main project that followed. Part of this, I think came from the fact that the language generated through the shared images constantly reappeared as the common, and to some extent secret language of the group.

The last image, "Journey to the Future," was sort of the icing on the cake. The group clearly enjoyed the freedom of going beyond the immediate problems of the region to picture and share a vision of what it might become. There was no little bit of laughter, but also some very serious ideas expressed. The actual content was almost beside the point (although we recorded the basic ideas); the major thing was the presence of that indefinable sense of possibility. . . shared possibility.

That evening we dined on a sumptuous seafood dinner (what else) and allowed the day to marinate in some excellent wine and cocktails well served. By the time everybody went home, some 13 hours after the start, I felt certain that they could never go home again. For sure, not all the pieces were there, and everything was just "possibility" . . . but everything was clearly different.

The second session, which occurred some two weeks later, took place in the Board Room of the Newport News Ship Building and Dry Dock. Again the location was superb and very important. From the windows one could look out over the enormous yard filled with the rising hulls of newborn ships and into the harbor itself. Since the subject for the day was the practicality of vision — nuts and bolts, real live opportunities for growth from the sea — the back-drop of this massive industrial operation was appropriate and very stimulating. The actual format was quite standard and straight forward, utilizing a "brainstorming" process which took the participants, in small groups and large, from their vision of the preceding session to the practical opportunities. By the end of the day we had flip charts full — more ideas than most regions could use in a millennium. The significant part, however, was not the ideas themselves but the excitement which had been generated in their production. I knew that real investment had occurred when I overheard some of the participants in heated argument as to the best way to raise capital for a special project they had just created.

The last session took place at the new Marine Research Center at Hampton University. It was designed to create a workable mechanism where by the whole venture might be carried forward, and simultaneously secure the commitment of those involved to whatever might happen next. In introducing the session I said, "Given the Vision as you all have experienced it, and the practical opportunities that you have identified and invented, the question is now, How do you share all this and make it grow bigger and richer? How do you tell this emerging story to 1,200,000 people who share this region with you, so that it becomes not just your story but our story?" To get them started, we proposed a simple organizational design which could provide the means for bringing a large number of regional residents together over time, in what would appear to be a collective self-study, but in fact was an orchestrated representation of the unity of Hampton Roads. We intentionally did not work out all the details of the design — doing just that was the business of the day.

To heighten the interest and build the dynamics, I intentionally appealed to the normal competitiveness of the area by dividing the group in two, and assigning each group the responsibility of considering the design and then either modifying it or coming up with something totally new which would accomplish the purpose. I asked Bill Mayer to chair one group and Admiral Train to take charge of the other. We allowed both groups to work for four hours, during which time they discussed, modified, invented and changed. At 2:00 we called everybody together, and each group presented their ideas to the other. The similarities of approach were obvious, but the differences were most useful, and it was apparent that each group was quite heavily invested in the way it had chosen to go. For several hours we negotiated and discussed, literally creating the design as we went. To aid in the process, I had invited Jim Channon, who has a marvelous ability to capture a group's thinking in graphic terms on what he calls "monster-grams" (30 foot long piece of butcher paper stuck up on the wall). As the group talked, the picture of who they were, what they might become, and how they proposed to get there all emerged on the wall.

By 4:30 it was all done, except for one very important piece. Would they really do it, was the commitment there? At that point, I took a direct leadership role, even though Henry Clay was sitting right at the table, on the grounds that consultants are always disposable. I stated the obvious and posed the question. "Gentlemen, you have created what I take to be a very workable design. The question is, Will you commit yourself in terms of time and funds to making it work? We need the answer before we adjourn, and cocktails will be served in half an hour."

While it might seem that such a direct and bold statement was ill-advised, I confess to have borrowed the whole scenario from Porter Hardy (see the story of EVMA), and in any event it was clear to me that commitment time was at hand.

There followed a moment of silence which grew longer and longer. But no commitment. Next, some generally approving comments, but still no commitment. Silence returned, only to be broken by an animated discussion on what to call the organization. There were those who favored "Tidewater's Future" (our working title) and another group that wanted "The Future of Hampton Roads." "Tidewater's Future" won by a show of hands, but as it turned out the name would later be changed to "The Future of Hampton Roads." But still there was no commitment.

At five minutes to five, I pointed to the clock and said something to the effect that either you go for it or just chalk it up to experience. By five o'clock everybody was in.

What happened immediately after that was just wonderful. Henry Clay took charge. Before cocktails were served, it had been determined who would draft the articles of incorporation and see to the creation of a nonprofit foundation, and who would be on the board initially. Harry Train had been approached about the executive slot, and William Mayer was to become first vice president (providing that "alternative place to stand"). The Story had been told, and the group was the Story. It now remained to be seen how it would play out in the region. But things were different, for never in the history of the region had such a group existed, nor committed itself to so much.

Within a month "Tidewater's Future" was legally constituted and the design agreed upon was being implemented. This design called for the creation of 10 (eventually 11) interest groups reflecting various sectors in the business and general community, such as transportation, finance, marine resources, health care and education. The definition of these groups was dictated by the current interests of the region and also those new areas where opportunity seemed to lie. Originally, these interest groups were called just that or sometimes "problem groups." But I prevailed upon the nascent organization to adopt the name "Opportunity Groups," just to remind everybody that we weren't out to solve problems so much as seize opportunity. That may seem like a small thing, but I believe it had major impact as the project went along, particularly when it got into the inevitable sticky places.

It is noteworthy that no political entities were recognized in the creation of the Opportunity Groups (as indeed there had been no elected officials in the core group),

240

and that was by design. It was felt that to achieve any kind of unity the existing political entities simply had to be "jumped over."

Chairpersons were designated for the several Opportunity Groups with the charge to expand the group, paying careful attention not only to gaining the necessary expertise, but of equal importance insuring regional balance. The function of each group was to start with the sea: identify or invent the opportunities available to each area; consider all that in the light of available resources; and develop a better way to go.

Once formed, the groups met intensely for the better part of the year. On a substantive level the contribution of the several groups varied all over the place, but there was no mistaking the emerging power and interest that was generated. Each time any group met or all the chairpersons gathered, the story of regional cooperation was told in the most powerful way of all, by demonstration. Henry Clay and Harry Train led the charge. Appearing together, or separately, they crisscrossed the region, speaking on the subject of Hampton Roads wherever opportunity presented itself. More than their words was their presence, for collectively they came to symbolize the emerging regional spirit, providing "cover" for those who might think regionally, but for whatever reason, fear going public. When the patrician figure and the four star admiral took the lead, it began to look more possible, not to say respectable.

For Henry Clay, such activity was but a natural extension of what he had done most of his life. He knew everybody, and was well known by all. Most of all, he knew how to operate in the unspoken and publicly ill defined power world of the region.

Harry Train, in contrast, found himself in a strange new world. As Admiral Train, he had commanded hundreds of thousands of men, assisted by a large personal staff. Now, as Executive Vice President for the Future of Hampton Roads Inc., he was in a position to command nobody, and had a personal staff of one secretary. Shortly before he took office, he asked me in a quiet moment, "Harrison, what have we gotten ourselves into?" My answer was something like, "Admiral, you have just assumed responsibility for bringing cohesion to a group of people about the size of the United States Army, which has been operating for 300 years as totally autonomous units. You must do all this without a shred of line authority." "Oh," said the Admiral. And that is precisely what happened — with excellence. As things moved along, the press picked up the story, and through a series of editorials, special features and two extended TV productions, told the tale yet another time.

One year after the original meetings (fall 1983), a symposium was held in the city of Norfolk at which the several opportunity groups conducted workshops and shared what they had found with the community at large. After that, it was decided to bring in the political jurisdictions, and a series of "road shows" were organized in each of the several cities whereby the "findings" of the Opportunity Groups were again put on public display and public comment invited.

In the fall of 1984 a second Symposium was held, which by virtually any standard was a resounding triumph, not so much in terms of the substantive offerings, although they were impressive, nor in terms of the number of attendees. The triumph was a palpable change in attitude and perception. Even though there were only 300 in attendance, they were fully representative of the region and the leadership of the region, and they came not so much out of curiosity as to participate. Something was truly different in the region. Whereas previously one would presume parochialism and argue (possibly at some risk) for a regional point of view, within a period of two years this had essentially switched. Regionalism was the accepted mode, against which one might defend a parochial view.

I have emphasized the change in view, and apparently down played the details and substantive accomplishments for the simple reason that the change in view (vision) was the primary objective of the whole enterprise. But this does not mean there have not been some very objective and impressive signs of this change. Perhaps most remarkable is the fact that the region went literally overnight from being the 143rd market area in the United States to becoming the 29th. This did not occur by mirrors or black magic, but through the simple expedient of stopping fighting. Previously, the various communities were so antagonistic that they would not allow themselves to be included in a single Standard Metropolitan Statistical Area (SMSA). As a consequence they splintered and were largely ignored when it came to looking at the big market places. The groundwork for the single SMSA had been laid, in large part, through many years of hard work on the part of Tom Chisman, a local television station owner from Hampton. Early on, he became a leader and strong supporter of the Future of Hampton Roads Inc., and the total effort paid off. Tidewater, or Hampton Roads as it prefers to call itself, is now very much in the top 50.

The SMSA is not the only change. The Chambers of Commerce have come very close to uniting, and the United Way is now one for the region. A regional sports authority, which had been created in 1963 and largely moribund ever since, has been revived, and is currently developing site selection plans for a regional stadium and sports complex. To the surprise of everybody, the mayors and city managers of three cities appeared on television and publicly said that it made no difference where the stadium might be placed, just so long as it was in the best site for the region. What will eventually happen, who knows, but that statement simply could not have been made two years previously. Tourism is now being approached on a regional basis, and the fragmented arts and cultural community has come together in a Regional Arts Council.

It might appear that concern for the Sea had dropped out, but not so. The Marine Resources Opportunity Group had developed solid plans for the culture and marketing of hard clams in addition to some profitable ideas about seafood marketing in general. And last, the Marine Industries Group had cast a hard and critical eye on the operations of the Port of Hampton Roads, to the point that the Port Authority — which had largely seen fit to work in a low-keyed, business as usual sort of way, suddenly found new energy, and has embarked on a major new effort to market the Port.

It would doubtless be incorrect to attribute all of these changes only to the existence of Tidewater's Future, or to the Future of Hampton Roads as it is presently called, but nobody that I have been able to talk to questions that the change in perception is real and that the Future of Hampton Roads Inc. has been very instrumental in the process. Perhaps the least earth-shattering but most graphic representation of the change of view appeared in a cartoon heading the editorial page of the *Newport News Daily Press*, following the second symposium. The cartoon shows the region as a puzzle with Newport News as the last piece being fitted in. To appreciate the impact of this particular editorial art, it must be known that over the years, the city of Newport News has resisted virtually every attempt at regional cooperation. Indeed when the whole project first started, there was real question whether any representation would appear from that city. Furthermore, it was the *Daily Press*, which editorially and in many other ways, championed the separation. The mere existence of this cartoon in the place that it appeared is taken by many as proof positive that hell has frozen over. The change is real, and that's the Story.

The bottom line is that the folks didn't let Henry Clay down. They did have the courage to dream — and the fruits of that dream are now becoming tangible. None of this is to suggest that all the battles have been won, nor that much does not remain to be done. But the fact of the matter is that the perception has altered, and nobody can go home again, even if they wanted to.

EPILOGUE AND WINDOW ON THE FUTURE

It may be said without fear of contradiction, that the future of any place lies with its children. As part of the second symposium, the 11th graders of the region were invited to participate in an essay contest on "The Future of Hampton Roads." The children were asked to imagine a future they would like to be a part of, and the report on it as if it were "really" there. No further instructions were given, nor was any suggestion made as to what the future might look like. It is interesting to note that all of the winning essays (one from each city, chosen by their teachers) presumed a unified region, and most of them went so far as to describe some form of consolidated government in the time frame they wrote about (usually 2010 or there abouts).

But beyond the specifics of their visions, which were rich and varied, there hovered a spirit of expectation and openness. Virginia Chin from Chesapeake took a "bird's-eye" view, and this is what she saw:

> "As I view this world today, I see a land of marked improvement. It is a land which has been uplifted by technology. The future holds much for Hampton Roads. One must allow it to grow. To do so, humanity must lend a helping hand. One must forget his limitations; instead, fly free and reach for the sky."

244

SELECTED BIBLIOGRAPHY

Bateson, Gregory. *Steps Towards and Ecology of Mind*, Ballentine, 1972.

Buber, Martin *I and Thou*, T&T Clark, 1937.

Burns, Frank and Nelson, Linda. <u>High Performing Programing: A Framework for Transforming Organizations</u>, *Transforming Work,* John Adams, Ed.., Miles River Press, 1984.

Campbell, Jeremy, *Grammatical Man*, Touchstone/Simon and Schuster, 1983.

Campbell, Joseph. The Masks of God (in 4 volumes), Viking Press 1962.

_____, *The Hero with a Thousand Faces*, Bolligen Series, Princeton Press, 1949.

Capra, Fritjov. *The Tao of Physics*, Bantum New Age, 1980.

Cassirer, Earnst. *The Philosophy of Symbolic Forms*, Vol I-IV, Yale University Press, 1955.

Collingwood, R.G. *The Idea of History*, Oxford, 1946.

Grof, Stanislav, *Beyond the Brain,* State University of New York Press, 1985.

Hall, Edward T. *Beyond Culture*, Anchor Press/Doubleday, 1977.

_____, *The Silent Language*, Doubleday, 1959.

Heidegger, Martin, *Being and Time*, Harper and Rowe, 1962.

_____, *On the Way to Language*, Harper and Row, 1971.

Jaynes, Julian, *The Origin of Consciousness in the Breakdown of the Bicameral Mind*, Houghton Mifflin, 1976.

Jung, C.G. *Symbols of Transformation* Bollingen Series/ Princeton University Press, 1956.

Keirkegaard, Soren. *Philosophical Fragments*, Princeton University Press, 1936.

Kenyon, Kathleen, *Digging up Jericho*, Ernst Benn, London, 1957.

Keubler-Ross, Elizabeth. *On Death and Dying,* Collier Books, 1969.

Kuhn, Thomas, *The Structure of Scientific Revolutions*, University of Chicago Press, 1962.

Laing, R.D. *The Politics of Experience*, Ballantine Books, 1967.

Langer, Susanne, *Philosophy in a New Key*, Harvard Univ. Press 1982.

Lovelock, James, *Gaia: A New Look at Life on Earth,* Oxford Univ. Press, 1979.

Maslow A.H. *Religions, Values and Peak-Experiences,* Viking press 1970.

Naisbitt, John. *Megatrends - 10 New Directions Transforming our lives*, Warner Books, 1982.

Nielsen, Eduard, *Oral Tradition*, SCM Press, 1954.

Pedersen, Jos. *Israel; Its Life and Culture,* Oxford Univ. Press 1959.

Peters and Waterman. *In Search of Excellence,* Harper, New York, 1981.

Prigogine, Ilya. *Order Out of Chaos*, Bantam New Age, 1984.

Russell, Peter. *The Global Brain*, Tarcher, 1983.

Tannenbaum, Robert and Hanna, Robert. <u>Holding on and letting Go; a neglected perspective on change</u>, in R. Tannenbaum, N. Margolies, and F. Mazorik, *Human Systems Development,* Jossey-Bass, San Francisco, 1985.

Toffler, Alvin. *The Third Wave*, William Morrow and Co.,1980.

Vaill, Peter. <u>Towards a Behavioral Description of High Performing Systems,</u> published in *Leadership: Where else can it go ?* Morgan McCall editor, Duke University Press, 1978.

Wilbur, Ken. *Up From Eden*, Anchor Press/Doubleday, 1981.

Yankelovich, Daniel. *New Rules*, Random House, 1981.

Young, Arthur, *The Reflexive Universe*, Delacort Press , 1977.